Life at Jericho

Jan Davey

In memory of my dear mum Evelyn Dewhirst.

First Published 2012 by Appin Press, an imprint of Countyvise Ltd
14 Appin Road, Birkenhead, CH41 9HH

Copyright © 2012 Jan Davey

The right of Jan Davey to be identified as the author of this work has been asserted by her in accordance with the Copyright, Design and Patents Act 1988.

British Library Cataloguing in Publication Data.
A catalogue record for this book is available from the British Library.

ISBN 978 1 906205 86 7

All rights reserved. No part of this publication may be reproduced, stored in a retrieval system, or transmitted, in any other form, or by any other means, electronic, chemical, mechanic, photograph copying, recording or otherwise, without the prior permission of the publisher.

Contents

Introduction   1

PART ONE: First Impressions   5

PART TWO: Opportunities, Possibilities and Uncertainties   11

PART THREE: From a Vision Emerged a Reality   212

Life at Jericho

Introduction

At the age of 56 I have come to a time in my life when I am reaping the rewards of or, depending on how you look at it, having to get on with the consequences of decisions that were made a number of years ago. There's nothing unusual in that of course it applies to us all as we get older. However the reflections of my life over the last 12 years or so are I feel a little different to the norm and therefore worthy of note.

The course of events which changed my life and that of my immediate family began to unravel towards the end of 1993.

To Julie

best wishes

Ian Davey.

Life at Jericho

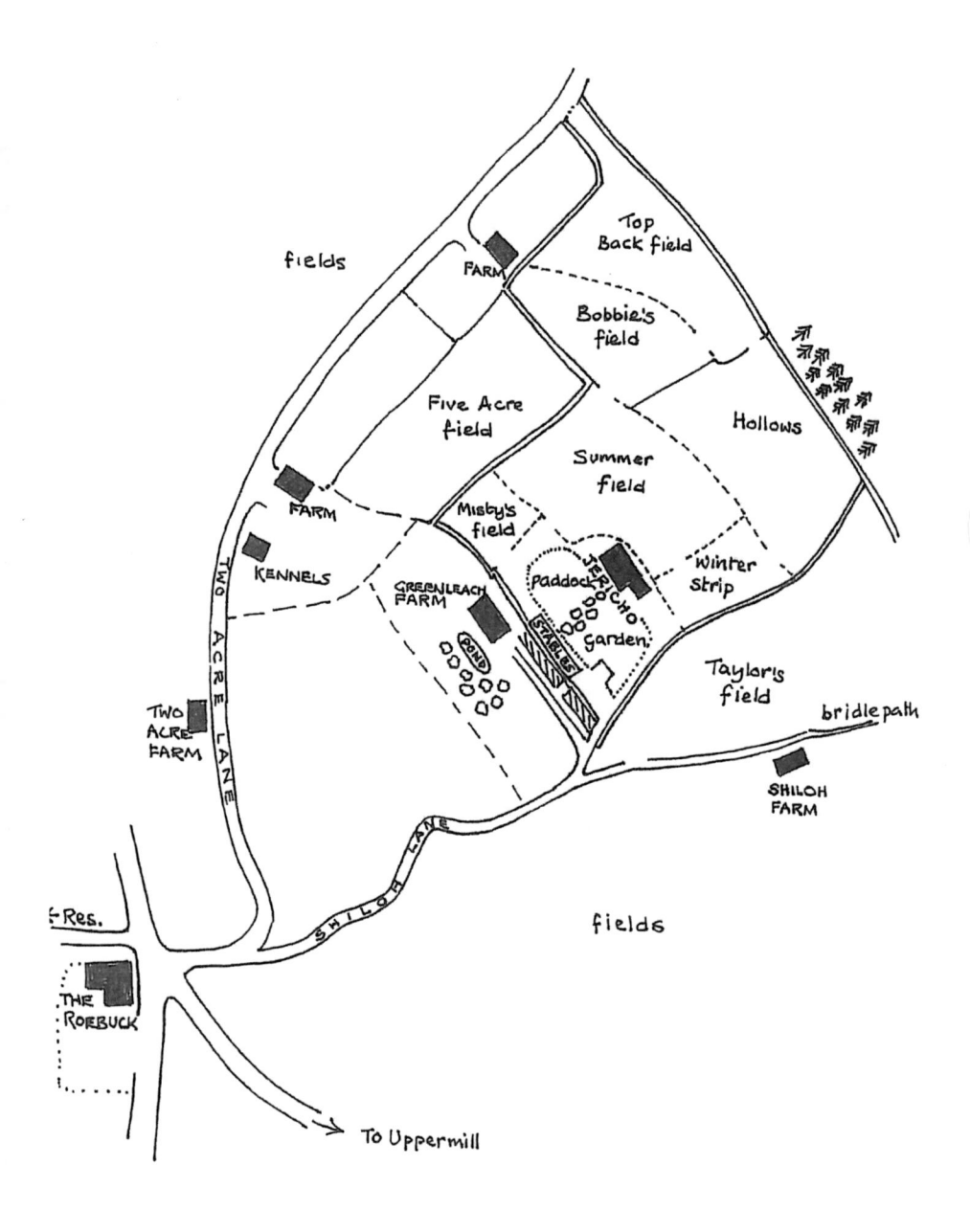

Preamble

October 27th 2002

The cold rain ran down my face and hair and trickled down my neck saturating my collar. The gale must have reached about 70 miles per hour by now. Every time there was a gust of wind I pulled down on the corner of the roof with all my strength - but I could still feel it lifting. The surface of the roof sheets was slippery when wet and it was hard to keep a firm grip on it and because it was so slippery there was no way I could climb on top of the roof to weigh it down. I had no option but to hold on until Alan and Sam got home. I daren't let go, if I did the whole lot could break free.

I reckoned that Alan had been gone about 10 minutes. I had been hanging on the roof for about five so I had at least another 15 minutes to wait. The time dragged by so slowly. My feet kept slipping on the roof of the rabbit hutch that I was standing on. My arms and shoulders ached with the constant strain of pulling down and all the time I was being battered by the wind. My wet hair was now plastered to my head and the water continued to trickle down my neck in a steady cold stream. I could feel it running down my back. My eyes were glued to the concrete area where I prayed Alan would park his car when he came home. If he parked there surely one of them would hear me when I shouted and then they would come and sort things out. If he parked at the front of the house I could be there for God knows how long! He'd probably go in and make himself a brew and turn on the telly assuming that I was down at the stables. Oh please don't let him park at the front!

We knew perfectly well how strong the winds could be at this time of year. Anchor straps should have been screwed to the walls of the stable, shippon and dairy to secure the roof spars. It was something that Alan had intended to do but he hadn't got round to it. As I clung stoically to the slippery roof I mused ruefully that over eight years had gone by and I was still finding myself in these ridiculous situations.

'Why does everything have to be so bloody difficult?' I shouted at the elements. I was nearly 52 years old for goodness sake what on earth was I doing hanging onto a slippery roof in the pouring rain and a howling gale? It just wasn't normal!

At that moment I realised that actually it was pretty normal for me. I had found myself in precarious, unpleasant and difficult situations before on several occasions since we had moved into Jericho Farm back in May 1994. Little did we know what we were letting ourselves in for on that snowy November morning the previous year when we had looked round Jericho for the first time. Despite its run down appearance and bleak situation the decision to go ahead and buy it as a long term project and investment for the future was an entirely mutual one. I could not therefore blame Alan for my present predicament – it was I suppose to some extent self inflicted…

PART ONE

First Impressions

1993

That November was very cold. Unusually, my husband Alan had been forced to take a week off school having succumbed to the flu or whatever bug it was that both our children had been struggling with since the beginning of the month. By Friday afternoon he was feeling much better and asked me if I'd checked recently if there were any suitable properties for sale.

'There's only Jericho Farm' I said. Three months previously I'd had a look at the place on my own, and rejected it because it overlooked two ugly, grey brick, derelict buildings belonging to the neighbouring property.

'Is that still for sale?' he asked. 'Have you looked at it?'

I nodded.

'Well what's wrong with it?'

I shrugged my shoulders 'There's an ugly derelict building in front of it. I don't know. It was a miserable day when I looked at it. I just wasn't keen.'

'Well, I'd like to go and see it for myself.'

A physically active man in his early forties Alan had played rugby since his early teens. Recreationally he had abandoned the rugby pitch some years ago in favour of the golf course and recently the classroom rather than the sports field had become his workplace now that his timetable was dominated by mathematics rather than P.E.

It was a lovely day. We took the opportunity to look at the farm while the children were still at school. Alan drove the three or four miles from Uppermill to Scouthead past the quarry and turned right at The Roebuck Inn into Shiloh Lane. After about half a mile we could see the farm in front of us. A narrow track pitted with potholes branched off to Jericho and the neighbouring Greenleach Farm. Slowly we made our way up the track and stopped about 50 yards from the farmhouse. We got out of the car and stared up at the long low building topped with Yorkshire greys. It was a traditional 18th century Pennine farmhouse built out of local gritstone. There was a row of small mullioned windows upstairs and a large arched doorway with pale yellow barn doors concealed the hay barn in the second half of the building. It was scruffy and run down but undeniably appealing.

'I like it. I can't believe you dismissed it.' Alan said. Let's arrange a proper viewing.'

'OK.' I agreed. We turned back to the car and immediately faced one of the derelict buildings. 'But look at that monstrosity!' I said 'Would you really want to sink all our money into buying this place and end up having to look at that?'

'It's 100 yards away from the house for goodness sake! Anyway we could grow some of those Leylandii trees in front of it.' He turned back to face Jericho. 'Look at it!'

I looked back and had to agree that it was much nicer than I remembered. 'OK.' I said 'I'll sort out a visit.'

On Monday morning I called in at the estate agents and asked them to arrange for us to view the farm. Later that week I received a phone call from the lady who lived there. She sounded nice and we arranged a mutually convenient time for us to visit.

The following Sunday morning when we set off to view Jericho Farm – officially this time - powdery snow was swirling about but not really settling in Uppermill. The Roebuck Inn was some 500 feet higher than Uppermill was however, and there the snow was settling thick and fast. We turned into Shiloh Lane. Our old BMW was less than ideal in these conditions and with spinning wheels we skidded and slipped our way up the narrow winding lane finally slithering to a halt about 100 yards away from the farm. Crunching our way up to the house we heard loud music blasting out from one of the upstairs rooms. Alan knocked at the door of the small front porch, but there was no response. He knocked again louder. The music stopped and a few moments later we heard the inside door being unlocked. The porch door was pulled open and an arm gestured us to come inside.

'Come in' said a woman's voice. Obediently we walked through the tiny porch and into the kitchen. I was completely taken aback by the sight of a short, dumpy, scruffy woman whose auburn hair - well most of it - was scrapped up in a slide. She looked as if she'd been out in a force ten gale! Her appearance was not what I had expected after having spoken to her on the phone. The next thing we saw was a cat busily washing itself on the work surface next to an open tub of margarine and a half eaten slice of toast. I found that a bit off putting - but not as off putting as the state of the work surface.

'This is the kitchen – the Aga is turned off at the moment because it's going to be serviced tomorrow. Usually it's very warm in here.' she said.

'It's a nice kitchen.' I lied trying to be objective and take in the general feeling of the room without focusing on the dirty cupboards, the dirtier Aga and the filthy floor.

'Come this way.' Again we were summoned through a doorway, this time into a dining room. A tall, thin, unshaven man who I guessed to be in his late fifties lay sprawled on a sofa beaming at us benignly.

'He's pissed!' I thought, smiling back. I looked around the room. The fireplace was built of artificial stone, totally incongruous in this old stone built property. A fire smouldered in the grate. The chimney-breast was clad with sheets of plywood which were painted deep purple. A dark oak dining table covered with newspapers and magazines stood in front of the window. Books, boxes and clothing were piled up against the walls. More cats were stretched sleepily on the backs of the armchairs. From the dining room we were shown into another room which was dominated completely by floor to ceiling dark wood cupboards that stood along one wall. Against the wall opposite the window stood a computer on a desk. Off the dining room another door concealed the staircase. We followed our guide up the stairs. A loose grubby rope served as a banister rail. The staircase and landing were dark with no natural light. When the light was switched on I stared at the dark purple corridor off which we were shown the master bedroom, a large room with four mullioned windows. Three walls and the ceiling were painted different shades of yellow. The fourth wall was papered with green hessian wallpaper much of which was falling off. A wardrobe, double bed and various boxes furnished the room.

'Big room! Long window sill!' was the only thing I could think of to say. I cringed when I heard Alan's over enthusiastic 'Oh yes!'

Next was the toilet. I stepped forward briefly to take a look. Alan took a step back. The next bedroom contained two single beds both of which I noticed were covered with course, hairy blankets.

'There's a big airing cupboard' we were told helpfully. The cupboard door was flung open to reveal – more hairy blankets. The final bedroom had a sheet of notepaper pinned to the door with a drawing pin, warning 'KEEP OUT'.

'My daughter's room - she's making potions'.

'I can well believe it!' I thought.

The bathroom completed the tour of the living accommodation. A narrow room with a curious bend in the wall allowing two windows to light the room where clearly there should only have been one.

Downstairs again and from the kitchen we were shown into the dairy. This was classed as an outbuilding, having a lean-to asbestos roof. A filthy old electric cooker, which looked as if it had not been used for years, stood on one wall along with an old sink and a cold tap the water pipe to which was lagged with a grubby red woollen scarf.

'We use this cooker in the summer when it's too hot to have the Aga lit – it's very reliable'. I looked at her in disbelief. She led the way through the dairy into the shippon. This room was full of junk. 'The layout of the property is excellent.' she continued. 'In very bad weather you can look after all the animals in the out buildings without having to go outside at all.' We looked with interest at the old, original stalls and chains which had been used for the cattle. A slurry channel ran down the length of the shippon. To the right was a door which led outside and to the left another door led into the hay barn. We turned left and stepped up through a low doorway.

'It's strange that you have to step up into the barn when the doorway is so low' I commented.

'Oh, it's not a step, that's just the shit that's accumulated over the years' she said airily. 'The hayloft is up these wooden steps' she gestured to her right 'but the goats have eaten them nearly away, so it's up to you if you go up there.'

We didn't. The inside of the yellow barn doors were in front of us now. The impressive arched doorway was one of the first things we had noticed when we saw the farmhouse that first time. To our right were two pigsties – no longer occupied but just as full of shit as the rest of the place!

'Well there you have it' she said and led us back to the kitchen. As we walked back through the shippon we looked out through low mullioned windows. There was little to see apart from a big old timber hen hut. Back in the kitchen the woman opened the door for us. 'Thank you' we both said. 'We'll be in touch' Alan added reassuringly. The door closed behind us. We slipped and stumbled through the snow back to the car.

'Well?' Alan asked as we opened the car doors.

'I love it.' I said.

'So do I.' Alan grinned 'I'm just glad she didn't offer us a brew!'

I had opted to stay at home to bring up our children until they both attended full time school. While they were little I earned a bit of money running a crèche in Tameside a couple of days a week until I was taken on as playgroup leader in Uppermill.

By the time our youngest child had begun primary school I had reached the stage of wondering what I should do with the rest of my life. Before starting a family I had taught art in a comprehensive school, and tentatively I returned to that environment. For several months I worked as a supply teacher, during which time I kept an eye on the 'Property for Sale' lists at the local estate agents.

There was nothing wrong with the house we were living in. On the contrary it was an impressive, spacious, stone built semi-detached property in a row of a dozen similar houses. At the front of the house was a footpath, which led to Saddleworth Comprehensive School. Behind was a cul-de-sac with a row of half a dozen brick semis. It was a safe, comfortable family home in the heart of Uppermill, a beautiful village in Saddleworth. We had lived there for 10 years during which time we had renovated the property throughout, with the exception of the attic. Had we stayed we would have converted that into a master bedroom with en suite. Outside however was restricted. There was a small, neat garden to the front, and an even smaller one to the rear, which included a cobbled area big enough to park one car.

Our two children Jessica aged eight, and Sam aged five, were very happy living there. I had recently decorated their bedrooms in colours which they had chosen themselves and they enjoyed the company of half a dozen children who lived nearby. Jess particularly was a very sociable child who loved spending time with her friends whether they were indoors playing in her bedroom or running around outside. Sam too was full of life. He enjoyed riding his bike and playing with his friends. Although he was just as happy on his own with his toy cars, trucks and tractors.

There were two more members of our family. Kim a handsome three year old Ridgeback cross who we had rescued from the RSPCA 18 months ago as a highly intelligent canine delinquent. Thankfully several months of intensive obedience training and endless patience had transformed her into a well-behaved, obedient – if a little boisterous – family dog. The other was Peanut a small elderly black cat who we had adopted a few years earlier and who had recently been diagnosed with feline alopecia and was rapidly losing her body hair.

As a teenager I had worked regularly at a local boarding kennels during school holidays and ever since then at the back of my mind had been a dream of owning my own boarding kennel business. Over the past few months we had discussed the possibility of making this dream a reality. From Alan's point of view he was ready for a challenge. Even though the kennels would be primarily my business he would be equally involved with the setting up and maintenance of such a project. Having been teaching for the past twenty years he had become, dare I say, bored and needed something different to focus on.

We had researched exhaustively into the pros and cons, regulations and restrictions of running a boarding kennel and cattery business. Finding the right premises was the first and most important step. The nature of the business restricted the type and location of the property we were looking for. Detached with at least three acres of land with no immediate neighbours were our criteria. In every respect Jericho Farm ticked all the boxes.

If we decided to move there it would be a huge culture shock for both children. I worried about how they would react. Jess in particular would miss her friends.

PART TWO

Opportunities, Possibilities and Uncertainties

1994

By the middle of January we had found a potential buyer for our house in Uppermill. Our first two offers for Jericho Farm had been turned down and offering more money would not only take us to our limit financially but would also commit us to doing the majority of the renovation work on the farmhouse ourselves. We weren't put off by that, over the last 20 years we had moved house three times and each time we had bought properties which were in desperate need of modernisation or repair. The prospect of renovating this old property appealed to me. I was not afraid of hard work and had always been a hands on sort of person. Jericho however was in need of considerably more renovation and repair than we had ever tackled before. Nevertheless we made the decision to go ahead and so it was with much anticipation and some trepidation that we put in our third and final offer. On the 21St of January we were delighted to hear that the offer had been accepted.

Throughout February and March I continued supply teaching part-time. All the while packing boxes and discarding anything which we could do without. By mid-March the mortgage for Jericho was organised and the sale of our house in Uppermill was going through fairly smoothly.

April was a month of endless packing and boxing up room by room. That month we bought an old SWB Land Rover. I'd had one years ago and had loved it. Moving to the farm had given me a strong argument for getting another.

As the time for the move got closer we gave a lot of thought to the filthy state of the farmhouse and the essential work which needed to be done before it would be safe for two young children to live in it. We decided that we had no choice but to hire or borrow a caravan to live in for the first few weeks. It wasn't long before Penny one of our friends heard of our predicament and generously offered us the loan of a small caravan belonging to her father. Up until the last couple of years it had been used regularly for holidays – now it was parked, cluttering up his driveway. We accepted the offer gratefully.

There was a discrepancy of two days between the completion dates of our house sale and that of Jericho so we made arrangements to pick-up the caravan on Monday afternoon and Alan booked us into a caravan site

I woke up early on the Saturday morning realising with an uneasy feeling that we had reached the point of no return. The removal men arrived and spent all day loading up all our worldly goods, taking them away and putting them in storage until further notice. When the men had gone I gave all the paintwork a final clean. We spent the evening with Cath and Jim - our friends who lived in one of the semis in the cul-de-sac behind our house. Their daughter Katy was six years older than Jess and she had always been like a big sister to both Jess and Sam. They were all very close. That night and Sunday night we slept in sleeping bags on the floor of our empty house along with Kim, Peanut and two tanks full of gerbils.

On the Monday morning after Alan and the children had gone to school, I took Kim for our last walk beside Pickhill Brook before stocking up with some provisions to keep us going for the first few days of living in the caravan. Early in the afternoon I took Peanut to 'Petsville' a boarding kennels and cattery in Uppermill where I had booked her in for a two-week stay. Alan got home from school as soon as he could and we loaded up the car and the Land Rover with the last bits and pieces and the gerbil tanks. Cath had made an early tea for Jess and Sam. While they ate Alan went in the Land Rover to collect the caravan and tow it to the 'Moorlands Caravan Park' in Denshaw where we were to stay for the next two nights. Half an hour later the children tearfully hugged Cath and Katy and having said their goodbyes they piled into the car with Kim. We set off. I looked at our lovely house and said a silent goodbye as we drove past. As we climbed the hill out of Denshaw we could see 'Moorlands' on our right, Alan had already arrived and was manoeuvring the caravan into a bay close to the entrance.

'There's Dad!' Sam shouted nudging Jess and pointing through the car window. I looked with horror at the scruffy little caravan. The side facing the road was completely covered in green algae – evidently it had been parked against a hedge at Penny's dad's house. It was far too cold to do anything about it then. It would just have to wait until morning.

I got up early and took Kim for a walk. The caravan park owner appeared as I returned and asked me, very politely, if I would clean the caravan as it 'lowered the tone'. He was dead right! Alan took the children to school on his way to work. I watched the car as it went down the hill until it disappeared from view. Feeling a bit abandoned to say the least I took the bowl of washing-up water outside and set about cleaning the caravan with a pan scrubber.

Cold Hard Reality

At 1pm on Wednesday the 11th May as arranged I arrived at the estate agent's to pick up the keys to the farmhouse. They weren't there. They still weren't there at 3 o'clock - or at 4 o'clock. I became more and more frustrated. We had planned to take the caravan to the farm as soon as Alan finished work. It had gone 6.30pm before we finally took possession of the keys. The previous owner had told the estate agent when they rang her that she was much too busy to bring the keys down to Uppermill. If we wanted them we would have to come up to the farm and collect them. Awkward woman! - I was livid. We drove up in the car passing a removal van in the lane. She was waiting for us outside the farmhouse in her car. Passing me the keys she fixed me with a surly stare.

'There you are' she said 'now the removal men have gone with the last load, the house is completely empty.'

I took the keys with a nod of my head. I couldn't trust myself to answer the wretched woman without telling her exactly what I thought of her. Having got the keys we drove back to Denshaw and paid the caravan park owner then we hitched up the caravan and towed it up to Jericho. By the time we'd finished positioning it next to the leaning Laburnum Tree on the patch of grass beside the kitchen it was going on for 8 o'clock. We unlocked the door of the farm house and showed Jess, Sam and Kim their new home for the first time.

Despite being told by 'that woman' that the house was completely empty the reality was very different. In the kitchen were several empty cardboard boxes and the waste bin was so full that the overflowing messy kitchen rubbish was piled up against the greasy wall. A half full tin of cat food with a fork stuck in it stood on the work surface. The children, so excited a few minutes earlier, were now struck dumb. We ventured into the dining room. The dirty old carpet was still there and also for some reason, was a single bed along with more old cardboard boxes. The next room was empty apart from another carpet and the floor to ceiling cupboards.

I opened the staircase door. Feeling for the grubby light switch I turned on the light and we went upstairs. A urine-soaked double mattress lay on the floor in the big bedroom and the wardrobe was still there. Apart from carpets and odd bits and pieces the other rooms were empty. We told Jess that as she was the eldest she could choose which one of the two smaller bedrooms she would like to have as her room.

'I don't care they're both horrible' she said quietly. Clearly there was no point in taking that discussion any further. Sam looked at Jess and linked his arm through hers. We went back downstairs. A quick look revealed the dairy and shippon to be as full of clutter and rubbish as they had been when we first came to look at the house back in November. Feeling angry and disappointed we locked the door and went back to the caravan for the night.

Living at Jericho for the next few years was to be a time of continuous hard work punctuated with regular intervals of pleasure, sadness, humour, worry and utter exhaustion. Jericho Farm was not just a house – it was a way of life.

Next morning when the others had gone to school I sat in the caravan sipping a hot mug of coffee with Kim by my side. I had zipped my fleece right up to my chin and was holding the mug in both hands to try and keep myself warm. Being quite slightly built I felt the cold easily. I looked out of the window at the trees swaying in the icy wind. I was worried and felt apprehensive. Had we done the right thing? There was so much that had to be done with this old farmhouse - had we taken on too much? What if the renovation cost more than we could afford? Wanting some attention Kim nudged my arm vigorously with her nose and the hot coffee spilt over my jeans.

'Dope!' I shouted standing up quickly to stop it burning my leg. I grabbed a dish cloth and tried to soak up the coffee. Kim stood with her head down looking up at me, unsure for a moment how cross I was. I stroked her head. She was a powerful dog and very protective. I was glad of her company.

The postman drove up our lane and pulled up beside the caravan. Kim barked loudly shaking me from my negativity. The postman got out of his van holding a letter. I leaned out of the caravan doorway and took it from him. It was from my mum as ever offering words of encouragement together with a cutting from the horoscope page of The Daily Mail newspaper. The star sign prediction for Sagittarius – my star sign – that week read as follows:

'Tonight's eclipse of the Sun occurs in your sixth solar house. It's the area that governs hard work and the need to be of service. It also has connotations with health and small animals – particularly pets. For most Sagittarians though, the impact will be felt in the work department. Out of the ashes of a project long pursued without success will rise the phoenix of a brilliant new enterprise.'

Feeling a little more positive I pulled myself together and got stuck into the immediate jobs of clearing out, sweeping and cleaning. After disinfecting the grimy phone I rang up and organised tradesmen to check, service or mend and over the next few weeks I endeavoured to sort out as much as I could before Alan and the children broke up from school for the summer holiday, when work would begin in earnest.

One of the first things I did was to order a large skip to accommodate the rubbish and junk that had been left in the house. I also arranged for the water quality to be checked along with the pumping and filtration system which drew the water from the well into the cellar and up into the house. Electricians had already been booked to begin rewiring the whole house and a chimney sweep was coming to sweep the dining room and kitchen chimneys next week.

That weekend Cath and Jim offered to come up and help. The loan of a tractor and trailer from Norman our milkman enabled Alan and Jim to make a start on digging out the muck in the barn. They made several journeys towing the loaded trailer up to the top field where they tipped the muck in a large hollow. The first time Cath had set foot in the house she had been horrified by the state of the kitchen. This time she had come armed with some extra strong bleach.

'You do the sink and work surfaces, I'll do this disgusting pantry and the tiles, and then we'll tackle the floor together' she ordered as she rolled up her sleeves and disappeared inside the pantry with the bleach and a bucket of water. I did as I was told and set about scrubbing the brown work surfaces – which turned out to be orange! Once I'd cleaned the surfaces I started on the dirty sink and polished the taps until they gleamed. Every few minutes various comments issued from the depths of the pantry. 'Dirty woman... Look at this muck! Dirty cow!' About half an hour later Cath emerged from the pantry her eyes red and streaming. 'That bleach is a bit strong!' she gasped blinking hard 'I think it's taken the skin off my throat!'

When we were satisfied with the kitchen we went up to the big bedroom which, with the exception of the urine soaked mattress, wasn't too bad. Between us we soon got it looking quite respectable. While we made a brew Alan struggled down the stairs with the revolting mattress, manhandled it into the kitchen and flung it outside, much to Jess and Sam's amusement.

Next day they came and helped us again - this is when you know who your real friends are. Alan and Jim shifted a substantial amount of the remaining muck in the barn. Cath and I and the children tackled the dairy and shippon. We struggled outside with loads of clutter and rubbish and practically filled the skip with it. Cath and I spent some time cleaning the Aga as well, although we didn't make much headway with it. We doubted that it had been lit in months. Alan had a go at lighting it with some anthracite which he'd found round the back of the house, but it remained stubbornly cold and unwelcoming.

That evening we were all tired and absolutely filthy. After we'd devoured a chippy tea I drove Jess and Sam down to Cath's so they could shower and get ready for bed. I took them in the car so they'd be more comfortable. Alan had warned me that it was low on petrol. Driving home I should have called at the petrol station but the children were so tired I just wanted to get them home and tucked up in bed. We turned the corner by The Roebuck, the car began to judder and we rolled to a halt at the bottom of Shiloh Lane. It had completely run out of petrol. I couldn't believe it; we only had half a mile to go. Stupid car! Stupid me! It was dark, cold and windy. At that time I didn't have the benefit of owning a mobile phone and so had no choice but to lock the car and walk the children home. Sam was wearing his warm coat, but Jess only had on her dressing gown. I put my coat round her shoulders and we trudged up the lane. I have no doubt that by the time we got home she was cold, but as soon as Alan appeared at the caravan door she developed extreme hypothermia and ran to him tearfully. Alan of course gathered her up and glared at me – his deep set eyes unblinking and accusing, his thin mouth set in a straight angry line. For goodness sake! Anybody would have thought I'd committed some heinous crime!

We waited until the children were asleep then we sneaked out of the caravan leaving Kim on guard. The caravan door had a stiff catch and we had to slam it to make sure it closed properly. Hurriedly we grabbed a small petrol can and hurtled off in the Land Rover to get some petrol. We put the petrol into the BMW and drove both vehicles back home. It didn't take very long, probably about twenty minutes, but when we got back the children were staring out of the caravan window with tear stained faces like abandoned waifs. Alan and I didn't speak for the rest of the evening. I felt like the world's worst mother.

I woke up at first light to hear the wind howling and the rain lashing against the windows. I looked at my two lovely children sleeping peacefully in their sleeping bags covered with outdoor coats. Kim wagged her tail when she saw that I was awake. Suddenly the air vent cover on the caravan roof pulled free from its catch. Battered by the driving rain it stood vertical threatening to break free at any moment. The cold wind rushed through the open vent into the caravan and snatched at the curtains. Shivering, I got out of my sleeping bag and grabbed the dog lead. Kim curled up even tighter in her basket evidently thinking I'd completely lost my marbles and was going to take her for a walk. I clipped the lead onto the vent cover and pulled it shut and then tied the other end to the cooker to secure it until morning. I got back into bed vowing that once we moved into the house I would never set foot in that caravan again.

It took several more sessions of earnest shovelling before the barn was completely empty of muck. We still had the pigsties to empty but at least now we could venture up the precarious wooden steps and begin emptying the junk out of the hayloft.

There was absolutely no way that any of us would contemplate using the toilet in the farmhouse. I completely ignored Alan's suggestion that 'we' could clean it and on Bank Holiday Monday he was busy all day fitting a new one. As I went backwards and forwards to Oldham getting the required plumbing parts the Land Rover became difficult to get into gear. Optimistically I hoped it just needed a top up of gearbox oil.

The following morning on our way to school it became apparent that my optimism had been misplaced. It was about a seven mile round trip to school and back and we had gone barely a mile when the gear box jammed. I had to do the rest of the journey in third gear. I couldn't shift the gear lever at all and had to rev like mad when going up hills. I was scared stiff I would stall it whenever I had to stop.

'Get out quick!' I bellowed when we arrived at school. Hurriedly the kids jumped out and Jess slammed the back door. I roared off aware of some very disapproving looks from other more responsible parents. It was with a huge sigh of relief that I arrived back at Jericho and turned off the engine. I thought maybe now that the engine was switched off, if I depressed the clutch and tried again, perhaps the gear lever would free itself. I pressed the clutch pedal and pushed the gear lever. No joy. I tried again, this time I pulled it back hard. Suddenly it freed itself – right out of the gearbox! Horrified I sat there with a gear lever in my hand. Carefully I pushed it back into its rubber housing and climbed out of the Land Rover feeling like a naughty child. Fortunately Alan knew a mechanic called Martin who worked on Land Rovers. That evening he went to see him and told him what had happened. Martin promised he would call up sometime in the next few days and sort it out for us at a reasonable price.

We had pretty much made up our minds to get rid of the old Aga. But as I had arranged for the chimney sweep to come we decided to give it one last chance. If we were still unable to light it after the kitchen chimney had been swept it would definitely have to go.

When the chimney sweep had finished in the dining room I explained to him that we'd tried to light the Aga several times but it would not stay alight. He said he would see what he could do and selected a small-headed brush which he began pushing up the bend in the flue. It seemed to be blocked and he wiggled and jabbed at the blockage. After giving it an almighty shove he announced triumphantly that he'd cleared it. I ran outside and cheered like an idiot when I saw the brush head sticking out of the chimney pot. Having swept the flue to his satisfaction he withdrew the brush – it got stuck at the bend. He pulled and pulled. Suddenly it became free. The chimney sweep shot backwards so fast he hit the back wall, dropped the brush and his cap fell off! I held my breath trying desperately not to collapse into giggles. He picked up the brush and the head broke in half. That did it. I burst out laughing, apologised and laughed again. Hurriedly I paid him. He put his cap back on and left.

Over the next two days I hacked and scrubbed at the hard baked grease that covered every surface of the Aga. When it was as clean as I could get it we tried lighting it again. This time we put charcoal in first and got that going before putting in the anthracite. Next morning the Aga was still lit. The kitchen was transformed. It was completely and wonderfully warm. We loved it. I wanted to curl up on the Aga like a cat. Kim lay against it. Sam sat on the simmering plate lid like a pixie.

Now that the Aga was lit providing us with warmth and hot water we used the kitchen to cook in and eat our meals. I decided to collect Peanut from the cattery. She had lost even more of her hair by this time but at least now she would be able to keep warm by the Aga.

At the back of the kitchen opposite the entrance to the dairy was a narrow door behind which was a steep flight of stone steps that led down to the cellar. The cellar consisted of one small room that extended beneath the kitchen; I thought it very impressive with its vaulted ceiling. Set into two of the walls were several small alcoves – probably used to store meat when the farmhouse was built about two hundred years ago. In the centre of the room was a massive stone slab supported by two chunks of stone which held the slab about two feet above the stone flagged floor. I didn't want to think about what the stone table had originally been used for. More recently the cellar housed the water pump which drew up water from the well and pumped it through the filtration system after which it was carried inside a black pipe across the ceiling then up beside the cellar door frame after which it disappeared from view through the ceiling to – I wasn't sure where. The water which ultimately spurted out of the taps in the kitchen was cold and clear and looked absolutely fine but nevertheless, bearing in mind the state of everything else in the farmhouse, I arranged to have the quality of the water and the filtration system checked before we dare use the water for drinking or cooking. The water system turned out to be a surprisingly good one, which only required a new filter and an ultra violet bulb to render the water completely safe and actually very nice to drink.

The following week the skip man came and took away the full skip and replaced it with another empty one. I cleared out any remaining junk – a lot of which had been bagged up – from the hayloft, barn, dairy and shippon and chucked it in the skip. Everywhere was swept clean and looked much better and I felt a lot happier. Jess decided which bedroom she wanted. She chose the one at the back of the house; it was a slightly bigger room than the other one and it overlooked the fields.

A celebrated date in the Saddleworth Calendar was and still is Whit Friday. A day when each village congregation is represented by a procession led by a brass band, and followed by a dozen or more smartly dressed young children and as many adults, carrying baskets of flowers or holding ribbons which are attached to a big embroidered banner bearing the name of the congregation at the head of each procession.

This year Whit Friday fell on the 27th of May. Jess and Sam walked with St. Chad's Church procession at Uppermill. Alan opted to stay at Jericho and spend the day pulling up the floorboards in the children's bedrooms while I had a day off with the children. I helped them get dressed up then we collected Katy on the way up to St. Chad's Parish Church where the congregation was meeting to form their procession.

The processions walk through village streets all over Saddleworth and congregate in King George V Playing Fields off Uppermill High Street. At 11 o'clock a church service is conducted by important church dignitaries who, wearing their flowing robes, stand on a flatbed trailer on the back of a lorry and speak into temperamental microphones. Hymns are sung and then the processions make their way back to their own villages. St. Chad's Church procession walks along the High Street through Uppermill to the viaduct and back to the Old School in Lee Street where some services are held and Sunday school meets on most Sundays. During the afternoon sport and entertainment is provided at St. Chad's Primary School for the younger children and their parents to enjoy. In the evening at 5 o'clock the Brass Band Competition gets underway in Uppermill. Bands from all over England and further afield take part. Throughout the evening they visit each Saddleworth village and play their selected offering to rounds of applause by the appreciative crowds that are attracted each year. The enthusiasm grows as the evening progresses partly due to the fact that the pubs are open for most of the day.

This particular Whit Friday was a very welcome break from all the hard work and we thoroughly enjoyed the day.

The following Sunday was a beautiful day. While Alan continued to work on Sam's bedroom floor, I helped Jess and Sam clear out the dog hut which had been left by our predecessors. It stood beside the farmhouse on a hard standing area which was surrounded on three sides by the remains of an old grey brick building. Once the hut was cleared out the children put their bikes and outdoor toys in it, so they were not left lying around outside.

Later that day I heard soft squeaking noises coming from one of the gerbil tanks. After a little delicate investigation I discovered that 'Triska' had once more had a happy event. Evidently before I'd separated them 'Moses' had had his wicked way with her – again! Separating the male babies from the litter would be tricky but in about three weeks I would have to do it or we would be over run with them.

Alan's father was a joiner and over the years Alan had picked up much of his expertise. He could tackle any job which involved working with wood. He was competent at plumbing and bricklaying too and could turn his hand to pretty much anything. By the end of the month he had ripped out the floors in both Jess and Sam's bedrooms and also the one on the landing and the joists had either been replaced or treated for woodworm. Pulling the boards up had revealed a large part of the plumbing system. The water from the well was pumped first into the cellar where the filtration system had been set up and from there it continued up through pipes in the kitchen roof space and in at the back of Jess's bedroom to the corner where the hot water cylinder stood. Finally it was taken up to the loft where the cold water storage tank was situated. More pipes went under Jess's bedroom floor to the bathroom and under the landing floor to the toilet.

Unbeknown to us over the years the acidity in the spring water had eaten into the copper pipes. When Alan had pulled up the old floorboards in Jess's room he must have disturbed some of the pipes. Overnight they began to leak like an efficient sprinkler system onto the dining room ceiling below. By the time we discovered it next morning the plasterboard was saturated and had begun to sag. The water pump worked on a float system like a toilet cistern so when the level of the water in the storage tank dropped – which it did because of the leaking pipes – the pump kicked in and refilled the tank. Sleeping in the caravan we were blissfully unaware of this particularly vicious circle! We turned off the water pump and because the water was heated by the Aga we had to let that go out as well.

Replacing the entire upstairs plumbing system including the hot water cylinder was going to be complicated and not a job to be done in a hurry. We spent time planning it so that we could work out what pipes and fittings would be needed. The dining room ceiling was divided into three sections by two beams. The plasterboard in the section beneath Jess's room and in the section next to it was all ruined. We had no option but to pull it all down. A new ceiling was yet another job added to the ever-increasing list of 'jobs to do'.

Typically, now that the Aga wasn't lit the weather turned cold again with wind and rain. I bought all the plumbing stuff during the day and when Alan came back from school we began replacing the old copper pipes with easier but bulkier plastic. Nothing was straightforward. Everything was awkward. Amazingly many of the things which went wrong were apparently my fault whether or not I was in the immediate vicinity. Alan's temper gradually became more and more frayed and by the time we stopped exhausted at 1am once again we couldn't stand the sight of each other.

After a good night's sleep we made an early start and continued where we'd left off the night before. This time everything went reasonably well. During the morning Jess was sitting in a camping chair below us in the dining room watching a children's TV programme on the little telly which we'd brought with us. Excitedly she ran upstairs to where we were working and balanced precariously on an exposed joist.

'Can I ring up and do the competition on telly?' she asked swinging on the bedroom door handle. She leant back so that her long hair fell loosely away from her shoulders

'Be careful! Stand up properly! Get off that joist. Go back downstairs you'll fall through the ceiling!'

'Please can I ring? It's the one with the two pink rhinos. It's really good and ...'

'Yes! Yes! OK. Anything - just go downstairs.'

Over the next half hour Jess tried continuously to get through to the TV programme. Suddenly we heard her talking down the phone.

'Jessica Davey...nine...yes...Saddleworth. Yes I'm ready...' At that moment Alan reached for a plastic fitting and accidentally nudged the bucket which we'd been using to drain water out of the pipes he was replacing. It teetered on the joist for a moment. He reached to grab it but knocked it over. Jess speaking clearly into the phone just underneath it was drenched with icy water. She screamed and dropped the phone, then glared up at us through the tangle of pipes.

'I don't suppose you've won then?' Alan asked unhelpfully. I shook my head at him and went downstairs to commiserate with Jess and find her some dry clothes. We finished the job without further mishap at about 6pm. Alan double checked each joint then I turned the water pump back on and re-filled the system. We kept everything crossed. Thankfully, there were no leaks so we re-lit the Aga.

Later that evening Martin brought back the Land Rover complete with new gearbox at a reasonable price as promised.

Norman, who had lent us his tractor and trailer, had been our milkman in Uppermill for the last 10 years. He was happy to continue to deliver our milk when we moved up to Jericho as he also delivered to both our neighbours. Our nearest neighbours were Steve and May Foster, a middle aged couple who lived at Greenleach Farm. They owned the grey brick buildings which we overlooked. Steve, amongst other things, was a dog handler and hopefully wouldn't object to our plans for boarding kennels. We had already met him briefly as we shared the access off Shiloh Lane to our houses but as yet we had not seen our other neighbours. According to Norman they lived at Shiloh Farm, kept horses and had three young children. The top end of Shiloh Lane ended in a bridle path well used by horse riders in the area. Shiloh Farm was right at the end of the lane to our left.

On Sunday my sister Pat came to see us for an hour or so. Slightly built like myself and my elder by six years Pat shares my sense of humour. Unlike me however she has always been a bit of a townie. The thought of living in a remote and draughty farmhouse which needed so much doing to it did not appeal to her in the least. She was accompanied by her husband John, their youngest daughters Dianna and Karen and by Matthew, Dianna's fiancé. We showed them what we had done so far in the house then walked up the fields to look at the views over Saddleworth. Although they recognised the potential Pat in particular thought we had taken on a mammoth task and was a bit worried about how we would manage. I reassured her that we would be fine.

When they had gone home we decided that it would be a good time to introduce ourselves to our other neighbours. Jess and Sam were excited at the prospect of having new friends to play with actually next door and couldn't wait to meet them. We set off towards Shiloh Farm. Hopping and jumping their way down the lane Jess and Sam chatted together. As we approached the farmhouse we could see a man and a child in front of us. Probably in his mid-forties with fair curly hair Steve Sloane greeted us with a friendly smile and introduced himself and five year old Stephanie, his eldest daughter. Tall for her age Stephanie was a skinny little girl with very long blonde hair. She was wearing a chunky purple fleece and her long legs clad in black leggings disappeared into a large pair of muddy wellies. Having met us she ran into their house shouting.

'Come and see Jess and Sam!' Within seconds she reappeared with her three year old sister Georgia a gorgeous petite little girl who smiled at us shyly from beneath a mass of blonde curls. The children took to each other immediately. Stephanie and Georgia held hands with Jess and took her to see the horses in the stables – Sam followed happily. Steve called his wife who within minutes appeared at the door wearing a dressing gown and a towel wrapped round her head. She was carrying their youngest child Lizzy, another blonde beauty who looked about 9 months old.

'I was in the shower' she smiled 'I'm Diane, pleased to meet you!'

Laughing and talking excitedly the children returned. When Stephanie and Georgia caught sight of Diane they ran to her shouting.

'Look Mummy, this is Jess and Sam.'

'Well, hello Jess and Sam!' said Diane. 'Would you like to stay and play for a while?' That day was the start of a long friendship between the five children. At weekends and during school holidays Jess and Sam frequently spent hours on end round at Shiloh Farm. This was a godsend for Alan and me enabling us to get on with renovation work without feeling guilty about not giving the children enough time and attention. Steve and Diane were happy with the arrangement too as Jess and Sam kept their three children occupied and being at their house meant that Lizzy was not left out.

As the weeks passed by I got used to doing the school run each day and when we reached Scouthead and turned into Doctor Lane I began to feel that we were going home. Driving up the hill we passed Doctor House Farm on our right. The first time that Jess and Sam saw the farmer he was walking along the pavement beside his farm. They were horrified when they noticed his shiny steel prosthetic hook glinting in the sunshine.

'It's Captain Hook!' exclaimed Sam in a hoarse whisper his eyes on stalks.

'It's Gerald Collins!' I said. 'He got his arm caught in a hay baling machine when he was a young man and…' Jess clamped her hands over her ears and refused to listen to any further information.

At that time Gerald Collins was a very active man in his late sixties. He and his brother owned and worked a substantial acreage of the land in the Scouthead area of Saddleworth the quality of which was renowned. They spread, harrowed, rolled, cut and baled the grass which grew long and lush and was the envy of many. Gerald was well known in the area as he sold hay, haylage and straw and also cut and baled for other people. He was a likeable character with a reputation not only for being hard working but also for being extremely careful with his money! Over the next few years we were to find Gerald helpful and courteous – if somewhat prone to relating long drawn out reminiscences of his early life.

The move to Jericho had been overshadowed from the start by the increasingly worrying condition of Alan's father. He had been unwell and losing weight since the beginning of the year and early in June he was diagnosed with inoperable cancer. The prognosis was about one year. The huge amount of work that we were involved in at Jericho to some extent helped to keep Alan's mind off the situation. Naturally, however the nagging sadness at the prospect of losing his father and the worry about how his mother was going to cope was always at the back of his mind.

By the middle of June the electricians had almost finished rewiring the house so I made arrangements for our furniture to be taken out of storage and brought up to the farm.

I washed all the paintwork and floors in the back room downstairs and in the big bedroom upstairs in preparation for the arrival of the furniture. These two rooms were chosen partly because they were both relatively clean and tidy and also because both of them had the luxury of an electric storage heater.

To give us more space in the back room we decided to move the big wooden cupboards and put them along the other side of the same wall in the dining room to store tools and such like. In addition to which one of the long open shelves provided a safe location for the two gerbil tanks with their numerous occupants. Apart from the big cupboards, a plastic bucket, some stepladders and a few lengths of timber that were leant up against the wall, the room was empty. Sam took full advantage of this and rode his small trike round and round at breakneck speed regarding the room as an indoor play area rather than a grubby and unwelcoming dining room.

To help prevent anything from getting damp until we were ready to bring it all into the house. I swept out the barn again and we put down some pallets for the storage boxes and furniture to stand on. All our furniture and boxes were brought up to Jericho in four loads. We put all the beds and chests of drawers in the big bedroom. The sofa and chairs and big TV we put in the back room. That night we slept in our beds for the first time in over four weeks.

At the weekend we plumbed the washing machine into the dairy and I put a wash through. It soon became apparent that we had a major problem with the drains. We found two areas of raw sewage, one at the back of the house and the other emerging from an inspection chamber about five yards away from the septic tank at the top of the lane.

Two men from the council arrived mid-week to sort out the sewage problem. They cleared the blockages which I'd told them about, but evidently didn't check to see if there were any more; in fact they couldn't get away quick enough! I discovered a few minutes after they'd gone that there was another blockage right at the entrance to the septic tank. The newly released build-up of raw sewage now flowed freely through the pipes but was unable to continue into the septic tank and was therefore shooting through a gap between two old clay pipes straight into the garden, creating a grotesque garden pond. I had to work quickly with a stick to free the blockage and was very close to having raw sewage flood over the top of my wellies. Most unpleasant!

Now we were well into June the weather had warmed up and the grass beside the house was getting very long and looked untidy – as did the rest of the garden. We bought a rotary petrol lawn mower and whenever we had time and the weather allowed we cut the grass and tried to keep up with it throughout the summer.

At the end of the month Cath, Jim and Katy came up for a 'demolishing the old hen hut party'. There was nothing Jim enjoyed more than having an excuse to get stuck into some serious demolition. He was a big man and armed with a sledgehammer he made short work of flattening the large dilapidated hut which filled the space between the shippon and the stone wall at the back of the house. Alan rived the wooden cladding off the timber frames with a crow bar and claw hammer and between them the hen hut was soon reduced to a large and smelly pile of firewood. At the bottom of the field behind the house we made a bonfire out of the biggest pieces of timber and panels of wood from off the roof. With constant warnings about rusty nails and splinters we all gathered up the remaining smaller pieces of wood and took it down to the end of the house where Alan put his boy-scout skills to good use and made a smaller bonfire. Because it was so windy he was concerned that the fire might get too big and out of control. So we were instructed to deposit the armfuls of wood into piles according to size from which Alan fed the fire.

Cath and I left them to it while we went inside to take the jacket potatoes out of the Aga, and heat up the chilli which I'd made the day before. Cath made a big bowl of salad and we piled all the food and plates onto two trays and went back outside to join the others by the small bonfire. I carried out the chilli and potatoes and Cath followed with the plates, chunks of bread and the bowl of salad. As she came through the shippon doorway a gust of wind snatched the lettuce out of the bowl and we watched it disappear over the wall and into the field.

'I didn't want lettuce anyway' Sam said, helping himself to a chunk of bread.

Progress

The rest of June and July were spent mainly working on the children's rooms. I worked practically every day rubbing down window frames, revealing and mortaring up the sides of stone mullions and stripping walls and ceilings. Alan worked after school most evenings and at weekends putting down floors, boxing in pipes and making the new partition wall between Sam's bedroom and the bathroom.

I had left it as late as I dared to extricate the male baby gerbils from Triska's new litter. We now had a third tank full of the wretched things!

As well as working in the children's bedrooms I started revealing the dining room beams. They were boxed in with plasterboard, which was plastered over. I levered off the plasterboard with a crow bar. Once I'd got some of it off the rest was not too difficult to remove but it was absolutely filthy. Dust and muck dropped in my eyes and down my neck. When all the boarding was off I was left with two beams covered in a dark treacly stain and peppered with dozens of nails, which try as I might I couldn't get out. Alan managed to pull most of the nails out and those he couldn't get out he hammered in. The next job was sanding. Even though I wore a dust mask and a woolly hat the thick sticky dust filled my hair, eyes and ears. All the hard work was worthwhile however when eventually the rich warm colour of old pine emerged as the dark stain was sanded off. The beams looked old and strong and felt smooth to the touch.

Sanding had revealed some evidence of previous woodworm infestation so I coated the beams with a woodworm treatment. Brushing the thin liquid generously onto the beams while balancing on a stepladder was tricky, because despite wearing rubber gloves I couldn't stop the caustic liquid running down the brush handle and covering my hand from where it persistently crept past the glove and down my arm. Having thoroughly brushed every surface of one beam my right arm was beginning to burn unbearably. I doused it with cold water, wrapped it in a wet towel and treated the second beam determined to get the job done. By the time I'd finished my arm was bright red and swollen. It took several days for it to get back to normal.

Both sides of the new dividing wall upstairs and some of the walls in Jess's bedroom all needed plastering. Thanks to the leaking copper pipes most of the dining room ceiling needed boarding and plastering too. Alan felt he was not skilled enough at plastering to tackle such a big job so we enlisted the help of Rob Jones, my friend Julie's brother-in-law who over the next two weeks did it all for us. Off-loading some of the work onto somebody else for a change gave us a welcome break and it was a real boost when the plastering was all done and everywhere started to look so much better.

At the beginning of July the BMW broke down – it had driven faultlessly throughout the day but when Alan wanted to go out in the evening the car was completely dead and he was plunged into a state of mourning. The main dealers informed him that he would need a new Electric Control Unit to rectify the problem and that it would cost in excess of £300. So the car remained where it was in front of the house until he could find a cheaper one from somewhere else.

All the following week I taxied Alan to work and the children to school and fetched them all back home again at different times! Alan mentioned our car problem to his mum and dad and they rang us later in the week offering us his mum's old VW Polo. They said they no longer needed two cars. If they went anywhere by car they tended to use his dad's Toyota. We appreciated the offer and made arrangements to collect both the Polo and the little wood burning stove which they had bought for us as a house warming present – quite literally.

Our parents lived in Ilkley. At the weekend we went over there in the Land Rover. We hitched up our little trailer which we had left at my mum's a month or so before then we collected the wood burning stove and various pieces of timber and tools from Alan's mum and dad. We stayed for a while and then set off home. Alan took the children in the Polo and I drove the Land Rover towing the trailer. Everything was fine until we stopped to put petrol in the Polo after which it refused to restart. Twice we pushed it off and twice it petered out after about half a mile. I couldn't tow it because I was already towing the trailer so I had to leave Alan and the children with the car while I drove back to Jericho. I unhitched the trailer and then returned to where they were waiting. Then we towed the Polo home. What a performance!

Fortunately the problem with the car was only a minor one and Alan was able to sort it out the following day.

The school holidays began in the last week of July. Sam stayed with Mum for a few days while Jess went to Brownie Camp. While they were both away we worked flat out trying to get as much done as possible.

As is often the case when renovating old properties, the walls inside Jericho were invariably not absolutely vertical and floors were often not level. Added to that where the efforts of previous occupants with little or no expertise - particularly in joinery - had to be improved upon or ripped out altogether or if things were particularly difficult or when he was tired Alan soon lost his patience. At such times he would often roar with rage when things went wrong or hammer an offending nail into a piece of wood with far more force than was necessary sending the dogs scuttling to their beds trembling with uncertainty. His bad temper in these situations annoyed me intensely.

It was a beautiful sunny day when I drove over to Ilkley to fetch Sam and spend some time with my mum and I enjoyed the break.

Next day we ripped out the fireplace in the dining room and took the artificial stone outside. The purple plywood soon followed. It looked a lot better without it but we were disappointed not to have found an old stone fireplace behind it. Alan and Rob discussed what to do. They had discovered that further up the wall there was a lintel. They decided to knock out the brick wall below it, open it up and then brick round and plaster over to create a fairly large but shallow space to house the wood burning stove. Carefully, Alan removed a few bricks from below the lintel and had given the remaining wall a few swipes with a sledgehammer when I called to them that I had made a brew. The men came into the kitchen for a break. Sam asked if he could have a go with the sledgehammer. As he thought he'd barely be able to lift it let alone hit the wall with it Alan said he could. Over the next few minutes we heard Sam bashing at the wall. Suddenly there was an almighty crash. We all looked at each other then hurried into the dining room. Sledgehammer in hand and covered in soot Sam emerged from a cloud of thick black dust grinning triumphantly. In front of the fireplace there were bricks all over the floor. He had demolished the wall completely!

Later in the week Rob re-plastered the chimney breast and the recess around the flue. Two heavy hearthstones were set in place and the new fireplace was finished. A few days later Alan stood the wood burner in position.

The following week I took Jess over to Ilkley. It was her turn to stay for a few days with my mum. We promised that her bedroom would be finished when she came home. One afternoon when I was rubbing down the woodwork in her bedroom Alan took a few hours off to watch a football match on TV. When I had finished I took Sam to Oldham in the car to buy him some new trainers. As we drove home up Shiloh Lane we could see the Land Rover in the distance parked next to the wall by the field near the house. I thought Alan was sitting in the driver's seat wearing a red t-shirt.

'The football must have finished, I wonder what your dad's doing in the Land Rover.' I commented. As we got closer I thought it was just the sun reflecting on the windscreen. Then as we drove past Greenleach Farm I realised with horror that the Land Rover was on fire! I pulled up in front of the house, jumped out of the car and hurriedly guided Sam into the kitchen. 'Alan we're on fire!' I shrieked. 'It's OK Sam don't panic!' I said panicking. Alan appeared bleary eyed having fallen asleep in front of the telly.

'What?'

'The Land Rover's on fire! Call the fire brigade!' I shouted. I really wasn't coping well with this latest crisis. Alan ran outside to look, then came back in and dialled 999. All we could do was wait for the fire brigade to come. After ten minutes or so the fire engine came into view. We watched with dismay as it went the wrong way after The Roebuck and had to reverse along Two Acre Lane. Standing in front of the yellow barn doors we waved our arms frantically to attract their attention. When the firemen finally arrived they coped quickly and competently with the blaze and soon put it out, stating quite definitely that it was an electrical fault as the windscreen wiper motor had been running as they had put the fire out. What a mess! I was devastated.

The rest of the week I spent wallpapering and painting in Jess's bedroom. Alan tiled the windowsill. On Sunday morning we laid the carpet we'd bought. As it was such a small room we'd been lucky and had managed to get a good quality 100% wool off cut. In the afternoon we went over to Ilkley, picked up Jess and spent a few hours with my mum and Alan's mum and dad before returning home to show Jess her finished room. She loved it.

There were three weeks left of the school holiday. During that time the back of the dining room fireplace was tiled; a new bath was fitted in the bathroom; the dividing wall in Sam's bedroom was fitted with shelving and I made a start on decorating his room.

The loss assessor from the insurance company came to look at the Land Rover – and wrote it off. Alan's brother Gary was interested in restoring it. We were in two minds whether or not to restore it ourselves but ultimately decided that we had enough to do and agreed to let him have it if he could collect it. Until then it would just have to stay where it was.

The bathroom was receiving more of our attention now. Alan clad the rough uneven ceiling with pine and boxed in the bath to match. When I had papered and painted the walls Alan made a start on the tiling. It was beginning to look clean and bright. While we were doing all this Jess and Sam were spending a lot of time at Shiloh Farm and Jess was developing an interest in horses.

By the end of the month we had fitted a carpet in Sam's bedroom. It was an L shaped room and we managed to cut and fit a reasonable piece of carpet from one which we'd brought with us from the house in Uppermill. Sam was in his own room at last. He was delighted. So were we, it had been four months since we'd had a bedroom to ourselves!

The fields at Jericho had not been grazed for years. They were overgrown and difficult to walk through because the grass had grown in thick tufts. We weren't sure what to do with them. We were going to ask Bill Dawson at Two Acre Farm to cut them for us until Steve Sloane suggested that his horses could eat them down instead, which would benefit him as well as us. He said that he and Carl, the young man who rode and looked after their horses, would fence behind the house to keep the horses safely in the fields. In return for the free grazing which not only fed and exercised his horses but also rested his own fields, he would arrange for Carl to give Jess and Sam riding lessons each week on Dolly their small pony.

All summer we left two camping chairs outside the kitchen door to flop into and soak up some sunshine whilst enjoying a brew between jobs. Every so often, seduced outside by the warmth, Peanut would lie on the flags beside us. Kim would take up her favourite position beneath the Laburnum tree, apparently asleep, but always keeping a watchful eye on us.

Alan managed to buy and fit a new E.C. unit for the BMW at a fraction of the cost that he would have been charged by the Main Dealers.

When Alan returned to school at the beginning of September the pace of work at Jericho slowed down. The first term of a new year is always particularly busy and Alan was no longer able to work on the house in the evenings due to the volume of schoolwork or sheer tiredness. He did what he could, mostly at weekends. Until the next school break the majority of the work in the house was done by me. When I had finished decorating the bathroom I stripped the wallpaper off the walls in our bedroom and then started work on the landing.

Despite all the space we had outside the house I still managed to give the Polo an almighty clout on the Land Rover bumper, denting the back wing badly as I swung the car round to the front of the house in preparation for taking the children to school. Sarcastic remarks from Alan like 'Isn't there enough room? Maybe you should park in the field!' didn't help.

Early in the morning on Saturday 17th September Alan received an urgent phone call and immediately drove to Ilkley. His father died that evening. He spent the next day in Ilkley with his family. Jess and Sam were stunned and upset at the loss of their Grandad.

Steve and Carl had already made a start on the fencing behind the house. That weekend they finished the job after which they walked their horses up to Jericho and turned them out in our fields.

Whether I worked inside or outside Kim was my constant companion. She curled up in the corner of the room when I worked upstairs or joined Peanut by the Aga when I worked downstairs. Outside she was in heaven whether she played with a ball in the garden or bounded tirelessly over the fields. She loved living up here and on the occasions when we were on our own on dark and dismal days I felt quite safe in the knowledge that she was always close by.

That September Jess and Sam had their first riding lesson with Carl, the first of many and Jess took to it like a duck to water. We also had our first introduction to show jumping. We went to watch Carl who competed on Steve and Diane's horses at Birchinley Manor (an equestrian centre near Milnrow) on Thursday evenings.

The first week of October brought a change in the weather from heavy rain and damp enveloping mist to ice and freezing temperatures. The second week continued to be very cold but we were treated to a few days of beautiful sunshine.

The little wood-burning stove was a great success. It had to be fed rather frequently with wood throughout the evening, but it kept the room comfortably warm. We found that if we banked it up with anthracite late in the evening and shut it up tight we could keep it in until morning, a luxury which we enjoyed at weekends. I found a pine furniture manufacturer in Oldham where I could bag up pine off-cuts. I tried to visit the place twice a week to keep us stocked up over winter.

It was around this time that Alan bought a white Land Rover Station Wagon. Usually we discussed this sort of large purchase and took our time over it. This, however, was an uncharacteristic impulsive decision. We went over to Bury in the Polo and Alan drove the Land Rover home. It looked really good from a distance but on closer inspection I had serious doubts. The fact that the top half of the passenger door was fastened to the bottom half with a sturdy rubber band did nothing to increase my confidence!

By the time winter set in Peanut's back and hind legs were practically bald and she only ventured outside when absolutely necessary. The rest of the time she lay against the Aga like a giant fridge magnet.

A lot of old timber had accumulated outside due to the removal of old floorboards, door-frames and doors etc. which we had replaced. All that, together with a few no longer needed pallets made a very impressive bonfire. We invited neighbours and friends old and new to spend bonfire night with us. Cath, Jim and Katy came of course so did Julie and Pete Jones with their children Lauren and William who were school friends of Jess and Sam. Other neighbours from Uppermill came and so did the Sloanes. Everyone brought some fireworks. I made yet another pan of chilli with some jacket potatoes and we borrowed the Sloanes' barbeque. To our relief the weather stayed dry and not windy. A very enjoyable evening – and we got rid of all the rubbish.

Throughout November I continued to strip and sand the five doorframes on the landing. It took me ages. I also painted our bedroom walls to brighten up the room until we had time to sort it out properly.

Throughout December we concentrated on the dining room. I stripped and sanded even more doorframes – I was becoming quite proficient at it by this time! The walls were flaky and uneven in places so Alan patched them here and there with plaster. I sanded whole walls before painting them and the ceilings between the beams. Alan completely replaced the old skirting boards and I lightly stained and oiled the new ones and all the doorframes. I treated the old beams with a nourishing coat of linseed oil – they absorbed it faster than I could brush it on – so I gave them a second coat, which left them with a rich sheen. I strung some cord across them and hung up our Christmas cards.

The two big window frames in the dining room were completely rotten. Back in October we had placed an order with a joiner in Uppermill for two new frames with double glazed units. They were ready for collection the week before Christmas. Alan and the children had just broken up from school for the Christmas holidays so they picked them up on their way home and I treated them with preservative. The weather that week was bright, cold and dry so we took advantage of the fact and decided to fit the new window frames. With my help Alan managed to take out both of the old ones, fasten in the new frames and put in the glazed units before dark. Next day I spent time with Jess and Sam and was kept busy with Christmas jobs while Alan gave the outside of the window frames a coat of paint.

What with one thing and another it was 2.30am on Christmas morning by the time I'd finished wrapping the children's presents and prepared most of the Christmas dinner. Our first Christmas Day at Jericho was a well deserved holiday. We had a relaxing family day, opening presents, eating far too much and playing endless games of monopoly.

On Boxing Day we went over to Pat and John's for the usual family get-together. A lovely day but I felt ill - very unusual for me. Next day Jess too was unwell. We stayed in the warm and watched 'Mrs. Doubtfire' on TV.

On New Year's Eve we decided to pay a visit to the Pike View Animal Shelter which was only a couple of miles away, with the intention of buying two kittens for the children. It hadn't occurred to me at the time that it was the wrong time of year for kittens to be born. However the man at the Shelter assured me that they would almost certainly have some by March.

I glanced at the car. The children's faces were pressed against the windows waiting for me to beckon them over; they were going to be so disappointed. Just then a black puppy with a small white patch on her chest trotted out of a shed into a run next to where we were talking. It was love at first sight.

'How old is she?' I heard myself ask.

'Six months.' he said. 'She hasn't been badly treated. The previous owner decided he couldn't keep her or her sister anymore, so he brought them both here. Her sister was re-homed last week so this one's a bit lonely. She's a Lurcher, a Whippet cross.'

'Can I have a closer look?'

Next minute the gorgeous, wriggling puppy was in my arms licking my face. I carried her to the car. 'Sorry, no kittens I'm afraid – but there's this puppy!' Jess and Sam immediately jumped out of the car and stroked her.

'Can we have her?' Jess asked. I looked at Alan who was sitting with his forehead on the steering wheel muttering something under his breath.

'I think that's a yes.' I laughed.

We bought her, took her home and called her 'Maggie'.

1995

Whenever the weather allowed Jess rode Dolly. Despite the fact that Dolly was a stubborn and lazy little pony Jess nevertheless was learning the basics of riding, and Carl was pleased with her progress. We were getting used to living in a generally windy environment, but it wasn't until the second week in January that we had a taste of the incredible strength of the gale force winds which frequently hammered Jericho during the winter months.

After an exceptionally windy night we woke up to a gale the force of which we had never experienced before. The trees were bowing down under the strain and the massive electricity pylon in the neighbouring field was groaning and whining as the cables threatened to break free. Anything not fastened down simply blew away. We set off to school. The children struggled to stay on their feet as we went out of the door. Once safely in the car we realized that the little bike shed had been torn off its base and blown over the wall where it stood at a crazy angle upside down about 10 yards away from the wall in Norman's field. The base of the hut remained on the ground with the two bikes, but the various footballs and other toys were nowhere to be seen.

The friendship between our children and the Sloane girls, inevitably led to many chats with Steve and Diane. The subject of our intention to start a boarding kennel business came up in conversation several times. Diane, never slow to express her opinion, thought that it would be a much better idea, less work and less tying to have a livery yard instead. I argued that I was experienced with, and knowledgeable about dogs and comfortable with handling them. The only dealings I'd had with horses, was occasionally tacking up Dolly for Jess and Sam's riding lessons!

Alan and I discussed at length the pros and cons of both businesses. Points *for* having kennels were not an issue but the points against had to be considered:

There was already a boarding kennel establishment less than a mile away.

Kennels at times would be noisy and would always be very tying.

Having a livery yard would mean that the children could be involved with riding. Having kennels would not involve them at all.

A DIY livery yard would in theory, provide a steady income from the stable rent with only a small amount of horse care. Although I was certain it would not bring in anything like as much income as a boarding kennel business would.

We had enough land for a small livery yard – more than we needed for kennels.

There were a lot of horse riders in the area, so we would have no problem filling stables.

We had close, easy access to bridle paths.

I would soon learn how to handle and look after horses, and Diane and Steve were only next-door if I needed help or advice.

However, a livery yard would mean we would have to learn how to manage the land. We would need a tractor and trailer to enable us to get rid of the muckheap regularly.

All these things and more went round and round in my head. As time went by I felt that my boarding kennel dream, so close to becoming a reality, was slipping away. Undoubtedly we were being inclined towards horses because of the Sloanes - but was it really our best option? We were unsure what to do.

January continued to be a very cold month carried along by icy winds. We got used to waking up to ice on the inside of the bedroom windows. I spent most of my time doing 'finishing off' jobs all over the house. The last two weeks of January were incredibly cold with ice, sleet and gale force winds. I worked indoors preparing surfaces for re-painting. It was too cold to have the windows open and working in such a dusty environment ultimately affected my chest which felt very tight and painful. I made a rare visit to the doctor who prescribed an inhaler - which was neither use nor ornament.

Snow fell heavily on the last few days of the month and I kept Jess and Sam off school. Alan got the Land Rover stuck in a snow drift at the bottom of the lane and had to walk to school and home again in the evening.

On the 31st January it was Jessica's 10th birthday. I made her a horse's head birthday cake.

The Shetlands

Steve insisted that we would soon learn how to look after horses; all we needed was practice. He had two Shetland Ponies and he suggested that we borrow them and Dolly and look after them for a month to see how we got on. Jess and Sam were very excited. I wasn't sure who was doing who the favour! We agreed, but told him that we needed a couple of weeks to prepare for them.

At the back of the house past the shippon was a large outbuilding which backed on to the barn, ideal we thought as a stable. Although the roof timbers were sagging under the weight of the stone slates they were not about to fall in. The original access door had been roughly bricked up and the present access was through a narrow door inside the barn. The first job was to knock out the brickwork in the original doorway. The building was of course full of muck and old bedding which had to be shifted. According to Bill Dawson at Two Acre Farm, geese had been kept in there. It took all weekend to empty it and sweep it clean. Dianna and Matthew came over and gave us a hand.

At the front of the house about 15 feet away from the yellow barn doors was a wired enclosure. It measured approximately 30 feet by

50 feet, and had previously been used as a goat pen. Alan made a new gate for it and we re-enforced two or three posts to make the enclosure secure enough to contain the three ponies.

As a late treat for Jess's birthday we collected Lauren and William in the Land Rover and took the four children to the swimming pool at Barnsley Metrodome. They thoroughly enjoyed it and to finish off the outing we intended to have our tea at Compo's fish and chip restaurant in Holmfirth. Not far from Holmfirth however, the Land Rover began to make unnerving, loud clunking noises. There was a loud bang and we ground to a halt. Alan and I got out. Alan lifted the bonnet and we stared hopelessly at the engine, he pushed and tweaked at various engine parts but couldn't see anything obviously wrong. I tried to start the engine again, but it was completely dead. In desperation we rang Pete and Julie. Pete was a member of National Breakdown. He rang them and made out that it was he and Julie who had broken down. He told them where we were, and gave us his membership number.

When the recovery vehicle arrived we pretended to be Pete and Julie. Pete also arrived and pretended to be Alan and took the children home. The Land Rover was winched onto the back of the recovery vehicle and Alan and I got into the cab with the driver. All the way home I was worried in case we called each other by our own names! Finally we arrived back at Pete and Julie's house. The Land Rover was deposited at the end of their road against a grass verge, and the helpful recovery man drove off. We apologised to the children who actually seemed to regard it all as a bit of an adventure, and we thanked Pete and Julie for their help, promising to remove the Land Rover as soon as possible.

On the Sunday Alan worked on the stable doorway. In the afternoon Jess helped him to hang the new stable door which he'd made. The following week I transferred the insurance cover from the Land Rover to the BMW which had been taken off the road for the winter.

Steve brought up some bales of straw to bed down the ponies. Soon after he helped Alan and the children lead them from Shiloh Farm to their new stable – there was plenty of room for them all. It snowed again overnight so the ponies stayed in the stable most of the next day. We turned them out into the enclosure to stretch their legs about four o'clock while we mucked out, after which we took them back to the stable. Jess led Dolly, Alan took one Shetland and I led the other. Shetland Ponies are deceptively strong and these two were no exception. They were almost identical in appearance but very different in character. One had been broken, could be ridden and was quite well mannered. The other was a thug. Unfortunately at first we could not tell them apart. That evening unwittingly I had taken hold of the thug. As Dolly and the other Shetland disappeared from view round the back of the house, my Shetland broke into a brisk trot in a bid to catch up. I was taken by surprise. Foolishly I had wrapped the lead rope round my hand. The pony bolted toward the stable door but there wasn't enough room for both of us to get through the doorway together – unable to free my hand quickly enough from the lead rope I hit the wall and spun into the stable cutting my face in two places!

The daily mucking out and regular handling of the ponies soon enabled us to distinguish between the two Shetlands. During the February half term we collected the ponies' tack from Steve. Several times that week we clipped a lead rope onto the bridle of the well mannered Shetland and Sam rode him while Jess rode Dolly.

Appalling weather - snow, sleet, heavy rain and gale force winds beset the rest of February. After much deliberation Alan and I decided to go with the idea of a livery yard instead of boarding kennels. The first step was to plan exactly where we would situate the stable yard on our land. The next was to design the stable block. Diane and Steve introduced us to a local man, who was not only involved with horses but also owned a business that produced stables, barns, field shelters and fencing. We discussed our ideas with him and he agreed to build whatever design we came up with once the Planning Office had approved the plans.

Throughout February the Aga had been giving off strong fumes and despite regular daily riddling and removal of the ash it had gone out on numerous occasions.

By the time the ponies had been with us for two weeks I had become used to dealing with them along with my other chores. One morning after I'd taken the children to school I put the ponies in the enclosure, and then mucked out their stable. I left them out while I went to the wood yard to stock up with wood for the stove, then I got on with jobs in the house. The weather deteriorated so I decided to bring them in before fetching the children from school. I went into the enclosure, put Dolly's head collar on her and led her to the stable. Returning to the enclosure I approached the nearest Shetland and began to put on his head collar. The other one – the thug – came up behind me with his ears back and sank his teeth into my arm. I screamed out in pain and he trotted off. I was wearing a thick jacket and thankfully his teeth hadn't broken the skin but it still hurt! Too late I remembered what Carl had said.

'Don't turn your back on the little buggers. If ever they bite or kick you – kick them back!' The injustice of having been bitten when I was bringing them in out of the bad weather infuriated me. I walked over to the unsuspecting pony and gave it a good hard kick then ran back to the other Shetland, grabbed the lead rope and took him to the stable.

On my return the thug stood still while I put the head collar on him and walked quietly beside me all the way back to the stable where he joined the others. I was well chuffed.

The indoor job that took up most of my time now was plan drawing. We had decided how much space we could allocate to the stable yard and also the design of it. There were to be eight stables each one with its own tack room accessible from inside the stable. A barn was to be positioned in the middle of the block to store hay and bedding. Diane and Steve agreed that it was an excellent idea to have individual tack rooms, as in their experience one of the main causes of arguments on a livery yard arose from items of tack or equipment going missing from one that was shared. Scale drawings of the floor plan, front, side and rear elevations had to be drawn up and copies of each submitted to the Planning Office in Oldham. Before going to university I had worked as a plan drawer and tracer for a fire insurance company in Leeds, an experience that now proved very useful. I finished all the plans and got them copied and despatched to the Planning Office by the first week in March.

Heavy snow fell repeatedly throughout March but never settled for long. In between we enjoyed some beautiful sunny days.

All the perimeter walls had to be checked for old barbed wire fencing and wire netting which had long since become rusted and brittle and lay stubbornly tangled beneath several consecutive years of new summer grass. We spent hours with pliers and crowbars pulling out yard upon yard of tangled wire and turf, cutting our hands and tearing our clothes in the process. By the time we were satisfied that we'd pulled it all out, we had created a tangled mound of sharp and rusty wire the size of a small car on the bank behind the house.

Fencing also was a seemingly endless task at this time added to which we had gates to hang and walls to mend. Once the field to the left of the one with the hollows was completely free of old wire, re-fenced and made secure with a gate we transferred Dolly and the two Shetlands into it. Now that the weather was improving they could stay out all day and some nights too.

Snow, sunshine, mist and drizzle were thrown at us during the last week of March and beginning of April. Jess struggled with a nasty dose of flu. Feeling shivery and weak she spent most of the week cuddled up on the sofa under her duvet, sleeping or watching TV. Thankfully Sam managed to avoid catching the flu. It was his seventh birthday on the 6th April and although the Aga continued to misbehave, barely reaching cooking temperature, I managed to stoke it up enough to make him a birthday cake by the time he came home from school.

Physically, Sam could best be described as being neat. He had a neat little face with dark hair and grey eyes and a well proportioned lean little body. From being very young he had always preferred to play outside and his skin tanned easily. Although he had several friends he had always been happy in his own company and could make his own entertainment. He was a quiet, sensitive little boy with a strong affection for his family.

Sam had enjoyed Bonfire Night in November so much that we thought a bonfire birthday party would be a nice idea, and a good way to get rid of even more unwanted old wood. I had managed to buy another box of fireworks, a rocket and a few packets of sparklers at the end of November and had put them away until now. We made a good sized bonfire with what remained of the roof and four sides of the bike hut which had been smashed to bits by the January gales and also from several pallets which we no longer needed now that the rest of the furniture and boxes had been brought into the house.

    The Sloane girls and Katy were invited, along with 10 boys from Sam's class at school. Before we lit the fire the boys ran, fought and chased each other all over the garden and in the field behind the house. By the time we lit the bonfire they had tired themselves out and were happy to tuck into hot dogs, jacket potatoes and drinks of pop as they watched the fireworks. It was a great success.

The first week of the Easter holiday coincided with beautiful dry, sunny weather. Outdoor jobs took precedent. Alan spent some time tidying up the antiquated septic tank. He pulled out the nettles, which had grown through the mortar, and re pointed it. Then he laid three new sections of clay pipe at the entrance to the tank. It was only a temporary measure, before long the whole thing would have to be replaced.

    The gutters at the back of the house leaked like a watering can whenever we had heavy rain. They were completely rotten. We pulled them down and bought new wooden ones to replace them. At least with the dairy and shippon roofs being immediately underneath, we could work without ladders. While I treated the insides of the new ones with an appropriate sealant and the outsides with preservative, undercoat and gloss paint, Alan pointed up the stone and set in new hangers for the gutters to rest on. They were heavy to manoeuvre but once positioned on the hangers it wasn't too bad and we covered the joints with lead to make them watertight. They looked loads better when we'd finished – and they didn't leak.

    The next job was to discover what we could do about the water which cascaded over the wall behind the house after days of heavy rain. After one particularly heavy downpour lasting most of the day, we found that the area at the back of the house had flooded and formed a sizeable pond. Once the rain stopped the water soon dispersed, so we decided to investigate. About 18 inches up from the bottom of the wall there was a square hole about six inches across. It looked as if that was the intended outlet for the water that at the moment was bubbling out of the grass about four or five feet back from the top of the wall. Alan decided to dig around the area carefully to see if he could find the underground spring. After a while he found it, two or three feet under the surface. A stone had become dislodged, probably due to the force of the rushing water, blocking the proper water course and forcing it to escape up through the grass and down over the wall. He removed the stone and poured water into the space that it left to check if it came out through the square hole in the wall – it did – so, very pleased with himself, he repositioned it, wedged it firmly and backfilled above it with soil and turf.

We still had to find out where the water was supposed to go once it had come out of the hole in the wall. The whole area was overgrown. When we had cut the grass down and cleared the area with a spade a very large slab of stone was revealed which I thought closely resembled a gravestone – I didn't dwell on that thought! Between that and the wall was a space where the spring water flowed. However, it couldn't cope with the volume of water which gushed down after very heavy rain and consequently resulted in a flood. This suggested that there was yet another blockage. Alan managed to lever up one side of the massive flagstone. I forced a brick under it. He levered it up higher, another brick went under - we carried on until we were able to grasp the stone and heave it upright. Having braced it with sturdy wooden posts we investigated what lay beneath. We were intrigued to discover a circular brick chamber, two feet six inches across resembling a small well. It was full of sludge. At one side we could just see the curved top half of a horizontal clay pipe which disappeared beneath the ground towards the gable end of the house. Evidently this took the spring water elsewhere. We went round to the little stream, which erupted from under the ground near the edge of the pony enclosure at the front of the house and realised that it was fed almost definitely from the spring behind the house. The silt and sludge that had been carried down with the spring water over a number of years had gradually filled up the chamber, which evidently had been built for that reason, and it now needed dredging.

I lay on the ground, put one arm down the clay pipe and cleared stones and debris from inside it for as far as I could reach. We ladled the sludge out of the chamber with a couple of buckets. It was very heavy and very messy and Sam got completely covered in it. Once we'd emptied the chamber Alan lowered Sam into it to check the depth – evidently a man thing - it was about three feet deep. Having cleaned it out we felt confident that we had solved the flooding problem, but just to make sure Alan fastened together the dozen rodding poles which we'd found in the shippon, and gave it a good prodding. That done we managed with some difficulty to lower the big stone back into position.

On the last day of the Easter holidays as it was such a gorgeous sunny day Alan and I decided to shift the muck heap which had accumulated at the bottom of the field. We borrowed Steve's tractor and trailer and laboriously forked the muck onto the trailer and made numerous trips to another spot at the very top of the backfield where it could stay and rot down before being spread next winter. Late that afternoon Alan's brother, Gary and his wife Jen came over to collect the old blue Land Rover. They stayed for an hour or so, and then Gary drove it home. I had some misgivings about that.

Next morning we woke up to a totally different day. We got up early and carried on moving the muck up the fields. We forked three or four more loads onto the trailer and took them up to the ever-increasing heap in the top field. The ground was becoming churned up and the tractor wheels were beginning to slide. The driving rain and icy wind seemed to get right through to my bones. I began shivering uncontrollably and had to admit defeat and go back indoors. The job was abandoned for the time being.

The last week of April I spent in the toilet – not being ill but decorating. The following week I worked on the outside of the dining room windows and finished the bathroom door and doorframe. After that I started work on the landing – a big job which took the best part of three weeks to complete - stripping wallpaper, scrubbing walls, applying filler, painting, sanding and sealing woodwork.

Life at Jericho

Me with Thomas, Ben and Reuben

Jess and Alan leaning against a snowdrift at the back of the house.

Life at Jericho

"Alan lowered Sam into it to check the depth"

Working on the stairs and landing all day was a bit claustrophobic. It was always a nice break therefore, around midday to take the dogs out. I loved walking through the fields. When the weather was nice I would walk up to the top field, sit down on the grass and watch the dogs play. They chased each other tirelessly. Kim was fast and powerful but had no brakes. Maggie was fast too but slightly built like a whippet she could swerve and change direction very quickly. She had grown quite a lot over the past three months but would never be a big dog.

The view from our fields was impressive. We could see beyond Oldham, Rochdale and Manchester over the Cheshire plain to the cooling towers at Warrington and the observatory at Jodrell Bank. On a really clear day we could see the Welsh hills. I remember when I was about twelve sitting in a field with my Labrador beside me hoping that one day I would have a field of my own. As I looked around me I realised how lucky I was.

Whenever I walked the dogs through the fields I always made a point of looking out for Steve's heavily pregnant horse Melody, to check that she was OK. Sometimes Alan brought the children home from school and it was on one of those occasions that we had a worrying episode with Melody. I was still working upstairs when Alan and the children got home. Sam ran in and shouted upstairs to me.

'Mum! Melody's upside down! Dad says ring Steve!'

I stopped what I was doing and ran downstairs. As I got there Alan rushed into the kitchen and grabbed the phone. He told Steve that Melody was on her back with her legs straight up in the air. He had tried to encourage her to roll over onto her side, but she had seemed unable to move. The weight of her unborn foal appeared to have pinned her to the ground. Steve said he would come round right away. Jess explained that as they had driven up the lane towards the house they had seen what looked like a table upside down in the field – and then they had realized that it was Melody.

Steve and Carl arrived with two ropes. We all went up the field. They attached one rope to Melody's left hind leg and another to her left front leg then they walked over to her right side and pulled as hard as they could. At first they couldn't move her at all. She just lay there. I stroked her head and talked to her. They tried repeatedly to pull her onto her side. All of a sudden she seemed to realise what was happening and tried to get up. The men pushed against her to give her some support as she struggled shakily to her feet. Steve was anxious to take her back to Shiloh but decided to give her half an hour to recover. Carl stood with her and stroked her while Steve went to fetch a warm stable rug. When they had rugged her up they opened the gate and set off walking, one each side of her. We watched as they led her slowly back to Shiloh Farm.

By the end of May I had finished painting the landing. It looked bright and clean and more spacious and I was pleased with my efforts. The plans for the stables were passed and Melody gave birth to a beautiful colt foal which they called 'Robbie'.

Alan spent the Spring Bank week working on the staircase putting new skirting boards up the sides. The existing skirtings were very bumped and battered and there were gaps in places which allowed horrendous draughts to blow through. The original stairs were stone and the wooden staircase had been fitted over the top. The stairs were not identical in size, which made fitting new skirting boards up the sides very tricky. He also fitted a proper wooden handrail to replace the old piece of rope, and clad the opposite side of the stairs with tongue and grooved pine. It was very time consuming and by the end of the week he was completely fed up with it. By midnight on Saturday we had hung the door at the bottom of the stairs, I had sealed all the wood and we were both completely shattered.

Whit Friday was a beautiful day. I went to Saddleworth Church with the children and watched the walks. In the evening we all went to Uppermill and listened to the bands.

Throughout April, May and June, Jess rode Dolly and had regular riding lessons with Carl. She was becoming a good little rider and was developing a genuine interest in horses and everything to do with them.

Our intention was to have the livery yard up and running by the end of September. We needed therefore to get stocked up with hay which could be bought straight off the field at this time of year at a relatively cheap price. Before we could do that we had to put a new floor in the hayloft. The existing joists were riddled with woodworm, so they had to be taken out and burnt. We managed to get hold of some reclaimed timbers that were a suitable replacement for the old joists and some 'oily boards' for the floor from an old mill in the process of being demolished somewhere in Manchester. We spent the last weekend in June stripping out the old floor and putting in the new one. It was one of the hardest jobs we'd tackled. The timbers were very heavy and most of them had nails in that needed to be removed before we could heave them into position. The oily tongue and grooved boards were filthy and rough and had to be cut to length and fitted tightly together. When the job was finished we swept the new floor thoroughly to ensure we'd left no nails. The loft was ready to store hay.

Now that the plans had been passed the next job was to prepare the area where the stables were to be built, dig it out and fill it with hardcore. We would then be able to get on with the concreting. Alan hired a local man to do the groundwork, his name was Mike. A short, stocky man with an alarming taste in Bermuda shorts, which he wore whatever the weather with a thick pair of socks and heavy work boots.

The stable at the back of the house was empty now that the three ponies were out in the fields all the time. We decided to alter it. It was much bigger than it needed to be for just one stable, so we decided to divide it in half and take three feet off the front creating a passage for access to both smaller stables. There would be room at the end of the passage to keep shavings forks and a feed bin. Each stable would measure 10 feet square – big enough to accommodate a pony quite comfortably.

In July Alan managed to enlist the help of three members of staff from school to help us unload a delivery of one hundred and fifty very heavy bales of new hay. Carrying them up the goat-chewed steps to the hayloft was really tricky. I stayed in the hayloft with one of the men and we stacked the bales while the other three men relayed them from the delivery wagon to the top of the steps.

The following day as I drove back home after taking the children to school, I decided to call in at the Pike View Animal Shelter to return the puppy collar that Maggie had outgrown. I'd had it in the front of the Land Rover for a week or so intending to drop it in. I don't know what made me take it that morning. I parked in the small car park. Nobody was about so I walked over to the office door. A couple of dogs came out to greet me, one was a large German Shepherd and the other was an elderly Border Collie who walked slowly towards me wagging his tail. He was very handsome despite being overweight and a bit scruffy. He leaned against me and looked up at me as I stroked him. I noticed that one side of his face was swollen. A woman came to the door. I gave her Maggie's collar and asked her about the old dog.

'Oh that's Pete, he'll probably spend the rest of his life here – nobody wants an old dog.'

'I do.' I thought. His eyes hardly left mine. The woman told me that Pete had been with them for less than a week and that the old farmer who he had belonged to had died. The person who had taken over the farm didn't want an old dog and had sent a young man who worked there to take the dog to be put down. The young man took pity on the gentle old dog and called at Pike View on route to the vet in the hope that they would take him. Thankfully they did.

Reluctantly I left Pete, assuring the woman that if at all possible I would give him a home and I would be in touch with her in about a week. Alan's sister Elaine, her husband Mick and their two daughters were booked into a campsite near one of the Saddleworth villages from that Friday intending to spend the next week with us. Although I was looking forward to seeing them, all I could think about was Pete and when I would be able to bring him home. There was no way I would be able to do that until after they had gone. Unable to get the old dog out of my mind, I rang Alan at lunchtime.

'Do you think having three dogs is excessive?' I asked. He hung up.

The following week we spent most of the time with Elaine, Mick and the girls. We showed them Jericho, took them to a local Pony Club show and gave the girls rides on Dolly. Mick was interested in canals so we showed them the canal which runs through Uppermill and the Portland Basin at Ashton-under-Lyne. We also took a trip out to Sowerby Bridge where a lot of work was being done there by members of the Huddersfield Canal Society who were renovating the canal basin and locks.

Alan had already started work on the alterations to the back stable. Mick gave him a hand during the week. Frequently, whenever we were on our own, I brought up the subject of Pete. Alan was very negative.

'We'd have vet's bills if we took on an old dog like that' he said. 'Kim and Maggie get on fine but having another dog might cause trouble' he added. 'Anyway, where would he sleep? You've already got two dog beds in the kitchen.'

I argued that if we didn't give Pete a home he would probably stay at Pike View for what was left of his life – surely he didn't want that on his conscience. I was certain Pete would be fine with the dogs and besides there was something special about him. I'd completely fallen for him and there was no way I was going to leave him at Pike View. By the time Elaine and Mick had gone home Alan was sick of hearing me wittering on about the old dog.

'If you want him so much you'd better go and get him!' He'd barely finished the sentence before I got in the car and went back to Pike View to pick him up. The staff there were delighted that I was offering a home to another of their dogs, particularly such an old one. They told me that he was having treatment for an infected tooth, hence the swollen face, and that he would need to see their vet again in a week's time. They had been told that he was 15 years old.

With a bit of help Pete got in the back of the car and lay down on the back seat quite happily. When I arrived home I let him out of the car. Alan was a bit taken aback by the size of him. I had to admit he was the biggest Border Collie I'd ever seen. He padded over to Alan and stared up into his face with those haunted eyes. Alan was won over immediately. I had said nothing about Pete to either Jess or Sam. Jess came out of the kitchen and Sam appeared from round the back of the house.

'Who does that dog belong to?' Jess asked.

'Us' I said. 'I've just got him from Pike View.' Jess immediately flung her arms around Pete's neck. He sat back on his haunches and thoroughly enjoyed the fuss and attention.

'Oh, no!' cried Sam. 'Someone's cut off his ears!'

'No they haven't, his ears just lie flat.' I said, showing him. Sam hugged the old dog. 'Once I've got all this weight off him he'll be a lot healthier.' I said.

We let Kim and Maggie out of the house to meet him. I didn't anticipate any trouble because at Pike View I hadn't seen him make eye contact with any of the dogs that were out with him. Kim bristled a bit at first and had a good sniff at him. Then she lay down and rolled on her back under the Laburnum tree. Maggie wagged her tail and licked his face. Pete just stood still and slowly wagged his tail. No problem!

Later I took Jess and Sam out to buy him a big bed with a soft duvet to go inside it. When we got home I put the bed in front of the cellar door. I tapped the bed and called Pete. He looked at it, then at me and wagged his tail.

'Come on Pete, get in your bed' I encouraged him. With a massive leap Pete jumped into the bed and lay down.

Towards the end of July Steve brought Melody and Robbie up to Jericho and put them in the fields with the other horses.

When Mike had began work on the foundations at the beginning of July he had come up here every day and dug out the area. As time went by however, although he worked hard when he was here, sometimes a whole week would go by and there would be no sign of him. Alan began to get very frustrated.

A lot of earth had been removed from the site. We needed several large wagonloads of brick and rubble to bring the area up to the right height. Coincidentally Steve Foster had decided to lower the grey brick buildings to a single storey, which meant that he would have a lot of bricks to get rid of. He suggested that if we could make use of them it would be a mutually beneficial arrangement if his demolition men could bring all the bricks across to us.

At the end of July demolition men began taking down the top storey of Steve's buildings. We were delighted because once our stables were built we would no longer be able to see any of the biggest building. The only one we would still see was the smaller one, which would be behind the car park and not as noticeable.

Throughout the whole month of July the water in the well had been very low.

Steve Sloane had rented a bungalow in Anglesey for the first week in August and was going to take the girls there. He said there was room in the bungalow for Jess and Sam to stay too, but there wasn't enough room in his car. If we could take them over there and fetch them back at the end of the week, they would be very welcome to join them. It was a kind offer and would give the children a beach holiday which we didn't have time to give them. I drove Jess and Sam across to Anglesey on Monday afternoon, stayed for an hour or so, and then returned home.

While Mike levelled the bricks and rubble, Alan and I put gutters up along the dairy, shippon and back stable. We also spent a lot of time collecting up large stones from the field behind the house where there appeared to have been some sort of animal shelter which was now derelict. We decided that the stones would be useful to put along the edges of the concrete shuttering at the back of the stables. We made numerous trips taking them from the field to the stable base in Mike's dumper, which he'd left at Jericho for us to use. It was heavy work. One morning I decided to have a go at driving the dumper to the field, it looked easy enough. I set off up the lane at a snails pace.
 'You can go a bit quicker than that surely!' Alan laughed as he walked past me. Irritated I pressed the accelerator. The dumper lurched forward. The metal seat shot backwards from under me throwing me off balance. Laying on my back clinging to the steering wheel my foot jammed against the accelerator pedal I hurtled up the lane almost knocking Alan over. Just before I reached the field I managed to heave myself upright and take my foot off the pedal. My heart was going like the clappers. Helpless with laughter Alan caught up with me. 'I

forgot to tell you about that seat - are you OK?' I got off the dumper and stalked up the field.

'You drive the damn thing!' I retorted crossly.

That summer was rapidly becoming the hottest, driest summer for several years. We worked for hours on end moving stone, shovelling hardcore and checking the level along the length of the base. Working day after day in such high temperatures was exhausting.

The Sloanes water supply had almost dried up. Horses require several litres of water each day and as Steve had eight horses the situation was becoming critical. In desperation he contacted the fire department who were very understanding and gave him permission to use the water hydrant opposite The Roebuck. They lent him all the necessary equipment which would enable him to fill large tanks full of water from the hydrant whenever the water situation became desperate.

At the end of the week I got up early and left for Anglesey around 7am to collect the children. The weather was gorgeous and being able to relax in the sunshine instead of work in it was heaven for me. We all spent the day on the beach then tidied up the bungalow after which Steve and the girls went home. We three decided to have fish'n'chips for our tea and travel back when it was cooler. We got home at about 8.30pm.to find that our next hay delivery – not expected until Monday – had arrived early. Alan had unloaded most of it on his own. Jim and Cath had come up at some point to help him. When we arrived Cath gathered up the sleepy children and gave them a hot drink before bed, while I went into the barn to help Alan and Jim. By the time all the hay was stacked Cath had got the children showered and in bed, and Alan was completely exhausted. The following week Mike came up and worked on the stable base.

...Concrete...Concrete...Concrete...Concrete...

The month of August was blistering hot and was dominated completely by the laying of a staggering 45 cubic metres of concrete for the stable yard. Alan made a 12 foot long tamper to help us to get it all level.

The first delivery of concrete was due on Saturday 12th August at 8am. We got up at 5.30am to see to any last minute preparations but despite the assistance of Mike and a friend of his, who arrived just before the wagon arrived, 12 cubic metres of concrete was far too much for us to cope with all at once on such a hot day. We managed with difficulty to level it all but it was very hard work and so subsequent deliveries were ordered in smaller, more manageable quantities.

On the Monday morning another load of hardcore was delivered for building up the level of the base. Alan went down to start shovelling it. When I went down to join him a few minutes later he was sitting down stroking Pete. Apparently when he had picked up a shovel Pete had dropped to the ground cowering in fear. Horrified, Alan had put down the shovel and tried to reassure him. When I got there Pete wagged his tail again slowly and stared up at us with those worried eyes. It knocked us sick. Between the death of the old farmer and being taken in at Pike View we guessed he had endured some cruel beatings.

On Tuesday we struggled to level the previous day's delivery of bricks and rubble. When we had finished we laid a plastic pipe across it to enclose the armoured cable which would provide electricity to the stable block.

The second concrete delivery arrived at 9am on Wednesday morning – four cubic metres this time. About half an hour later Steve Foster arrived unexpectedly and helped us to put it down. It was a very hot day. In the afternoon we had forty tons of limestone chippings delivered to blind off the hardcore and level up the rest of the base. That evening Mike came up and levelled a lot of it with his mini-digger.

The following day Mike arrived very early and worked on the levelling before it got too hot – he disappeared at midday. Alan and I carried on in the afternoon. We shovelled limestone chippings into the dumper then when it was full we tipped it in piles along the length of the base to rake over and level up. We did this about four times. Having raked out the last of the piles we returned to the dumper to fill it with more chippings. Alan began chucking them everywhere, completely missing the dumper. I stopped and watched him.

'What *are* you doing?!' I exclaimed.

'I'm filling the dumper – well one of them.' he said.

'What do you mean – one of them?'

'I mean I can see three of the bloody things! I think I've had too much sun.' With that he threw down his shovel, meandered up the garden and went to bed.

Next day we laid four metres of concrete. On Saturday Pete Jones came up and helped us to lay another four metres. We laid another four on the Monday.

The following Saturday Alan borrowed a van and we went to Ilkley. We left Sam with my mum and Jess with Alan's mum for a few days. Then we went to a saw mill in Ilkley where we bought a large quantity of post and rail fencing.

Towards the end of August we had noticed that Melody didn't seem to be grazing. She was just standing still for long periods or lying down. Steve came and took her and Robbie back to Shiloh Farm.

Always ready to try out a moneymaking scheme Steve had come across a bright yellow British Telecom van which was for sale at a very reasonable price. He and Alan decided to buy it between them and use it to collect wood shavings and sawdust from various furniture manufacturers in Oldham. The idea was that they could collect bags of pine shavings from some places and hardwood sawdust from others. They would mix it all together in a stable at Shiloh or in one of our pigsties at Jericho bag it up and sell it. This project turned out to be quite a long-term arrangement that helped us make some extra money, but it was an unpleasant job and very time consuming.

It was our twenty second wedding anniversary on 1st September. We got up at 6am and laid four cubic metres of concrete in the morning and another four in the afternoon. Next morning we were up early again to prepare for the last concrete delivery. When it was all done we took the children to The Roebuck and celebrated with a family meal.

Earlier in the summer we had sold the Land Rover to somebody we knew. At the beginning of September he brought it back because his wife didn't like driving it! He asked if he could swap it for the Polo. We took a few days to decide then finally we agreed. We hoped we had made the right decision.

Life at Jericho

It was a depressing start to the month when Melody was diagnosed with cancer and had to be put to sleep. Robbie was only three months old and not yet weaned. It was a difficult and distressing time for the Sloanes.

Around this time Jess began riding Tic-Tac a small bay Show Pony belonging to one of Diane's friends.

At 10 years old Jessica was quite small for her age. A pretty girl, with large blue grey eyes and long fair hair bleached blonde by the summer sun. She was able frequently and without too much effort to wrap Alan around her little finger. Happiest when in company she had never been very good at occupying herself – unless she was watching TV. She enjoyed the company of adults as well as that of her peers and her sense of humour and generous nature made her popular and fun to be with. In many respects she was mature for her age.

A new school year began in September and Alan, Jess and Sam returned to school. I felt completely drained. I think the concreting must have taken more out of me than I had realised. Over the next few days I felt really ill and tired. Between bouts of dizziness I worked on the concrete base brushing dry cement into any cracks and I soaked all the new fence posts in creosote. By Friday I felt no better. Sam said he felt ill too so I let him stay at home and Alan took Jess to school. By 10am Sam had made a miraculous recovery. I hadn't so he had to stay off school.

Over the next few weeks Jess rode Tic-Tac whenever possible after school and at weekends. Work on the stable block continued. The back of it was creosoted, the roof was felted and all the catches, bolts and tethering rings were fastened on.

Alan and Steve collected shavings and sawdust on most Saturday mornings. Some loads went to Steve other loads came to us. We mixed and bagged it late in the evenings – a horrible dusty job.

At the end of September Steve took all his horses back to Shiloh except for Dolly.

Up and Running

I put an advert in the Oldham Chronicle at the beginning of October advertising stables and grazing. There were four enquiries that evening. Next day there were three more, and the day after another two.

The first person to call and see the stables was a teacher called Shelley. She was very impressed and wanted the first two stables in the block for her own horse and that of a friend.

At the weekend Jane – a nurse – called and confirmed that she wanted the third stable. Another woman with four horrendous children, who ran riot all over the garden shouting and fighting each other, also came to look and said she would like a stable too. She seemed fine but the thought of those children coming up to the yard regularly once the stables were occupied was a definite 'no-no'. I told her I'd have to check how many stables were already taken and ring her back.

We had bought a 75metre drum of armoured cable to connect electricity from the house to the stable block. After taking the children to school on Monday morning I spent much of the rest of the day unwinding the armoured cable from the heavy, cumbersome drum. I dragged the cable through the barn and continued through the shippon laying the cable along the bottom of the wall; then I had to feed the end of it through a hole in the dairy wall, above part of the kitchen ceiling and down to the electric consumer unit over the cellar steps. It was a really difficult job to do on my own, but I did it and was very pleased with myself.

Alan had already dug a trench from the barn at the front of the house down to the concrete base. When he got home from work we rolled the drum back out of the barn and guided the remaining cable along the trench. We threaded the end of the cable through the plastic pipe, which we'd laid under the concrete, and out at the back of the stable block. From there we fed it into the back of the barn to where the RCD unit for the stables was going to be connected.

Life at Jericho

The evenings were getting shorter as regards working outside. We put fence posts along the perimeter of all our land and beside all the dividing walls and then strung a combination of barbed and straight wire between them. Although we didn't like using barbed wire it was necessary to protect the walls from being knocked down by the horses scratching and rubbing themselves against them. We removed Steve's temporary barbed wire fencing which was behind the house and replaced it with the posts and rails that we had bought from the saw mill in Ilkley. We fenced behind the house from the wall bordering Taylor's field right across to the far wall on the opposite side of our land, leaving gaps for the field gates which we hung later. There were enough posts and rails to do the same at the bottom of the garden to separate it from the stable yard. What we didn't get done in the evenings we had to finish at weekends.

My days were spent weather permitting, treating the fronts of the stables with a preservative stain and coating all the doors and window frames with yacht varnish. Sometimes it was too windy for that sort of job. On those days the stain was practically blown from the brush onto the stable walls before I had a chance to brush it on and my hair was forever being blown across my face so I couldn't see what I was doing. I kept pushing it behind my ears because it wasn't long enough to tie back. The rubber gloves I was wearing were splashed with stain so my face was soon covered in dark brown streaks and my hair became stuck together in clumps that wouldn't wash out. Having resorted to cleaning it with turps on more than one occasion I decided to have my hair cut short.

At the weekend Shelley and her friend Andy hacked over from Mossley on their two horses 'Thomas' a four year old coloured 14.2hh Cob and 'Bonnie' an attractive and very fine 15.1hh Hanoverian mare. They had arranged to bring the horses over for grazing only until all the jobs on the stables had been finished. On the Sunday Alan and I trowelled a cement fillet against the front of the stable block along its entire length.

The following week I finished treating the last of the stables with preservative and on the Friday Shelley and Andy moved their horses into their stables and Jane arrived with 'Katie' her 16hh. Danish warm blood and settled her into stable three. We now had Tic Tac on a temporary loan for Jess. He lived with Dolly at the back of the house in the second of the two stables.

The next weekend we made an area for the muck heap; we laid 20 flags and fenced round them on three sides. Jess rode Tic-Tac out on a hack with Andy and Bonnie and a young woman called Karen brought 'Knowsley' a handsome ten year old Arab and put him into stable five. Our water situation had not improved so Alan and I had to fetch water with Steve's tractor and trailer to fill the field baths and the water tank at the stables.

During the half term week, with Alan's help, Steve Foster wired the whole stable block for us. When they had finished there was one light in each stable, one in each tack room, two in the barn and five outside the front of the block beneath the overhanging roof.

The Sloanes went away for half-term and left Carl in charge at Shiloh Farm. A strong, dark haired, good looking young man in his early twenties he called round to Jericho early in the week and asked if I wanted five Black Rock hens. I told him that although I'd like to keep poultry at some point I wasn't ready for any just yet. I had nowhere secure to keep them and at the moment I was too busy to sort anything out. He rang me several times throughout the week and on Friday he called round again.

'You could keep them in the stable with Dolly' he suggested hopefully. 'Steve'll go mad if he comes back and finds hens in his barn. I bought them cheap intending to ring their necks and put them in the freezer' he confessed 'but I couldn't do it. Please will you have them?'

I said I would but told him he would have to give me time to sort out somewhere safe to keep them. About an hour later Carl brought round a large cardboard box which he deposited outside the back stable with a bag of corn.

'That's for your mum.' he told Jess hurriedly then he beat a hasty retreat!

Alan helped me to construct a sturdy partition out of some pallets to create a separate area for them in Dolly's stable as a temporary arrangement. We put down some sawdust and then installed the hens in their new home with some corn and a bowl of water. They seemed quite happy.

On Bonfire Night, a young single mum called Nicola, brought 'Solitaire' her 18 year-old Thoroughbred bay mare to the yard and put her into stable four. That evening we took the children to the local cricket club bonfire.

Jess thoroughly enjoyed the social life which the stable yard provided. In particular she enjoyed the company of Shelley who took her to shops which sold endless bits and pieces of 'horsy' merchandise. Shelley and Andy were quite happy for Jess to ride out with them occasionally which was nice for Jess as Tic-Tac was often a difficult pony when on his own, but generally he behaved impeccably when hacking out in company.

Sam too chatted to Shelley and her husband Lee who appeared from time to time with sacks of feed for Thomas. Karen was also a favourite; Jess happily talked to her while she mucked out Knowsley's stable. Inevitably while enjoying the social chats, Jess learnt a lot about horses from people who were experienced in dealing with them.

An Irish odd job man, who had been laying some tarmac for Steve Foster, came up to Jericho on several occasions. He asked if he could tarmac our lane or our car park or anywhere really that didn't have grass on it! I kept saying no and eventually he gave up. A week or so later 'Tarmac Jim' as I called him knocked on the door again. He told me that he had a caravan base which we might find useful for transporting hay bales from the hay barn down to the stable block. I decided that it would be a really good idea because I could hitch it behind the Land Rover and not only transport hay and shavings but also probably shift muck up the field. If we had that we wouldn't need to borrow Steve's tractor and trailer so often. He only wanted £30 for it so I bought it.

Throughout November I concentrated on getting a coat of Yacht Varnish on each stable door and on the two barn doors. Sometimes however the weather was just too cold.

Life at Jericho

The five Black Rock hens settled happily. Once they got used to us we let them out of the stable during the day to potter about. They were very easy to look after and readily returned to their stable at about four o'clock when we got back from school and it began to get dark. In the sunshine their black plumage shone blue and green. We gave all of them names. One had a particularly large comb, she was bigger than the rest and her plumage was especially nice. We called her Queenie. The others were called Cilla, Peggy, Annie and Blanche. Sam liked the hens and helped me to look after them. He gave them corn and clean water when he got home from school, and made sure they were all shut in before dark in case of foxes. Kim liked them too – she had a rather disconcerting habit of singling out one hen and following it closely whilst licking her chops!

As time went by I got used to handling the horses. I fed them in the mornings, changed their rugs and led them up to the top field with the hollows, which we used for winter turn out.

At the end of November I felt really rough. I couldn't seem to get warm and I ached all over. Early in December we woke up to heavy snow which stayed with us for about a week. I kept Jess and Sam off school for a couple of days because the lane was blocked. Alan had to walk to school on both mornings and back home again late in the afternoon. Towards the end of the week having turned out Thomas and Bonnie, mucked out both of their stables and done various other jobs I felt so ill that I went to bed at five o'clock finally having to accept that I had probably got flu. Next morning I didn't get dressed all day, in fact I didn't do much of anything! At the weekend Alan and the children scraped the remaining snow off the concrete and took hay and shavings down to the bottom barn on the new trailer. Sam and Kim hitched a ride on the hay.

By the end of the following week I felt much better and on the Thursday morning I went round to let out the hens as usual and found Queenie dead in Dolly's stable. Dolly must have knocked the partition and made a gap big enough for a hen to get through. Queenie evidently went into the stable and got kicked. It made me sad. I had become fond of the hens and I felt bad that we hadn't made somewhere safer for them.

The closer it got to Christmas the colder it became. On Christmas Eve Alan went over to Ilkley in the Land Rover and fetched my mum who was to spend Christmas with us. That afternoon it began to snow and continued to do so all evening. We woke up to a picturesque but very cold Christmas Day. That night was the coldest we'd experienced at Jericho. At 3am on Boxing Day morning according to Steve Foster it was minus 20 degrees! By 7am it had risen to minus 7. The Land Rover wouldn't start. The diesel had frozen in the fuel pipe. Thankfully it thawed out later and Alan got it started enabling us to go to Pat's for our usual Boxing Day family get together.

At the end of December Sue, a police woman, rang to ask if we had an available stable and if so, would we be able to make provision for her pregnant horse? She would need a separate grazing area for her from April and for a month or so after the birth of the foal. Alan and I discussed it and decided that we could fence off about half an acre of the summer field quite close to the stable block. I rang Sue and told her. Later in the week she called up to see the stables and confirmed that she would definitely like one and would bring her horse up to Jericho in a week's time.

1996

On the first Sunday of the New Year Sue came up with Misty, a light grey Arab x Welsh and settled her into her new stable. The following day I turned out Thomas and Bonnie, mucked out Tic-Tac and Dolly, took two containers of water up to the winter field in the Land Rover, loaded 10 bales of hay and 9 bags of shavings onto the flatbed trailer and took it down to the stable block. It was the first time I'd towed the trailer. Driving along to the barn was no problem. I unloaded the hay and shavings and stacked them in the barn. Reversing the trailer however proved more difficult. Try as I might I couldn't reverse the damn thing in a straight line. I must have gone backwards and forwards a dozen times before in desperation I un-hitched it and pushed it back by hand into the car park. I then re-hitched it and towed it back up to the house. After that I swept out the shippon, fetched the children, made the tea and took Sam to swimming club. I slept well that night.

The next two weeks or so of January were very cold with freezing temperatures and frequent heavy snow falls. Every morning I trudged up the fields with some of the horses and brought them back down again late afternoon. I mucked out the ponies and carried endless buckets of water down to the stables because the rain water in the tank at the end of the stable block was frozen. Hay bales and bags of shavings also had to be carried down the garden because the lane was too full of snow for me to take the trailer down.

The wind picked up and after more heavy overnight snow we woke up to snow drifts as tall as Jess! A gale force icy wind made it difficult to work outside. I had to muck out all the horses because no-one could get up the lane. Alan felt ill and was unable to help me. Next day the snow remained deep and difficult in places. I fed and watered all the horses in the morning. Gradually throughout the day everybody managed to make their way through the drifts and get up to the yard.

In narrow lanes like Shiloh a snow plough can cause problems. The snow which is pushed to one side by the blade creates a continuous mound of hard packed snow. The narrower the lane the less room there is for the snow and the higher the mounds become. The alternative to a snow plough is a snow blower, a vehicle with wide rows of rotating paddles, resembling a water wheel, mounted at the front. As it drives along, the snow is cleared off the road by the paddles and is blown several feet up in the air and out at one side through a flue. No mounds of hard packed snow are created like there are with a snow plough, instead the snow is blown well clear of the road falling in a powdery form over a larger area.

Apparently at the time the council didn't own one of these but a farmer who lived near The Roebuck did. It was highly unlikely that the council would clear Shiloh Lane with a snow plough or employ the farmer to clear it with his snow blower. So together with Steve Sloane and Steve Foster we decided to ask the farmer to clear Shiloh Lane and our access road, and share the cost between us. Early that evening the snow blower cleared our lane right up to the house. It was an unusual and impressive sight and we watched it with the children at a safe distance.

Life at Jericho

The Land Rover was proving to be very unreliable, sometimes refusing to start at all. On those days I took everyone to school in the car and kept my fingers crossed that I could get back home up Shiloh Lane which was very icy in places.

Every morning I did my stable jobs. I saw to the horses, did any mucking out that I had been asked to do and made sure that the barn was stocked up with hay and shavings. Once the outside jobs were done I tried to stay in the warm, but there was little warmth to be found. The icy wind penetrated the kitchen through the ill fitting doors, and the Aga struggled to reach cooking temperature let alone heat the kitchen.

It was Jess's 11th birthday on the 31st January. Karen had unexpectedly left the yard with Knowsley, so we let Jess have the stable for Tic-Tac.

There was a blizzard warning the following week and on the Tuesday it snowed all day. Alan had taken the children to school but when they came home he could only get the car as far as The Roebuck. They walked home up the lane through the snow drifts. Next morning armed with shovels and accompanied by the dogs, we made our way down to the car. After digging some of the snow away we managed to get the car out and Alan was able to take the children to school again - much to Sam's disappointment.

At the weekend Alan bought some new glow plugs for the Land Rover and got it started; which was a good thing as even more snow fell in February which drifted in the icy winds. The snow and freezing temperatures stayed with us until the end of the month.

When our lane was finally free of snow I loaded up the low trailer with hay and shavings and re-stocked the barn. At this time we had a new arrival on the yard - a young woman called Christine rode up to Jericho on 'Jake' a 16hh chestnut gelding and took the eighth stable.

Life was proving to be very hard living at Jericho especially for me working outside so much. I was cold most of the time and completely exhausted.

After Queenie's untimely demise I was anxious to get the remaining hens out of the stable as soon as possible. Alan said that he would build a hen hut for them if I designed one, until then we made another temporary home for them. Behind the kitchen there was a make shift car port made out of timber and roofing felt. We had used it for the Polo but it wasn't big enough for the BMW. It was now just used for storage and had become an untidy dumping ground. It was open fronted so all we had to do once we had emptied everything out of it was make a timber and wire netting front panel. We covered the floor with a thick layer of sawdust, put up a perch where the hens could roost and provided a secluded area to serve as a nesting box. As soon as it was finished we transferred the hens into it. They had more room there than they'd had in the stable and they settled into their new accommodation very quickly.

Reuben

Quite unexpectedly Alan announced that he had bought me a horse! Chatting over a brew one day I had commented that it must be nice to have a foal and bring it on yourself so that you knew exactly what had been done with it and how it had been treated. Apparently he had mentioned my remark to Carl who bought and sold young horses from time to time. Carl had seen a particularly nice colt at Holmfirth market, bought it and brought it back to Shiloh Farm. He and Steve were of the opinion that it would be ideal eventually for Jess to ride. They all thought it would be nice for me to look after it and by the time it was old enough to be broken and schooled Jess would have become a competent rider. I couldn't believe that they had conspired to do this without discussing it with me! A young horse is a total commitment. I didn't know anything about rearing young horses, and I was already very busy with the stable yard and the house.

After doing my morning jobs I went down to Steve's to see the colt for the first time. He was a 10 month old Cleveland Bay x Cob with a thick rich russet brown coat and a white star on his forehead. He was looking over the stable door as I approached, watching me with his big beautiful brown eyes. As I came closer he raised his head sharply and took a step back, obviously suspicious and nervous of me. I felt the same way about him.

Steve came back to Jericho with me and collected Dolly. When they'd gone I mucked out her stable and prepared it for the colt, putting down plenty of new shavings. In the afternoon I went down to fetch him. Steve clipped a lead rope onto his head collar and asked if I was happy to lead him home by myself.

'Yes fine!' I'd said, hoping I sounded more confident than I felt. We set off quite briskly. Half way along the lane something caught his eye and he stopped dead snorting noisily. I encouraged him to walk forward and we set off again. I felt apprehensive. I could feel his pent up strength and energy and knew that if he wanted to get away from me he could do so easily and I wouldn't be strong enough to stop him; but he didn't and we arrived safely at the stable door. Before setting off to fetch him I'd put a handful of carrots on the floor and hung up a hay net. Much to my surprise and immense relief I was able to lead him inside with no problem. When I unclipped the lead rope he glanced around the stable then began eating the carrots. I went outside and bolted the door. I watched him for a few minutes then left him to get used to his new surroundings.

It was unlikely that he'd had much human contact. He was difficult to handle, tending to throw his head about and pull hard on the lead rope. He was very jumpy and unsure of everything and I was quite scared of him. There was no way I could muck him out while he was in the stable. I had tried to do that on the second day. As I forked some muck into a skip bin I had been talking to him quietly – he was fine until the wind caught the shippon door and slammed it shut. He flew round and fired out with both back legs missing my knees by a couple of inches. I got out of there very fast! It shook me. I realised that I had to be very careful and take things very slowly. I understood that he was as nervous as I was and that there was no malice in him. He was just young and scared. After that incident for the next few days Alan walked him out whenever I mucked out.

Frequently each day I stood and talked to him, and went into his stable to stroke his head and run my hands over his back to reassure him and get him used to human contact. Several names were suggested for the colt but I stuck to my original choice and called him 'Reuben'. The following weekend we had him gelded and hoped that he would become more placid in a week or two.

I began work on the little back sitting room. A ceiling moulding ran around the top of the walls and along both sides of each beam. If it had all been the same size I might have been tempted to leave it on but unfortunately it was not. The moulding in one third of the room was larger than the rest so it all had to come off. I managed to remove the larger moulding fairly easily. The next day I made a start on the rest. The smaller moulding however proved much more difficult – in fact I broke a hammer trying to lever it off! The two beams were plastered over like the ones in the dining room had been, and that too had to be levered off.

Later that day I carried countless buckets of water down to the horses.

Jess and Sam had been invited to a swimming party. It was a cold, miserable Saturday but nevertheless Alan and I decided to take the opportunity to empty some of the muck heap while they were gone. Alan fetched the tractor and trailer from Steve and I dropped off the children at the swimming pool. When I got back we worked hard filling the trailer and took a couple of loads up the field. By the time we'd filled the trailer for the third time the weather had deteriorated and it started sleeting, so Alan took the trailer up the field and I went back indoors. The phone was ringing. I answered it. It was Jess.

'Where've you *been*?'

'Shifting the muck heap, I was just going to get changed and come and collect you. Are you OK?'

'No, not really, it was the wrong party!'

I was horrified. It was the first time I'd ever just dropped them off at a party without going in with them. Jess was not happy!

'I went into the changing room and realized I didn't know anybody.' she continued. 'They were all looking at me. I went up to a lady and asked her where Rose and Josh were. She said I must have come to the wrong party and took me to the man at the desk. He looked in his book and told me that Rose and Josh's party is *next* Saturday.'

'Sorry' I said lamely 'was Sam upset?'

'No, he jumped in the water and played on the floats and refused to come out!'

Once again I felt like a bad and neglectful mother. I thought I would never hear the end of it.

Over the next two weeks we continued from time to time to bag up shavings in the evenings. We managed to empty the muck heap completely and I continued to work on the back room. I fetched wood from the wood yard and took rubbish down to the council tip.

More New Arrivals

Carl asked Sam how the hens were doing. He suggested that we should get a cockerel to take care of them. Sam really liked the idea. I made some enquiries. It just so happened that a local man had recently lost all his hens to a fox and all he had left was the cockerel. Not wanting to get any more hens he had taken the cockerel to Pike View.

I took Sam to see the cockerel and told him that if he liked it he could have it as an early birthday present. I explained before we got there that the cockerel would be smaller than our hens were because it was a bantam. So if he thought it was too small he didn't have to have it.

The man at Pike View took us into a shed where the small animals were kept. The cockerel was perched on a thick branch in a large cage. He wasn't as small as I expected, his richly coloured shiny plumage was predominantly orange and brown and his red comb flopped over to one side. He was very alert and with his head on one side he looked at us out of a dark beady eye.

'What do you think Sam?' I asked.

Right on cue the cockerel crowed – very loudly. Startled, Sam laughed then looked at me and nodded. The man had no idea what to charge for a cockerel. He had never re homed one before, so I gave what I thought would be a suitable donation and the man put the cockerel into a cardboard box. We set off home in the Land Rover with the box between us.

'You'll have to think of a name for him' I commented.

'Eric' replied Sam without any hesitation.

We knew that a few feathers might fly when we introduced Eric to the hens. But he had to meet them sooner or later so as soon as we got home we opened their door and put him in with his new harem. Blanche immediately strode across and gave him a good battering. The others left him alone as long as he kept away from them. That night all the hens roosted on their perch as usual – Eric roosted on the feed barrel on his own. This continued for the next three nights.

We kept them all in the pen for four days to give them time to get used to each other before we opened the door and let them potter outside. Although he was now free to roam Eric stayed close to the hens and constantly made quiet chuntering noises in his throat while he scratched about busily with his claws. Whenever he succeeded in uncovering an unfortunate bug or worm he growled noisily and one or more of the hens would sprint across to him and devour the wriggling morsel. He fed each hen in this way before indulging himself. If we threw any tit-bits out for them he waited until all the hens had eaten something before he would eat anything himself. What a gentleman! I was well impressed.

Next morning when I went round to feed them Eric was perched right in the middle of the hens looking very pleased with himself!

Early in April Alan and I made a start fencing off the bottom section of the summer field in preparation for Misty and her foal. By the end of the week the fencing was complete. I tied strips of plastic tape along the wire to ensure that the horses could see that there was now a barrier where it had once been open. We hung an extra gate to allow separate access to the small field henceforward known as 'Misty's field'. As soon as we had finished Sue began turning Misty out in her own field to get her used to it, and to keep her away from the other horses just in case she dropped her foal while she was out. She was huge, just like Melody had been.

Alan had spent most evenings since Eric's arrival, working in the bottom of the hay barn constructing the new hen hut. He followed my design very closely and made the hut in panels which we would bolt together on site. The roof would be put on afterwards.

It was the middle of May before the new hen hut was fully assembled. It had a small fox proof safety run for occasions when we didn't want the hens roaming free. It was six feet by four feet and tall enough to stand up in. Inside, down one long side there were four laths on which the hens could roost and on the opposite side there was a window to give them light. Next to the window there was a full size door and there was also a separate small access for the hens at the front of the hut which led into the safety run. This access was blocked up each night with a big concrete block. Alan had made two nesting boxes at the back of the hut, access to which was through a dark brown curtain that I'd secured with elastic wire. The curtain had vertical slits in it so the hens could push their way through into the nesting boxes and lay their eggs in the dark. The boxes extended out from the back of the hut and could be opened from the outside so we could retrieve the eggs without having to go into the hen hut. Sam loved it. He put sawdust on the floor, gave them a tub of fresh water and a generous bowlful of mixed corn. He then installed Eric and 'the girls' as he called them much to our amusement.

It was time for our septic tank to be emptied again and this time on Bill Dawson's advice I asked Gerald Collins if he would empty it for us. That morning Gerald arrived on the dot of eight o'clock as arranged. Nodding wisely he performed the unenviable task and informed me gravely that our septic tank was very old and in need of attention. His sharp eyes noticed too the abundant healthy shoots of rhubarb which were growing a little further down the garden and as he packed away his equipment he commented on his liking for rhubarb crumble. Needless to say I pulled several long sticks of rhubarb and gave them to him along with his payment. He accepted both with a huge smile and drove up into the top of the summer field to spread the contents of the tank over the land before driving off down Shiloh Lane.

I learnt afterwards from Bill that when Gerald had emptied the Sloanes tank the previous year he had attempted to spray the contents surreptitiously onto Bill's field as he drove down the lane. A small proportion of which failed to reach the field and instead spattered rather unpleasantly all over the dry stone wall for quite some distance down the lane!

Starting from scratch running a livery yard, especially when we had no prior knowledge of horses, meant that making decisions was very much a case of trial and error. The subject of winter turn out was no exception. We wanted to keep the big field behind the house as a summer field and so had decided to use the hollows field – which was behind the summer field - for winter. The advantage of using that field was that it was surrounded by dry stone walls, which although not in fantastic condition at least provided a substantial visible barrier. There had been a few areas where the walls had started to collapse or lost a few stones and we had re-built most of them, any larger gaps we had fenced until we would have time to mend them properly.

Now, as the end of the first winter season was almost upon us I could reflect upon the disadvantages of using that field and how we could improve things for next time. One disadvantage was that the winter field was a good two hundred and fifty yard walk up hill from the stable block through the summer field. In bad weather with a horse which was raring to go I was aware of every one of those two hundred and fifty yards every time I made my way up to the hollows!

Another disadvantage was that some people on the yard brought in their horses after work in the evening. This meant that in the depths of winter they had to walk their horses down the field in total darkness often in awful weather conditions. Sometimes if they were delayed at work for some reason they would ring me, often after 7 o'clock, and ask me to bring in their horse and on occasions muck out their stable as well. Having finished my outdoor jobs, made and eaten our evening meal the last thing I wanted to do was plod up a muddy field in awful weather to lead down a horse which had been left on its own in the field and was excitable to say the least. In addition to all that was the terrible condition of the field, particularly at the gateway where the horses congregated as soon as the first horse had been brought in at the end of the day. I decided that before the next winter season began in November some changes would have to be made.

People come and go on stable yards and as soon as we had a vacant stable I took Reuben out of his stable at the back of the house and installed him in the one on the yard. I was sure that he would like the close proximity of the other horses and it would be good for him to get used to people walking past his stable every day. Since being gelded he had calmed down considerably and I was no longer nervous of being in the stable with him in fact I had become very fond of him. I spent more and more time with him and picked out his feet with a hoof pick every day. He got so used to it that he lifted his feet up automatically as I went round to each leg. I never allowed him to put his head down and eat grass on our way to the field and I taught him to stand back and wait when I gave him his feeds in the stable. He was becoming well mannered and pleasant to handle and also much more gentle. He had long since stopped throwing his head about and I could now put my face against his as he blew softly through his nostrils.

The farrier had agreed to look at Reuben's feet every time he came to the yard so that when the time came for him to be shod he would be more at ease. In the middle of May the farrier came to the yard to shoe Thomas and Reuben had his feet trimmed for the first time. He trembled and leaned against the farrier to keep his balance. The farrier was a quiet young man with a kind and gentle manner. His head was shaved and tanned golden brown. As he bent to trim Reuben's first front hoof Reuben began to lick his bald head – and continued to lick it until the farrier had finished both his front hooves. After which with a grin the farrier pulled up his tee shirt and rubbed his head dry.

Early on the Saturday morning Alan got up and made me a coffee. He said he'd go down and feed Tic-Tac and Reuben so that I could have a bit of a lie in. I got up half an hour later and went downstairs expecting to find Alan having his breakfast – but he wasn't there. I went down to the yard. Tic-Tac was eating his hay. I looked over Reuben's stable door wondering if Alan had decided to muck out as well but he wasn't there and more surprisingly – neither was Reuben. I called Alan's name as I walked along to the end of the stable block and looked up into the field – but Reuben had not been turned out. Puzzled I returned to the stable to see if his head collar and lead rope were still there. As I walked into the stable I heard Alan's voice.

'Jan, I'm in the tack room.'
'Where's Reuben?'
'He's in here as well.'

'What!?'

I walked across to the tack room. Alan opened the door about half an inch and peered at me through the gap.

'He was already in here when I came down to feed him.' he explained. 'He must have fiddled with the bolt and managed to push the door open. He probably climbed in to get at his hay net then as he moved around his bum must have pushed the door shut again. He's OK though, he's not panicking – yet. But I'll have to make room for him to turn round before we can open the door and get him out. I'll try to pass things out to you.'

Over the next few minutes I could hear Alan talking quietly to Reuben and evidently feeding him carrots to keep him happy. After an assortment of rustling and creaking noises Alan managed to pull the door open about six inches and began to force things through the gap; a shavings fork, a yard brush, one half filled hay net and two crushed feed buckets. He then closed the door again. I heard him slide a bag of shavings and a feed bin across the tack room floor hoping to create enough space for him to manoeuvre Reuben's rear end away from the door. Meanwhile I hung up the hay net and put the rest of the stuff outside. After numerous encouraging clicking noises and general scuffling sounds Alan announced that he had managed to persuade Reuben to shuffle round until he was facing the door. The tack room door opened into the tack room and Reuben squirmed uncomfortably as the edge of the door scraped hard against his flank but as soon as he could see into his stable again he stepped forward eagerly and stood right up to the two foot high wall which divided the stable from the tack room beneath the door way. As Reuben moved forward Alan pushed the door open as wide as it would go against the inside wall of the tack room. Gingerly he ducked beneath Reuben's neck and stepped over the low wall encouraging Reuben to follow him into the stable.

'Come on Reuben, come on boy!' I called. Alan patted him encouragingly. Reuben clearly wanted to come back into his stable but was unsure how to do so as he repeatedly banged his forelegs hard against the top of the low wall. Suddenly he went for it and jumped out through the doorway hitting the top of his head against the top of the doorway and bashing first his forelegs and then his hind legs against the lower wall as he did so. Clumsily he landed in his stable but settled down almost immediately and began to eat from his hay net.

We put things back into the tack room and then Alan tied up the damaged bolt with baling twine as a temporary repair until he could replace it. We examined Reuben's legs and despite the bashing he'd given them they seemed fine so after a few minutes we turned him out into the field with Tic-Tac so he could chill out.

The tack room was only six feet square and Reuben had pretty much filled it. Thankfully it had no fixed shelving – everything was moveable and Reuben's temperament was such that he had remained calm. Although we had no way of knowing how long he had been in there before Alan discovered him, we guessed that it couldn't have been very long. If it had happened several hours ago and he had become distressed we could have faced a much more serious problem.

The following Thursday Peanut pottered out of the house heading slowly towards the field. I saw her go but thought nothing of it as it was quite a mild day. Half an hour later I realised that she hadn't returned to her spot against the Aga. There was no sign of her. I called her and called her all that day and the next and searched for her everywhere. She never came back. We never found her.

At the weekend Misty went into labour. Sue kept her in and spent most of the day with her convinced that she was about to give birth – but nothing happened. She came back again later in the evening to check on her and still nothing had happened. I checked on Misty at 11pm and this time something was quite definitely happening! I rang Sue and she came straight back and rang the vet. By the time he arrived Misty was well into labour. By 2 am she had given birth to a beautiful brown colt foal. Alan and I watched the whole thing. It was amazing.

The next new arrival on the yard was Ben, a 9 month old colt. His mother was a Shetland pony which had been rescued and lived at an animal shelter near where Shelley worked. The pony had dropped her foal unexpectedly as the people who ran the shelter were unaware when they took her in that she was pregnant. They didn't have room at the shelter to keep the foal now that he needed to be weaned so Shelley wanted to bring him here. Her plan was to get him broken eventually so that her eldest daughter, Natasha could ride him when she was a bit older. Shelley asked us if we had any objections. As we had two empty stables at the time we had no reason to object so she decided to rent another stable and she rescued the foal from the shelter.

Ben was a rather unattractive black colt. When he arrived he behaved as if he was 15hh instead of 10hh. He was very bolshy and Shelley booked him in to be gelded as soon as possible.

It was a sunny afternoon when the vet came to geld Ben. He decided that it would be best to geld him outside in Misty's field where he could recover from the anaesthetic without risk of harming himself rather than in the confines of his stable. Shelley and I stood either side of Ben and supported him as the anaesthetic took effect and he slumped to the ground. The vet did the business and then to our surprise tossed the two testes into the long grass.

'A treat for the foxes' he laughed as we stared at him. Without hesitation Maggie who had watched the whole episode with interest, trotted over and ate them!

Sue called the foal 'Trader'. At eight days old he had become very lively in the stable so as the weather was warm and dry Sue decided to turn them out into Misty's field for the first time. She took Misty out of the stable and Trader followed wearing a tiny, bright orange turn out rug with a fleecy edge and lining. He looked very cute. I opened the field gate and as Sue led Misty to the field Trader trotted along close behind her. They both went into the field without a problem.

Jess had never been keen on the hens but after one particular incident she was put off altogether. She and I were sitting outside the kitchen chatting and enjoying the sunshine. I had brought out a drink and a snack and within minutes the hens had noticed and rushed across to where we were sitting clearly hoping to be given a tit-bit or to find some fallen crumbs. I broke up a slice of bread and threw the pieces as far away from us as I could. Jess noticed that one of them was wiping each side of her beak on the ground.

'Oh my God! It's sharpening its beak!' she exclaimed.

'No she's cleaning it.' I laughed. Just then Blanche, evidently

Life at Jericho

a little short-sighted mistook one of Jess's painted toe nails for a tasty morsel and pecked it hard with her sharp beak. Horrified Jess screamed and fled into the house.

We had invited Pat and John and all the family along with my mum and Alan's mum to Jessica's confirmation at Manchester Cathedral on the afternoon of Saturday 15th June. Jess had been attending Confirmation classes with her Sunday school group for months and wanted her grandmas and family to share the day. We were all going on a coach from Uppermill and I had made a buffet to have with a barbeque afterwards.

Alan and I were sitting outside enjoying a brew when the bomb went off in Manchester that morning. We heard it and saw the smoke. I turned on the TV and it was confirmed on a news flash. Very soon afterwards our vicar rang and told us that the cathedral had been damaged in the blast and that the area had been sealed off. We would be given an alternative date for the Confirmation in due course. I rang the family and explained the situation. As it was such a beautiful day they all came over anyway.

At the end of the month Shelley and Natasha arrived at the door with a tiny, long haired black and white kitten which they had seen in a pet shop window and had been unable to resist buying. They had called him Joe and had intended to keep him but apparently Lee had got really angry when they had taken him home

'You've already got two horses, two dogs and three cats and now you want another mouth to feed! Are you mad?' he had shouted and stormed off. Not wishing to push her luck Shelley asked if there was any chance that little Joe could live in the barn on the stable block. Sam overheard the conversation and complained that the kitten was much too small to live in the barn and asked if he could have him in the house instead. I had no objection and Alan didn't mind so Joe became Sam's cat. He was very small but very feisty and not scared of the dogs at all. If anything I think the dogs were a bit scared of him!

On the first Sunday in July a horse show was held at Churchill Playing

Fields in Greenfield. Jess rode Thomas and Jake and jumped a clear round on both of them.

Later that day I tethered Reuben outside his stable for the first time while I groomed him. He was very unsure and a bit jumpy as I expected he would be. I kept him there for just a short time. He didn't attempt to pull away so I praised him, gave him a tit-bit and put him back in the stable. I intended next time to leave him a little longer and continue slowly to build his confidence.

In the middle of July we joined forces with the Sloanes and collected six hundred and thirty bales of hay straight off the fields from a farm in Milnrow. We used Steve's horsebox, the yellow van and a flatbed trailer to collect them and shared them between us. Dianna and Matthew came over and helped us unload the first two hundred bales, along with two of Alan's teacher friends from school. The other four nights we did it between us with help from Steve's friend Alec. We finished on Sunday night with a barbeque at Steve and Diane's tired out but very pleased with ourselves.

At the beginning of the school holidays I took Jess to her friend Tom's house where she and some of her friends rode a pony that his mum had on a temporary loan. At the end of the month she was confirmed at Manchester Cathedral.

During August while Alan was at home we worked hard and got a lot of outside jobs done. One of the most labour saving jobs Alan did was to lay a pipe down the garden to provide water to the stable block. He hacked his way through the road in front of the kitchen with a pick axe and then dug a narrow trench from the top of the garden to the bottom of the garden opposite the barn and built a small stone pier on which he attached a tap. We laid a water pipe in the trench and then connected it up to our water supply in the kitchen. No more carrying heavy buckets of water down the garden or fetching water in the big tank on Steve's tractor when there wasn't enough rain water stored in the tank at the end of the stable block!

While Alan dug the trench I continued the mammoth task of creosoting the stable block a job which I had been doing on and off over the last few weeks. The weather had given the back of the stables a real hammering over winter and now the sun was taking its toll as well. It was essential to get it protected again before next winter.

Ever since his arrival on the yard Ben had occupied a full-size stable. He was so small that we decided to build a smaller lean-to stable for him at the end of the block which would free up the one he was presently living in for a larger horse. We dug out the footings and managed to get the concrete base down the same day. Over the next few days Alan made a sturdy framework for the stable and clad it with heavy timber boards. We roofed it with timber and felt and to complete the job Alan made a small replica of the other stable doors low enough for Ben to be able to stand with his head over it. The new stable measured 10 feet square. It was plenty big enough for him and he seemed very happy with it.

To avoid the situation which we had last winter when we had to walk each horse all the way up through the summer field to the hollows field gate to turn them out, we decided to fence off a 30 foot strip of the summer field as an additional winter field, the gate to which would be just to the right of the farm house. It was a very tiring job because the ground was so hard but well worthwhile as it would make my work in winter so much easier.

Whenever Alan and I went into the fields to erect or repair fencing, invariably Reuben would wander across to investigate. He would push his big head between us as we drove in a new post or fastened on a new rail, so that we had to stop what we were doing to avoid hitting him with the hammer. If we left it within reach he would pick up the bag of nails and sprinkle the contents on the ground then run off like a mischievous child. He was curious and comical and I loved him to bits.

We took a day off toward the end of August. I got up extra early, took the dogs for a long walk then mucked out Reuben and Bonnie. We took the children to Blackpool for the day and spent some time on the beach and at the amusements before going into the Pleasure Beach to have a go on some of the rides. We finished the day sitting on the promenade wall beside the beach with our legs dangling over the edge eating fish'n'chips out of the paper and sharing a big bottle of pop.

Ebony

Tic-Tac's owner had taken him back at the beginning of summer leaving Jess with no pony to ride over the holidays. Shelley let her ride Thomas quite a lot but he was much too big for her. After making some enquiries I rang up about a 13hh pony called Ebony that was available for loan. Next day I took Jess to see him. He was a striking jet black pony with a glossy mane and flowing tail. He was tethered outside his stable and we had a good look at him. Jess brushed him and picked out his feet then had a ride on him with his owner and myself walking alongside. His owner told us that her son had ridden him regularly and had competed at local shows. Ebony was good in traffic and well behaved in the stable. Jess really liked him. We agreed to collect him the following day.

Alan and the children went back to school at the beginning of September. It was Jessica's first day at Saddleworth School so I took a photo of her in her new school uniform – shivering outside the front door.

Sam came off his skateboard on the concrete in front of the stables that weekend. He skinned his chin and nose and bit his top lip. His face was a real mess.

I continued creosoting the stables and in an attempt to get as much done as possible I put off going shopping for as long as possible. The cupboards were practically bare by the time I finally went to the supermarket. I loaded up the Land Rover with a huge trolley load of shopping but the wretched thing refused to start.

Fortunately Cath and Jim happened to be there and they brought me home with most of my shopping. That evening we towed the Land Rover back home with the car. Alan made several unsuccessful attempts to start the engine.

Progress in the back room was slow. Outdoor jobs continued to take priority when the weather was good. However we worked on it now and again. The chimney breast had been blocked off by a sheet of ply which had been wall papered and a skirting board had been fastened at the bottom. We ripped it all out expecting to find a bricked up hole in the wall, but were pleasantly surprised to discover an old stone fire place. At each side there was a massive piece of stone standing about four feet tall which went back into the chimney recess about 18 inches. Another large piece of stone lay across the top of them. Whatever mantelpiece there might once have been, had long since disappeared, so Alan decided to make something simple but bold to complement the stone.

When we got married Alan's dad had given us a length of solid oak to put on top of our first fireplace. It was 7 feet long 10 inches deep and 5 inches thick and it was as straight as a die. Every time we moved house we had taken it with us. Alan decided to mount it on the wall above the horizontal stone. He had two other big pieces of oak that he had hoarded for years and now shaped them into two chunky supports which he bolted to the wall at each side for the length of oak to sit on. Finally he laid three stone flags to make a hearth. When he'd finished the whole thing looked solid and old as if it had always been there and we were very pleased with it.

Matthew was a monumental stonemason. We told him about the fireplace and asked if he would bring his chisels with him next time they came over and do a bit of work on the horizontal piece of stone for us. They came across the following weekend and Matthew worked on the stone to give it a 'punched finish' to match the two side pieces which were already faced like that. While he was here he had a look at the Land Rover with Alan and they came to the conclusion that the engine was beyond repair and we needed a new one.

Unfortunately the loan of Ebony was not a success. Jess enjoyed looking after him in the stable and he was fine to turn out and easy to catch. Several times I had walked with her down the lane to The Roebuck and back, or up the lane to the Sloane's paddock and everything seemed fine. But it wasn't the same as going out on a proper hack.

Unable to ride myself I had to rely on other people on the yard to take Jess out. I knew it was a big responsibility to put onto somebody else but in my defence I had been told that he was very well behaved and up to then he had given me no reason to doubt it. Both Shelley and Jane had taken Jess out at different times when they had hacked out and each of them had expressed concern about Ebony's behaviour. He behaved well enough when walking along a road but if they reached an open area he would become wilful and would spin round trying to tank off and Jess apparently struggled to control him. On Jane's advice I bought a different bit for Jess to try.

One particular time a few of them decided to go out on a long hack across the moors above Castleshaw reservoir. Apparently at one point they decided to have a canter and all set off together but Ebony veered off to the right and jumped over an unsuspecting sheep! The final straw however occurred when she hacked out with Shelley and Thomas. At the end of the bridle path near the Sloanes there is a quiet, narrow lane bordered by a small stone wall, when they reached this point and turned right to go down the lane Ebony suddenly whirled round and tried to jump over the wall. Jess was terrified as beyond the wall was a drop of about 50 feet. That evening I rang Ebony's owner and asked her to come and collect him.

Jess had been more frightened of riding Ebony than she cared to admit. She had completely lost her nerve and was reluctant to even sit on Thomas. We needed to find something steady and reliable – a school master or school mistress as they are called.

I had finally finished creosoting the stables and now, on my own again throughout the day my time was spent re sealing all the doors and window frames. It was a big job and very time consuming but I managed to get it finished by the end of the month.

The next time Dianna and Matthew came over Matthew took Alan to Wigan where they bought a re-conditioned diesel Land Rover engine. When they got home they managed to lever it from the back of Matthew's Land Rover into the back of our Land Rover. A few days later Martin towed it away to sort it out.

The first week of October was cold and wet. I worked down at the stables doing my usual jobs each morning and depending on the weather got other maintenance jobs done in the afternoons. I levelled the ground in front of the hen hut where it was getting muddy and managed to manoeuvre a large stone flag in front of it. As I lowered it into position I trapped my finger between the flag and the corner of the hut taking a big chunk out of it. Very painful!

In the middle of October Martin returned the Land Rover. Later the same month, Nicola sold Soli to Ann, a friend of Shelley's husband.

Alan no longer wanted to spend his time collecting and mixing sawdust and shavings with Steve. We forfeited our share in the yellow van as Steve had taxed it and put it through its MOT and instead I began to collect pine shavings in the Land Rover to sell just on our yard. I bought a large quantity of big plastic bags and called at two or three different places each week to bag up shavings. I could cram up to six of the bulging bags in the Land Rover which made for some awkward gear changing but I managed to drive home and covered in a layer of fine sawdust I stacked them all in the bottom barn. I expected to sell between 10 and 15 bags each week over winter depending on the weather.

During the half term we finished Ben's new stable and Shelley moved him into it. Andy left the yard with Bonnie and the following day a lady called Diane arrived with her teenage son Mark to enquire if we had an available stable.

A few days later Diane and Mark brought 'Zulu' a 15.3hh Thoroughbred bay gelding onto the yard. Two weeks previously they had been involved in a road traffic accident. The trailer in which Zulu had been travelling had overturned and he had been trapped inside it for over half an hour. The fire brigade and three vets attended the scene and after what must have been a traumatic time for all concerned Zulu was extricated from the trailer with only minor cuts and abrasions. Mark who had injured his back in the accident walked Zulu the half mile or so back to the yard where he was stabled. Under the circumstances it was understandable that Zulu was a little nervous when he arrived on our yard and it took him a day or so to settle.

Blizzards

The following Tuesday began cold and clear. Alan took Sam to school. Jess hadn't felt well the day before so I kept her at home. I turned the horses out and mucked out Reuben and then I went for shavings. By the time I got home the wind had whipped up and it had started to snow. The sky had become incredibly dark and I knew we were in for trouble. Hurriedly I began to bring the horses back in. I had only brought one of them in when the blizzard hit us.

I ran into the house and rang Saddleworth School. I spoke to Alan and urged him to pick up Sam and the Sloane girls and get home quick. He said he couldn't leave yet, it wasn't that bad. Frustrated, I told Jess I was going to fetch the children myself and I'd be as quick as I could. I started the Land Rover but only got as far as Steve Foster's when it began to slide and skid. I tried to reverse but the wheels spun and I couldn't do that either. The snow was coming down incredibly quickly and the more I tried to drive the more I skidded until finally the Land Rover became firmly wedged across the lane blocking it completely.

I ran back up the lane to resume bringing in the horses. The snow was coming down so thickly that I couldn't see properly. I tried to shield my eyes as I walked. Each time I brought a horse down the field the rest of them cantered down to the gate with me but by the time I returned to the gate for the next one they had all galloped back up to the top of the hollows again to seek shelter from the pine trees behind the wall. I slipped and struggled up the field. The snow blinded me and froze on my face. I was becoming very tired and my progress up the fields was slow. The cold air hurt my throat as I struggled to get my breath. I had brought in four horses when Steve Foster appeared and grabbed my arm.

'I've been watching you from my window' he said 'you shouldn't be doing this on your own. I'll help you.'

I was absolutely exhausted by this time and accepted his help gratefully. We fought our way up the fields again and clipped our lead ropes onto two more horses. Once more the remaining horses came down to the bottom gate with us. All the horses by this time were excited and agitated and difficult to handle. Steve led Soli. Once they had reached the concrete she calmed down and went into her stable eagerly. I was leading Katie who was very jumpy and was shivering uncontrollably. By the time we reached her stable the shavings were coated with a light covering of snow which had blown over the door. She snorted nervously and refused to go in. It took me several attempts and some gentle encouragement from Steve to eventually lead her safely inside. We trailed up to the top field again for the last two horses who by this time were shivering and shaking and more than happy to be led to their stables and out of the appalling weather. We shut all the top doors. I thanked Steve and couldn't help but laugh at his moustache which had been transformed into a block of ice.

I went into the kitchen and practically climbed on top of the Aga. I was so cold I couldn't stop shaking. Jess ran upstairs and fetched me a couple of towels which I warmed on the Aga while I took off my wet clothes. I rubbed myself dry, got changed and had a hot drink. By this time it was about 2.30pm. I rang Cath and asked her if she could pick up Sam from school and keep him overnight. Hopefully I'd be able to fetch him home in the morning. I remembered Steve Sloane telling me that he was working somewhere the other side of Manchester that week so I knew I wouldn't be able to contact him. I rang Diane's dental surgery in Milnrow but I was unable to speak to her as she had just left work to try and get home. It was most unlikely that she would manage to get home in the next hour so I had to sort something out quickly for the children. I decided to ring Pauline a friend whose little girl was in the same class as Stephanie. It was a big ask but I explained our predicament and asked if she would collect the three girls and take them home with her when she fetched her own daughter and keep them until I could arrange for someone to pick them up. She was a little taken aback as she'd only met Stephanie once and hadn't even seen the other two! To her credit she agreed to help. I was relieved and rang Alan again to tell him what arrangements I'd made for the children and advise him to stay overnight in Uppermill. He wouldn't hear of it and said he would be setting off to walk home very soon.

I knew nobody would be able to get up here to see to their horses that night so I went back down to the stables skipped them all out, fed and watered them.

The hens had all retreated to the hen hut when the snow began to fall. I gave them some corn and clean water and put the block in to secure the hut for the night. Cold and tired I went back indoors lit the stove and made some tea for me and Jess.

Having walked the three miles or so from Uppermill to Scouthead without too much difficulty Alan turned into Doctor Lane and began to tackle the hill towards the quarry. It was then that he encountered the blizzard. He struggled through the driving snow and climbed over the snow drifts that filled the roads. Some three hours after he had set off from school – a walk which would normally have taken him about an hour - he arrived at The Roebuck completely exhausted and extremely cold. He went inside to get warm in front of their open fire and rang to tell me that he would stay there for another 20 minutes then he would start walking up Shiloh Lane. Jess and I watched out for him through the dining room window. When we caught sight of him in the lane I took the dogs with me and went to meet him. He was numb with cold and couldn't believe how bad it was up here. At 7pm. I had to ring Pauline to tell her that I had been unable to contact either Diane or Steve. She agreed to keep the girls overnight and take them to school in the morning. Diane got home about 7.30pm and Steve about an hour later.

Next morning the wind had dropped. The snow was incredibly deep in places. Driving down the lane in the Land Rover was not an option and Alan rang school to tell them that he was unable to come in to work. We fed all the horses and let the hens out – they didn't venture very far. We cleared the snow from the concrete in front of all the stables then mucked out all the horses. We dug the snow out of the shippon and back stable where it had blown through the gaps in the doors and we brushed it off the hay bales where it had blown into the top of the hay barn. We dug away the huge snow drift that had formed behind the Land Rover and managed to reverse it into the car park. The next job was to dig out our access road. Steve Foster joined us and the three of us spent the rest of the day shovelling back the snow until we reached Shiloh Lane. Nobody came up to the stables so we settled the horses for the night with a feed and fresh water. Now that the wind had dropped the dogs enjoyed the snow. Kim and Maggie careered about the garden chasing each other and swallowed mouthfuls of it.

Shiloh Lane was completely filled with drifted snow which in places towered high above the walls. There was absolutely no possibility of any vehicles getting up or down the lane unless a snow plough or snow blower was sent to clear it. Sam had to spend the night at Julie's with William. On Thursday we woke up to find that the snow blower had cleared Shiloh Lane during the night. Alan went to work in the Land Rover. I turned out the horses and mucked out. That evening Sam came home. He was very upset at having been away from Jericho when there had been so much snow and angry with us that we hadn't fetched him! I promised him that he could have the next day off school whether it snowed again or not! Another week went by before we were able to drive the Land Rover up to the house. The BMW still struggled to get any grip on the icy ground so we left it in the car park by the stables.

At the end of November Pat John Dianna and Matthew came over with my birthday present; a big chunk of sandstone with one smooth face on which Matthew had carved 'JERICHO FARM'. I loved it and we positioned it on the first patch of grass on the left as you come up our lane

Up to this time Misty and Trader had been living together in Misty's stable. Trader was now six months old and it was time he was weaned. We put him in one of the stables at the back of the house. Over the next six weeks he and Misty were turned out alternately so that they could not come into contact. At first Trader stood and called loudly and persistently for his mum but before long he got used to her absence and grazed quite happily without her.

December was a very cold month. I saw to most of the horses every morning and got stocked up with as many bags of shavings as possible to keep us going over the Christmas break. Just before Christmas Soli went on loan and left the yard.

Christmas day and Boxing Day were nice family days as usual.

The weather was cold and dry over the whole Christmas period and we managed to shift most of the muck heap using the Land Rover and the low trailer.

1996 went out with high winds and heavy snow. On New Year's Eve the wind brought heavy snow from the North which continued to fall throughout the day. Light powdery snow blew into the stables and coated the horses bedding. We mucked them all out as best we could then shut all the top stable doors for the rest of the day and overnight.

1997

On New Year's Day the lane was impassable by car. Jane was the only one who managed to get up to the yard and she saw to Katie. We mucked out the rest of the horses. At about 4 o'clock that afternoon we were relieved to see the snow blower coming up Shiloh Lane.

Throughout the day everywhere was blindingly white in the winter sunshine. Late that night the snow was bathed in moonlight so everywhere was still quite light which must have confused Eric as he crowed loud and long at midnight!

Next day all the horses were turned out at different times for a bit of exercise while their stables were mucked out. By early evening it was bitterly cold again.

Another blizzard hit us during Friday afternoon and evening. Once again Shiloh Lane was full of drifted snow. We knew that the Sloanes had been visiting family and that when they returned they would be unable to drive up the lane. All evening we watched out for them. At about 10 o'clock we saw car head lights at the bottom of the lane near The Roebuck. The lights didn't come any closer and then they went out. Looking through binoculars Alan could make out figures in the snow. It was still snowing heavily and the wind made it difficult and unpleasant to walk. Hurriedly I gathered up some warm coats and hats for Alan to take with him then he set off to meet them as they struggled up the lane. The sleepy children were in their pyjamas ready for bed. Alan helped Steve and Diane carry them home through the snow drifts.

At the weekend Alan, Sam and Steve Foster began digging the snow out of our access road. When I had finished my stable jobs I joined them. It took us most of the day to get to the end where it joined Shiloh Lane. Tired and hungry we were scraping up the last bits of snow when we saw a snow plough coming. As it cleared the lane hard packed ice and snow built up against the huge blade forming a high wall of gritty snow. When it reached our access road it deposited the lot in the space we had just created completely blocking off what had taken us all day to clear. Hardly able to believe our eyes we hurled abuse at the driver as he continued up the lane. On reaching Shiloh Farm the driver turned the snow plough round and came back. I climbed onto the offending pile of snow which he had dumped there and gestured to the driver to stop and shift it for us. He gestured back with two fingers and drove past.

Snow continued to fall and make life difficult for another two weeks. The icy temperatures froze the water tap at the stables. I couldn't free it with boiling water and had to resort once again to carrying seemingly endless buckets of water from the kitchen down the garden to the stables.

Driving continued to be hazardous as gritters appeared rarely if at all. Cars at times blocked the lane causing more problems and fraying tempers. It was with immense relief that we welcomed the arrival of warmer weather.

After Soli's departure from the yard at the end of December we had some maintenance work to do on her stable in preparation for the next occupant – which turned out to be Trader. Sue took him out of the back stable and turned him out in the field to be re-united with Misty for a while, after which she put him in his new stable on the yard.

Bobbie

Jess and Mark got on well and shared a similar sense of humour. At 16 years old Mark was tall and skinny with short dark hair. He was a competent rider and looked forward to the new season when he would compete on Zulu in show jumping and cross country competitions at Northern events and local Pony Club and Riding Club shows.

Mark's mum Diane mentioned to me that Mark's first pony was at present on loan to a family in Saddleworth. They had recently told her that they no longer wanted the pony and had asked her either to take him back or find somewhere else for him to go as soon as possible. Over the last month or so probably due to her friendship with Mark, Jess had started to show an interest in riding again and as we had an available stable we talked to her about 'Bobbie'. It turned out that this was the pony that she had ridden the previous summer with a couple of her friends at the place where he was on loan. The prospect of loaning him appealed to Jess as he was very well schooled, so we spoke to Diane about it. She was delighted at the prospect of having Bobbie on our yard and made arrangements for us to collect him.

The following Saturday morning Jess got Bobbie's stable ready and we collected him in the afternoon. Bobbie was a 14.2hh middle weight bay gelding. He was twenty three years old and hadn't been ridden for some time. His fitness had to be built up slowly as did Jess's confidence. To begin with Jess rode him in Misty's field just to get used to him, but her confidence returned very quickly and soon she was hacking out with both Mark and Shelley. Bobbie was forward going but sensible and Jess felt safe on him, he was just what we had wanted for her and we were very pleased to have him.

Around this time I bought a bridle and a training bit for Reuben. Gently I encouraged him to take the bit into his mouth. He responded well and very soon accepted it quite readily. I put the bridle on him every morning before mucking him out and left it on him while I filled his hay nets and water. He mouthed the bit quite happily with his head over the stable door. I also began taking him for walks down the lane, each time taking him a few yards further than I had the time before. At first he would stop and snort at anything he was unsure of. If a car came down the lane behind him he would turn right round and take a good look at it as it approached. He remained rooted to the spot until it had gone past us and disappeared from view, only then could we resume our walk. After a while however he no longer turned round and instead he just put his ears back, turned his head and watched the cars as they passed by. I felt encouraged that he was progressing so well.

The weather was misty, cold and dismal throughout the first half of February. I continued to work on the backroom sanding the beams and trying to clean the stone at the back of the fire place which was partially covered in black paint.

By this time I was well and truly into the winter routine as regards looking after the horses. The winter strip made my life so much easier. I no longer had to walk all the way up the field to turn out and bring in the horses. Now, I only had to walk as far as the gate beside the house. The other gate which led into the hollows field was wedged open so that the horses had that field too for grazing and exercise. At the end of the day when they were ready to come in they all tended to accumulate at the bottom gate by the house. It made life easier for everybody having the field gate so much closer to the stable block.

The freezing temperatures throughout December and January had made life difficult as regards frozen water taps and slippery surfaces but they were conditions when at least everywhere was clean. This all changed in February the latter half of which was horrendous with heavy rain and gale force winds. The winter fields took a terrific hammering from the horses and the lower half of the winter strip resembled a quagmire particularly by the gate. Working at the stables was unpleasant. Everyday I got dirty, wet and cold. The continuous rain was depressing and made every job I did more difficult. One of the worst jobs I had to do in wet weather was the twice weekly shavings collection. The sawdust stuck to my wet clothes and hands and was transferred into the Land Rover coating everything with a thin layer of fine dust.

Working indoors I persevered with my efforts to remove the black paint from the stone fire place in the back room. In between applications of paint stripper I rubbed down the paint work on the window frame and the cupboard door.

By early March, Reuben had been with us for one year. As a rule, unless the weather was really bad, I tethered him outside his stable while I mucked out. He was becoming very relaxed and was happy to stand and munch the hay in his hay net while I got on with my jobs. I regularly strapped a numnah across his back with a sursingle, and now and again I lay across him to get him used to the feel of some weight on his back in preparation for introducing him to a saddle. He was a little worried about that! I intended to send him away later in the year to a local man who would back him and give him some intensive schooling. Hopefully by then Jess would be able to continue to bring him on. In the meantime I planned to have lessons on Bobbie and learn to ride properly myself.

Bobbie was a pleasure to look after. He stood still while his feet were checked and while he was being groomed. He moved over in the stable when he was asked to, and waited until he was told before he ate his feed. He walked quietly when being turned out or brought in from the field. He was no problem with other horses and he behaved well when out on a hack. He was full of character and played tricks on me regularly. When I changed his rugs I tended to hang his stable rug over the stable door while I got his outdoor rug from the tack room. As soon as I turned my back he would get hold of the stable rug with his teeth and pull it on to the floor then he would turn away as if he'd had nothing to do with it. He did have one fault and that was his reluctance to be caught once he had been turned out. We spent many a frustrating half hour trying to entice him to come to us with carrots or apples when Jess came home from school wanting to ride. On one occasion Jess and Mark hacked across to Castleshaw Moor. At one point they jumped over a low stone wall, Jess lost her balance and fell off Bobbie. It took them 40 minutes to catch him!

The weather throughout March was mixed but was mainly dry and very cold. After having done the usual stable jobs each morning I carried on working in the back room. Having successfully removed the paint from the back of the fire place I turned my attention once more to the beams. When I had finished sanding them I brushed them with linseed oil. I sealed the door and door frame then painted the cupboard door and window frame. I decided to wallpaper the room as the plaster on one of the walls was particularly poor. The room looked loads better - I just needed to find time to get it painted.

We needed a paddock where people could school their horses. Although we couldn't afford a proper surface we could provide a flat area for them to work. During March our milkman Norman Taylor and his brother Jim began work with their JCB and mini-digger. They set about levelling and squaring off the area of ground that included the enclosure which we had used for the two Shetlands and Dolly between the hay barn at the end of the house and the stable block.

The Taylor brothers were farmers well known in Saddleworth and renowned for their frequent and bitter arguments. Norman was a big friendly man who towered over his elder brother. Jim was a slightly built polite little man who always wore a jacket and tie when working and was never without his flat cap.

Before they started work I made a point of showing Norman where we had laid the armoured cable to the stable block and he assured me that he would tell Jim. However a couple of days later Jim Taylor cut through the armoured cable with the JCB – so there was no power to the stables. This sparked a furious row between the two brothers. Norman's face was as red as a beetroot as he shouted at his brother and accused him of being careless. Jim shouted back just as angrily that Norman had not told him that there was a cable to avoid let alone where it was!

At the weekend Steve Foster mended the cable and we managed to reroute it a little further away from the edge of the paddock.

Zulu's trailer had been sent away soon after the accident to undergo tests which would determine whether or not the chassis had been twisted or distorted. Fortunately it turned out that the damage was only cosmetic and when the necessary repairs had been done the trailer was brought up to Jericho and parked in the stables car park. Mark had no idea whether or not Zulu would load into the trailer again – we all thought it unlikely.

During the Easter break his mum manoeuvred the trailer into the middle of the car park so that Mark could begin to gradually re introduce Zulu to it. Mark had intended at first to just walk Zulu up to the open trailer then next day perhaps take him part way up the ramp or maybe feed him in the trailer depending on how he had reacted to it initially. He dropped the rear ramp and also the side ramp so that Zulu would not feel enclosed, then he lead him from his stable and approached the open trailer. To Mark's complete astonishment Zulu eagerly walked straight up the ramp and stood inside the trailer. He then followed Mark calmly out through the side door. Over the next few days Mark did this several times. Zulu remained calm each time so Mark hung up a hay net, closed the side ramp and walked him in again. Zulu appeared to be completely unconcerned and began to eat the hay so Mark closed the rear ramp also. Keeping everything crossed his mum drove off and they towed the trailer for a few miles then came back and unloaded him. Zulu behaved as if nothing traumatic had ever happened and has continued to do so ever since!

Around this time a man arrived at Jericho in a transit van selling unbelievably cheap carpets. The van was crammed with rolls of different coloured plain carpets. They were all the same type and all apparently very hard wearing. The price was so reasonable that I bought two rolls for the back room. I paid cash and asked no questions!

When the Easter break was at an end all the others went back to school. I started to ride Bobbie quite regularly, not very well but there was plenty of time to improve.

I continued to spend time with Reuben each day. I tethered him outside his stable to pick out his hooves and groom him. He was losing his winter coat and the summer one was coming through with a healthy shine. I thoroughly enjoyed looking after him and seeing him develop into a handsome and well-mannered young horse made me feel proud. Although I knew that I would need some help and guidance over the next year or two, I didn't feel anything like as out of my depth as I had twelve months ago. I regarded Jane as probably the most knowledgeable person on the yard as far as horses were concerned. Although she kept herself to herself much of the time every now and again she would impart words of wisdom or make some meaningful remark. One morning I was grooming Reuben outside his stable.

'He looks well. You're doing a good job with him.' she remarked then disappeared into her stable. I was well chuffed.

Julie asked if she could bring her horse up to Jericho for a short time until some grazing near her home in Uppermill was available for her to rent. We had an available stable so a few days later she rode up to the yard on Kristie.

A Pony Club team show jumping competition was to be held at Woodnook in Meltham the following weekend. Jess had been enrolled as a member of the Saddleworth branch of the Pony Club and was asked to take part. Throughout the week after school Diane Sloane helped her work with Bobbie in their arena to prepare for it.

Early in May we had problems with the Aga. Our water was heated by the Aga and somehow air had got into the system. One evening the water began bubbling in the pipes, which soon after started to vibrate violently. The Aga sounded as if it was going to explode. I was scared out of my wits. Alan bled the system at the point where the pipes went into the hot water cylinder. It seemed to help but not for long. He had to keep bleeding it every two hours throughout the night.

Next day was a dry, cold and sunny day. Early in the evening, accompanied by Mark riding Zulu, Jess hacked Bobbie to her first Pony Club rally at the Pony Club field in Friezland about three and a half miles away. Towards the end of the rally the weather deteriorated – they hacked home through sleet and snow. When we got home, the Aga was still making bubbling noises. Alan continued to bleed the system throughout the rest of the evening.

The following Monday was a lovely bright, crisp day. After taking the children to school I turned out the horses and mucked out Reuben before getting on with some outdoor jobs. Later on I collected the children from school and as usual Jess went up to her bedroom to listen to music before getting changed and seeing to Bobbie.

Mark came to the house very upset. He had gone up the field to bring Zulu in so he could ride. As he walked up the field he noticed that all the horses were clustered together. As he approached them he saw that one of them was laid down. It was Bobbie. He was dead. Straightaway Mark turned and ran back to the house. I walked back up with him. The horses had wandered away from Bobbie by this time. We think that he may have had a heart attack and dropped dead - probably just before Mark had found him.

Mark caught Zulu and took him down to his stable. I returned to the house and went upstairs to tell Jess. She was heartbroken and insisted on going to see Bobbie. We walked up the field together and cried when we saw him. Jess knelt down beside the old pony and stroked his head. When she was ready we left him and walked back to the house. With tears streaming down her face she went back up to her bedroom and stayed there until morning.

We told Norman what had happened and asked him if he would dig a big hole with his JCB. We buried Bobbie where he had died. Matthew made us a small headstone with his name on and we put it near the wall close to where he was buried in the field henceforward known as 'Bobbie's field'.

During the Whit week holiday at the end of May we enjoyed a settled spell of glorious hot sunny weather. On the Thursday we decided to have a barbeque. We invited my mum and Alan's mum over for the afternoon. My mum was very fond of animals and always made a fuss of the cat and dogs and liked to see the poultry. I took her to the field gate to show her Reuben as she had only seen him in a photo. I called him and obligingly he ambled across to be stroked. Mum thought he was very handsome and commented on his beautiful light brown tail which was streaked with silver and black. We walked back to the others who were sitting outside enjoying the sunshine. Reuben walked with us as far as the water trough. We laughed when we heard him blowing noisily in the water.

'It's a bit hot for them today' I said 'he's probably trying to cool himself down.'

About 6 o'clock after our mums had gone home I went to bring Reuben in from the field. Unusually he was lying down. I went right up to him and put his head collar on him while he was still lying down.

'C'mon Reuben it's time to go in' I said, giving him a push. He got to his feet and walked with me to his stable. It was warm in there too. I gave him his feed. He looked at it then walked to the back of the stable and lay down again. I was a bit worried and told Alan.

'He's probably had too much sun; he'll eat when he's ready'.

'Yes but he's lying down, he never does that when I'm in the stable'.

'Honestly Jan I think he's just got overheated but if you're really worried ask Steve and Carl to have a look at him.'

Steve and Carl came over and looked at Reuben. They couldn't see anything obviously wrong and agreed with Alan that he had probably had too much sun. When I took the dogs for their last walk about 9.30pm I checked on Reuben again. He was looking over his stable door and seemed OK – but he still hadn't eaten his tea.

I got up early next morning and went straight down to check on him. He seemed very subdued, his food was still untouched and he had done no droppings at all. I was really worried and rang the vet.

The vet examined Reuben very thoroughly and was concerned that he had not passed anything since at least six o'clock the previous evening. He gave him an anti biotic injection and told me to keep him in. Before leaving he gave me his mobile telephone number and told me to ring him in the morning if there was no change. I spent most of that day with Reuben. He seemed to appreciate my company and nudged me every so often for a stroke.

Next morning there was no change. The vet came back about 9.30am. Once again he put his stethoscope against Reuben's flanks and listened intently. After what seemed like ages he looked at me. 'I'm going to have to refer him to Leahurst Equine Hospital in Liverpool' he said. 'I don't know what's wrong with him but I do know you've got a very sick horse.' With that he went to his car to make a phone call. I felt sick. Tears pricked my eyes. I hugged Reuben and told him everything would be OK.

The vet came back to the stable. 'You need to take him across to Leahurst for about 12 o'clock' he said stroking Reuben 'they'll be expecting you.'

Alan went over to Shiloh Farm to ask Steve and Diane if we could borrow their horse box. I went up to the house to make some hurried arrangements for the children. After a couple of phone calls I took Jess and Sam down to Uppermill to spend the day with friends. When I got back the horse box was already in our car park. I borrowed some travel boots from Shelley and we loaded Reuben into the box quite easily. The vet had given Alan some directions to Leahurst for when we left the motorway. The journey took about an hour and a half. I was worried that Reuben would be scared. The last time he had been in a horse box was to travel to and from Holmfirth market fifteen months ago. I would have liked to have been able to check on him during the journey so that I could have comforted him but the horse box was an old one and there was no access into the back of it from the cab. As soon as we got to Leahurst Alan went to find somebody to let them know that we had arrived. I went into the box through the small side door to see Reuben. He was sweated up and trembling. I talked to him softly and stroked him. A few minutes later I heard the catches on the ramp being unfastened.

'OK Jan' Alan called 'the vet's going to look at Reuben before we get him off, then they'll tell us where to take him.'

The ramp was lowered. Reuben was wide eyed and nervous. The vet walked up the ramp. He related the information which our vet had given him and asked if we had anything to add. We hadn't. He looked at Reuben briefly then told us to unload him. I untied the lead rope and guided Reuben out of the stall. He came down the ramp quickly then stood quietly beside me at the bottom. The vet listened to Reuben's belly.

'Too quiet' he said. 'I hate this time of year. We get about 15 young horses sent to us each year from all over the North West with these symptoms. If your horse is one of these he has grass sickness which means he has ingested something which his immune system is too immature to cope with. Whatever it is has paralysed his gut preventing him from digesting food. Despite years of research we still don't know what causes it. If that's what it is he could recover to some extent but he will never be as he was, he will always be a sickly animal. There is however a possibility that he has an obstruction or a twist in his gut but we would have to operate to find that out. Is he insured?' I shook my head.

'He's hardly been off the yard. I intended taking out insurance for him this summer when I would be doing more with him.'

The vet was sympathetic. 'You need to know one way or the other.' he said. 'If you want me to operate I will just charge for the medication and use of equipment - not my time.'

We thanked him. He nodded and walked away. A veterinary student called to us to bring Reuben across the yard to a small stable block. She opened the door to the first stable and we took him inside. It was cool and roomy and Reuben soon became happier and more settled. The stable next to his was empty and the last two in the block were occupied by quiet horses. Reuben looked over the door, he looked so strong and healthy I couldn't believe he was desperately ill. After about an hour another veterinary student came to the stable. My stomach was churning.

'We're ready for Reuben now' she said. Struggling to stay composed I hugged Reuben and kissed his soft nose.

'Good boy, see you soon' I said as I clipped the lead rope onto his head collar and passed it to her. The girl smiled.

'Come on Reuben' she said kindly. He turned for a moment and looked at me with his beautiful trusting eyes.

'Go on Reuben, its OK.' I said trying to sound cheerful. He turned and walked away with the girl. We watched them make there way across the yard. The girl talked encouragingly to him as he walked quietly beside her, his beautiful tail swayed from side to side shining silver and black in the spring sunshine. That was the last time we saw him.

Some time later a veterinary nurse walked across to us and told us the news. There was no obstruction. No twist in his gut. She asked us if we wanted the vet to bring him out of the anaesthetic or to put him to sleep. We both felt that we could not let him live a weak and sickly existence after having been so healthy and full of life. We told her to ask the vet to put him to sleep. We left soon after.

Neither of us spoke on the journey home. There was nothing to say. When we got home the children were shocked and upset when we told them - as was everybody on the yard. It had all happened so quickly. That night I couldn't sleep I was too upset.

The following morning I got up early and blinking back the tears I emptied Reuben's stable and was back in the house before anyone arrived on the yard. I didn't feel sociable. For days I felt completely empty and miserable. It was unfair. It was wrong. He was a gentle intelligent creature we had all loved him and he should have lived a long and happy life with us.

At the beginning of June the paddock was finished. By the end of the month we had fenced round it and seeded the bank at the bottom which dropped down to the end of the stable yard. Mark used it frequently so did Jane and Shelley. Julie did too until the grazing she was waiting for in Uppermill became available at the end of the month and she left with Kristie.

A few days later Kristie escaped from the field in Uppermill. I received a frantic phone call from Julie early in the morning telling me that Kristie had been seen trotting down Uppermill High Street followed by the No.183 bus at 7am heading North West out of Uppermill! I received a second phone call from her a few hours later. Apparently somebody had caught Kristie on the bridle path not far from the Sloane's. She was evidently heading for Jericho! I was touched that she regarded our yard as home and wished she had made it to her stable without being caught.

Maintenance work on the stables took up most of my time in July. Mark decided that he had achieved as much as he could do on Zulu and he began to look for a new horse. Zulu was put up for sale.

We acquired an old livestock trailer from a friend of Steve Sloane. The trailer was in very poor condition and we had to strip it right back to the chassis. We enlisted Matthew to help rebuild it. He and Dianna came across on two consecutive weekends. Matthew welded lengths of angle iron onto the old chassis to reinforce it and create a strong frame. Alan fastened in a new timber floor and side panels. They took off the two old wheels with the perished tyres and replaced them with two Land Rover wheels which Matthew had brought over and the renovated trailer was finished.

'The job's a good un!' Matthew announced beaming from ear to ear.

Hay Making

Some months earlier we had been approached by a neighbouring family whose land was adjacent to ours. They no longer had cattle to graze their land and there was too much grazing for their three ponies. They asked if we would be interested in renting their large hay field which they referred to as the 'Five Acre field' on condition that we fertilized and harrowed it each year. We jumped at the chance as our fields had a long way to go before they could be considered to be good grazing. This summer we had the use of the Five Acre field for the first time. Because there was so much grass on it we decided to make hay before letting the horses in to graze.

In the middle of July Bill cut the grass. We needed at least five dry, preferably warm, sunny days to make good quality hay. Because we had no farm machinery of our own we were completely dependent upon other people to cut and bale it for us. Stacking the bales and bringing them in was down to us. Never before had weather forecasts been so important. I found myself staring anxiously up at the sky and watching the appearance of clouds with renewed interest.

Twice during the previous week Mark and his mum had been to see an eventing horse. He was a handsome 16.3hh bright bay gelding called James. They decided to buy him and he arrived on the yard on the Sunday.

After having cut the grass Bill turned it twice to help dry it out and mid morning on the Wednesday he came again and rowed it ready for baling. Gerald arrived with the baler attached to his tractor and made a start on the baling early in the afternoon. When he had finished there were four hundred and sixteen small hay bales scattered all over the field.

As soon as the baling was finished Alan, me, Jess, Sam and William went into the field to stack the bales into piles of four or six ready to be thrown up onto the trailer. Twice we loaded our trailer with 30 bales then unloaded them and carried them up into the hay barn. The weather was very warm and the children were flagging, all of them were quite small and found the new bales very heavy. Alan and I did the bulk of it between us, it was slow going. There were so many bales to collect we were worried that we wouldn't get them all in before dark without some help. We rang Matthew and Gary to ask if there was any chance they could come across and give us a hand.

As we returned to collect the next load we saw the man who owned the field driving his tractor and trailer through his farm gate with his son to help us. Half an hour later Julie and Pete arrived then Matthew and Dianna and Gary soon after. Bill Dawson also came later with his niece.

Now that there were two tractors and trailers we split up into two groups. Some of us flung the hay bales up onto the trailers and some of us stood on the trailers and stacked the bales as they were thrown up. The children thoroughly enjoyed riding on top of the hay bales on the trips back to the barn to unload. With so many more hands the job became much easier and quicker and all the bales were off the field and stacked in our hay barn before dark. We were taken aback by all the help which was so readily given and felt bad about having asked Gary to come and help us. We had forgotten that he suffered from hay fever and he apparently sneezed constantly for the next two days!

There was a change in the weather the following day with torrential rain late in the afternoon. I breathed a huge sigh of relief that our hay was safely inside the barn.

At the beginning of August Beth, a member of Pony Club and a friend of Mark's moved onto the yard with her Thoroughbred mare 'Bliss'. Right from the start Beth adored Pete. The feeling was mutual and as soon as Beth's car arrived in the car park Pete would make his way down the garden and stay with her while she mucked out or groomed Bliss. Pete was very aware of the horses and always kept a respectful distance from them when down at the stables.

We desperately needed a rest and also wanted to take the children on holiday. A month or so earlier we had booked a chalet in Cornwall for the last week in August. Beth offered, while we were away, to collect Pete early in the mornings and keep him with her during the day and then bring him back in the evening and leave him in the house overnight. I booked Kim and Maggie into kennels and Jane said she would feed the cat and look after the hens. It was the first time we had been away from Jericho since we had moved there in 1994.

Having returned from our holiday we woke up to the sad news that Diana Princess of Wales had died in a car crash in Paris in the early hours of the morning.

That week Sam had his first riding lesson at Stamford Riding School in Mossley and I turned out the horses into the Five Acre field to graze for the rest of the summer.

Kim started to limp very badly so I took her to the vet. She had torn a ligament and I was told that she needed to rest it. Living where we were with an active dog like Kim that was easier said than done!

Bill Dawson at Two Acre Farm was about the same age as me. He was a wiry man with bushy ginger eyebrows and thick ginger hair that stuck out from beneath his flat cap. On his farm he had reared a good sized herd of cows and kept a variety of poultry which pottered freely about the yard. He was a compassionate farmer where his animals were concerned and I had taken to him immediately. As well as rearing cattle he sold hay and straw, cut and rowed grass ready for baling, spread fertilizer, sprayed weed killer and harrowed people's land. He always knew what was going on in the local area and we found him to be totally dependable. As soon as we got back from our holiday Bill asked me if I would give a home to a large white goose that had unwittingly got herself between a cow and its calf in his yard and had taken a battering. At first the goose had been unable to walk at all but having been isolated in a shed for a week she had recovered quite well. I said I would have her if he would give me another one to keep her company. Bill suggested that he could give me a young Chinese goose which had lived at Jericho before we had moved there. I agreed and the children came with me to collect them in the Land Rover.

'What are they called?' I asked Bill.
'Lucy'
'Which one's Lucy?'
'The white one' he laughed 'all the white ones are called Lucy. The other one doesn't have a name.'

My look of disapproval just made him laugh even more and chuckling to himself he wandered off and found a wire crate to put them in. Understandably the geese were extremely annoyed at being bundled into the crate and hissed at us loudly. Bill put the crate in the back of the Land Rover and Jess sat on one of the seats in the back with them. Every time one of them jabbed its beak between the gaps in the wire crate she squealed. She was petrified of them and the more she squealed the more they hissed. Sam was helpless with laughter in the safety of the front passenger seat. By the time we got home Jess was sitting with her knees up round her ears and couldn't get out of the Land Rover quick enough!

The geese soon got used to their new surroundings and settled happily in a small make shift hut behind the house. An old pond liner which had been left in the back field by our predecessors was still on the bank at the back of the house. We had never got round to getting rid of it. I dragged it out of the long grass, dug away some of the turf and soil on the bank and set the liner into the hole to make them a small pond. Lucy was the first to get in and float about. She flapped her wings hard on the water, ducked her head under the surface and gave herself a thorough wash. The Chinese goose, now called Mabel, took her turn a bit later. The pond was only big enough for them to be in it one at a time.

By mid September I had finished painting the back room. We put the carpet down that I'd bought from the man in the transit van and moved the furniture in.

The last of the gerbils had died so I cleaned the three tanks and gave them to a local pet shop to house various rodents.

James proved to be a very bad buy. He was a bully in the field, difficult to handle especially by men and in particular he appeared to have taken an instant dislike to Mark. He barged him repeatedly when in the stable and did his best to prevent him getting into the saddle. When Mark did manage to mount him riding at times became downright dangerous. From my point of view the last straw was when Soli returned to the yard having been away on loan for the last nine months. Sadly she came back in a poor neglected state and we put her in the field for an hour or so on the second day. James chased her and bit her twice before we could get her away from him. Mark was as upset about it as everybody else was and replaced all James's conditioning and high protein hard feed with a very basic mix hoping it would calm him down. It seemed to work almost immediately as regards his behaviour in the field, not however in his demeanour in the stable or, unfortunately, when Mark rode him.

Regularly throughout the summer we took trailer loads of muck from the muck heap at the stable yard to the one in the field where it would continue to rot down ready for spreading during the winter. By the end of October weather permitting; the muck heap would be practically empty.

One of Julie's neighbours had a new kitchen fitted that October. When Julie heard that the old one was to be thrown into a skip she mentioned to her neighbour that we only had one kitchen cupboard and a horrible old sink. Her neighbour was more than happy for us to take the lot if we wanted it as she just wanted rid of it. We went up to have a look. The cupboard doors were solid pine and although they were old the kitchen cupboards were clean and quite tidy and would be a luxury for us after what we had been managing with. We told her that we would come up and take them as soon as she was ready to get rid of them.

The previous week had been depressing with heavy rain and thick mist. The summer grazing was about to come to an end in less than three weeks and until then everyone was taking advantage of what time there was left and continued to turn out their horses as often as possible. As a result the path between the stable block and the summer field gate was ankle deep in thick sticky mud. This Sunday however was a beautiful sunny day. During the afternoon Sam had been amusing himself in the paddock playing with the dozen or so empty fertilizer containers which we used as supports for the jumping poles. As the time approached 4.30pm people had begun to arrive on the yard to bring in their horses from the field. Sam, still playing on the paddock was now stacking the fertilizer containers one on top of the other as high as he could reach, and then whacking the bottom one as hard as he could with a baseball bat sending them all flying and making a terrific din. Ann called to him as she went to bring in Soli.

'Sam, stop doing that now please. I'm bringing Soli in.'

'OK' he shouted back and obediently stopped what he was doing. Ann brought Soli onto the yard just as Sue set off to get Trader. Sam didn't notice Sue putting Trader's head collar on him at the gate. Nor did he see her lead him past the paddock entrance, he was too busy picking up the containers. Sue had set off to fetch Trader as soon as she had arrived on the yard. She had noticed Sam on the paddock but was unaware of what he was doing. Trader was very strong and excitable at the best of times and it didn't take much to make him unmanageable. Sue led him round the corner and they made their way through the thick mud along the track below the paddock just as Sam placed the last container on top of the unsteady pile.

Completely unaware of the unfolding situation I walked down the garden to speak to Ann. Mark and Jess were chatting on the yard. Sam grabbed the baseball bat and gave the bottom container an almighty whack. There was a terrific crash! Trader bolted. Sue tried to hold onto the lead rope but her feet got stuck and she fell flat on her face in the sticky mud. There was silence for a moment then...

'SAM!!' Sue's shrill and angry scream rent the air. As I arrived on the concrete Trader shot past me. I looked down the yard and saw Sue struggling to her feet, her white jodhpurs and pale blue jacket plastered in thick mud. She was furious. Ann caught Trader and led him to his stable. Mark and Jess hid in their tack rooms trying to suppress their laughter. Sue was small in stature but not one to be trifled with - when he heard her shout Sam fled!

I watched as Sue tried to wipe the mud off her nose and chin with hands that were covered in mud. I managed to keep my face straight as she complained about Sam's stupidity. Nodding in agreement I assured her that Sam would be down to apologise shortly. I ignored Mark and Jess who were grinning at me over their stable doors and went back up to the house to find Sam. It took him several minutes to pluck up the courage to go down and apologise to Sue who, fortunately by that time, had begun to see the funny side.

At the end of the week I began to make a more substantial hut for the geese. After having slipped on goose poo several times when hanging out the washing I wanted it to be as far away from the house as possible and decided to position it at the bottom of the garden. I hardly ever seemed to get any time to spend on it but I worked on it whenever I could throughout October and November.

The first Saturday in November was the start of winter turn-out. Due to the damage sustained each year by the winter field I decided to reduce the number of hours that the horses were turned out. I brought all the horses in no later than 4.30pm free of charge. It was pointless to expect people to bring in their own horses by that time as most of them were still at work, but doing it myself meant that I could be flexible and could vary the time according to the weather conditions. It worked well and to a large extent stopped people ringing up at all hours asking me to see to their horses. It also gave me an end to my working day.

One morning as I loaded up the low trailer with muck from the muck heap I heard a commotion. The geese were honking loudly. I looked up to see Lucy hurtling down the garden honking and flapping her wings like mad. To my complete amazement a third of the way down the garden she became airborne! Still honking she ploughed through the top of one of the small trees in the flower bed at the bottom of the garden and flew over the stable block barely missing the apex of the roof. Left on her own at the top of the garden, Mabel honked miserably as she watched her fat friend disappear through the trees in front of Steve Foster's house.

I was horrified and set off down the lane in the Land Rover fully expecting to see Lucy in a dishevelled heap in one of the fields. I drove to the bottom of Shiloh Lane and turned right past Bill Dawson's farm, all the time scanning the fields for Lucy. There was no sign of her. I carried on past the boarding kennels and up the hill. Puzzled I pulled in and stared over the fields. Jericho was now on my right. There was no way she could have flown any further but I couldn't see her anywhere.

I went back home and walked round to Steve Foster's. At the front of his house there is a fairly large pond sometimes visited by wild ducks. Goodness knows why I hadn't thought of it straight away. Sure enough there was Lucy at one end of the pond swimming happily. I called her but she completely ignored me. Steve was not particularly pleased about the arrival of his new visitor but I assured him that she would return home early that evening to be fed. I was wrong. She appeared to have no intention of returning home at all. I tried to encourage Mabel to honk loudly in the hope that Lucy would hear her and come home. I tapped her food dish and repeatedly went down to the edge of the pond with tit-bits to try and entice her close enough to the edge for me to be able to grab her. Lucy however had no intention of leaving this spacious pond which put ours to shame, and she kept well out of my reach. As darkness fell I had no choice but to leave her there. I lay awake all night worrying that she would be caught by a fox. At 5.30am. I heard her honking loudly. Mabel answered her enthusiastically. I cringed at the thought of Steve and May trying to sleep.

I racked my brains trying to think of a way to get her off the pond. Then I had an idea. A couple of weeks ago some workmen had been digging up the road near The Roebuck and had been using some thin yellow rods which were about 30 feet long. Sam had tied one to the back of his bike and dragged it all the way home. By the time he admitted where he had got it from the workmen had packed up and left.

I got up early and searched beside the walls and along the edges of the paddock, and before long I found the rod. It was thin and whippy. If it was long enough to reach across Steve's pond from side to side I reckoned that if each of us held one end of the rod at opposite sides of the pond we could skim Lucy across it and out of the water as we walked along. The land beside the pond was very overgrown and Lucy was not good on her feet if the ground was uneven, so hopefully if we could get her out of the water I'd be able to grab her.

I called round to Steve's told him my cunning plan and asked him if he would hold one end of the yellow rod. He agreed resignedly mumbling that he didn't think it would work and even if it did she would probably come straight back again at the first opportunity. I refused to be put off and clutching one end of the rod I told him to get hold of the other end while I fought my way through the undergrowth to the other side of the pond opposite him.

Lucy was roughly in the middle of the pond, we set off walking holding the rod between us just above the level of the water. The rod was just a bit short so I had to wade through the icy cold water up to my knees. As we approached Lucy I pulled the rod taught and it made contact with her just under her tail. Looking a little surprised she skimmed quickly across the water and onto the bank and then set off across the grass in an ungainly fashion flapping her wings and stumbling awkwardly through the thick vegetation. I let go of the rod and heaved myself out of the pond. With water sloshing out of the tops of my wellies I hurtled towards the startled goose. As she fled in fear

I launched myself at her with a rugby tackle the British Lions would have been proud of. Steve stood open mouthed. After a struggle and much honking from Lucy I stood up holding the errant goose in my arms and looked across at Steve. He was helpless with laughter but managed to congratulate me as he passed me the yellow rod. With Lucy pinned securely under one arm I dragged the rod behind me and sloshed home whereupon I locked her in the stable at the back of the house with Mabel who was delighted to have her friend back. I kept them there for four days before I dare let them out again.

Kim was still limping badly despite being kept on a lead since her last visit to the vet two months ago. I took her back and the vet decided she needed to have an X-ray to determine exactly what was wrong. It turned out that she had damaged her Crucoid ligament and would probably be left with a permanent limp.

The kitchen was very basic to say the least and in desperate need of modernisation. The ceiling was covered in polystyrene tiles which we loathed. After we'd knocked them off we decided to clad it and bought some reclaimed pine boards which would tie in well with the 'new' kitchen cupboards. Throughout November we worked on it in the evenings and at weekends. We clad the ceiling and Alan repositioned some of the electric sockets and re plastered some of the walls.

Towards the end of the month I planted fourteen of the one hundred Hawthorne saplings which I had sent off for earlier. Before I had the chance to plant any more the temperature plummeted so I dug a hole and put the rest of the saplings into it and then covered the roots with straw to protect them from the frost until I had time to plant them properly. I hoped they would survive as I wanted to create a hedge against the fence behind the house.

It wasn't until the first week in December that I finished the new goose hut. Woodwork has never been my strong point and although the hut was sturdy and weatherproof I had to admit it was not attractive. Shelley commented rather uncharitably I thought that it looked like an outside toilet! The geese however were very happy with it and settled in very quickly and thankfully there was no reoccurrence of Lucy's bid for freedom.

Just before Christmas Alan plumbed in the sink and put the kitchen cupboards in place. There were still some fiddly jobs to finish off but it all looked nice and it was good to have plenty of storage space at last.

Christmas Day and Boxing Day were spent with family as usual, although this year they all came to Jericho on Boxing Day for a change.

On New Year's Eve we were invited round to Julie and Pete's to see in the New Year. We had a good evening – until we ran out of petrol on the way home – not my fault this time!

1998

January was a dismal month with heavy rain and waterlogged fields. Despite the reduced turn out the winter field gate way was a quagmire.

I began working on the dairy and cellar doors and doorways in the kitchen. I stripped off the old paint then sanded and sealed them both. I also finished sealing the kitchen ceiling.

Sam was selected to swim for Saddleworth Swimming Club's junior team and began competing in local competitions which boosted his confidence no end.

Alan had heard that there was an old David Brown tractor for sale at one of the nearby farms. We decided to have a look at it. It was time we had a tractor of our own, we couldn't borrow Steve's tractor indefinitely. The David Brown was big and scruffy but in good working order and wasn't a bad price. Old Mr. Longden was a likeable character. It didn't matter to him whether we wanted it as it was or when he had done it up. He also showed us a 3 ton tipping trailer which he had re-floored and re-painted.

Over the next week I continued to work on the dairy and cellar doorways. The Land Rover failed its MOT miserably and cost us a lot of money to get it through.

A nice surprise arrived in the post. I had let it slip when talking to Mum that the Land Rover had failed its MOT and I had also told her about the tractor and trailer. She sent us 'a little gift' in the form of a large cheque which would pay for both the tractor and the trailer.

'You'd be getting it eventually' she had said when I phoned to thank her 'you might as well have it now when you really need it.'

Alan went back to Mr. Longden and confirmed that we would buy them both. We collected them the following week.

On the last Saturday in February we woke up to thick snow. I wasn't pleased to see it but Jess and Sam were and spent most of the weekend with the Sloane girls sledging down the fields beside the bridle path just past Shiloh Farm.

Shelley had found looking after both Thomas and Ben very time consuming and had enlisted the help of an acquaintance of hers called Samantha to part-loan Thomas. Samantha enjoyed riding and being around horses and also rode Misty when Sue was very busy with work. Samantha's daughter Gemma had recently started to have riding lessons at Mossley with Sam once a week. Gemma was a year younger than Sam and the two of them got on well. Shelley was happy to let them loan Ben between them until Natasha was old enough to ride him.

Sam and Gemma spent a lot of time together on our paddock trying to persuade Ben to do as he was told. He was very lazy and often Jess got on him to make him work. When he was particularly difficult Mark also had a go which was comical as being tall his feet almost touched the ground.

All through the previous summer whenever Mark had competed anywhere on Zulu Jess had accompanied him. Despite numerous adverts and having been successful at local shows Zulu had remained unsold. Several people had come to see him but nobody wanted to buy. The probable reason for this was that he had a four beat rather than a three beat canter – like a trotter or pacer – which let him down in equitation and dressage.

During the last week in March Jess and Mark plucked up the courage to ask us if Jess could loan Zulu. An excellent solution they thought, Jess would have a horse that she knew and Mark would be able to keep him on our yard. I was against the idea at first. Jess was only small and although she was a competent rider I felt that at 15.3hh Zulu was too big for her. Alan and I discussed it and agreed to let her have a couple of lessons on him then hack him out and see how she managed. Needless to say she managed extremely well and began loaning Zulu officially at the end of March.

Early in April 10 tons of crushed brick and 20 tons of crusher run were tipped in the car park. Our intention was to dig off the surface of the track between the stable block and the summer field and put down a layer of crushed brick and then cover that with a layer of crusher run. This would solve the problem we had last summer of having to walk through thick mud when turning out or bringing in the horses after heavy or prolonged spells of rain. We were prevented from starting work on it that weekend by a heavy snow fall which stayed with us into the following week.

A couple of weeks later Bill Dawson brought his tractor with a loader on it and helped us put down the first few loads of crushed brick. It was a back breaking job as the track had to be wide enough for the tractor to drive along it.

More rain fell before the end of the month. It had been the wettest April since records began! Each weekend we persevered with preparing the track and Bill continued to help us by filling his trailer and then tipping it along the path for us to level out. It took us until the middle of May to finish the job.

Jessie Pony

Sam's interest in riding had not fizzled out as we had expected it to do. Quite the opposite in fact. His riding continued to improve and he not only spent most of his time on the yard helping people with their horses but also attended all the Pony Club rallies and shows, where he helped put up the jumps in the show jumping competitions and generally made himself useful.

He enjoyed loaning Ben but found his laziness frustrating. When hacking out in company Ben would keep up quite well but if either Sam or Gemma were trying to ride him on the paddock he was bone idle and would only grudgingly break into a trot. A canter only materialised if either Jess or Mark ran behind him threatening him with a crop. Sam was strong enough to get him to jump over a pole but Gemma was not. Ben invariably trotted up to a jump and then at the last minute put his head down and tipped her onto the ground.

Sam wanted to join Pony Club and have his own pony on which he could compete in show jumping competitions. I discussed this with Alan and as Sam had shown so much interest and had looked after Ben so well on the days that he loaned him we decided to look for a pony for him. After studying dozens of adverts in various newspapers and magazines we arranged to go and see a couple of ponies which were for sale in the Bolton area. Mark came with us to give us his opinion. The first pony was not suitable but we were interested in the second one which was a 13hh dark bay Show Pony. She was 19 years old, which was older than we wanted really, but she was fit and healthy and both Sam and Jess rode her and Jess took her over some jumps. We arranged to go and see her again so that Sam could take her out on a short hack. After the second visit we were even more impressed with the pony and Sam liked her. We decided to buy her subject to a satisfactory vet's report.

Matthew heard that we were looking for a pony and told us that his boss in Leeds had a 13.2hh pony for sale which excelled at show jumping and cross country. We asked him to make arrangements for us to go and see it.

We all trooped over to Leeds that weekend to look at the 15 year old Welsh X Arab mare. She was chestnut with a white blaze and one white foot and she wasn't anything like as fine as the Show Pony in Bolton. Her name was 'Jessie' and we all liked her immediately. The owner's daughter had been reluctant to part with Jessie despite the fact that she had completely outgrown her; in addition to which she now had two other horses on which she competed leaving Jessie ridden only occasionally. Recently however she had been persuaded that it would be fairer to the pony to sell her to somebody who would ride her regularly and competitively.

Sam rode Jessie and took her over some jumps and then Jess took her over part of their cross country course. Jess was very impressed as was Sam but we were unsure if Sam was competent enough at this stage to control the pony as she was strong and very fast. Jessie's owners suggested that we take her on trial for a couple of weeks to see how Sam coped with her. They offered to bring her over to Jericho so that they could see where she would be living if we decided to buy her. We agreed and cancelled the vetting of the other pony as Sam was adamant that he liked Jessie best.

During the first week of the trial Sam had lessons on Jessie and also hacked out with Jess on Zulu. The hack ended badly as Jessie overtook Zulu on the bridle path and Sam banged his knee on a fence post. She stopped at the end of the bridle path but it was due more to her common sense than Sam's ability to stop her.

I worried constantly. I didn't want to let a good pony slip through our fingers but at the same time I didn't want Sam to get hurt. I sent Mark out on Jessie with Jess on Zulu to repeat the hack to see what he thought. Mark admitted that the pony was strong but said she was sensible and not unsafe. He felt that the pony would be fine as Sam's riding improved and he suggested that in the mean time we bought a different bit and a flash nose band to give Sam more control. A couple of days later Jess and Sam repeated their hack using the different bit and nose band. Sam remained in control and rode home much happier.

Sam with Jessie, July 1998

Sam looked after Jessie every day and mucked out the stable with commendable thoroughness. Jessie was very well mannered in the stable and safe to be around. She was cheeky and full of character and Sam felt comfortable with her. Alan liked her very much and was not worried about Sam's safety.

'Boys grow quickly at Sam's age' he said 'He will soon get stronger and as his riding improves and he gets used to her I'm sure he will cope with her alright on a hack.'

As the end of the trial period approached Sam was absolutely certain that Jessie was the pony for him. My constant worrying was beginning to drive Mark up the wall and apparently he avoided me whenever I came down to the yard! I rang Jessie's owners and asked if we could extend the loan until after the coming weekend so that we could take her to a show - they readily agreed. I felt much happier about the pony when we watched her in a competition environment at the Pony Club show. Jess did extremely well on Zulu and competed on Jessie too in one show jumping class. Sam also jumped her in the practice ring. She was steady and honest with no ducking out or sudden refusals. Sam thought she was great and we went over to Leeds on Sunday afternoon and bought her.

To give him some confidence before he began hacking out with other people Jess rode out with Sam several times in the first two or three weeks after we'd bought Jessie. On one occasion Sam was laughing when the two of them came into the kitchen after their ride.

'I've just seen a bare bum!' he said and collapsed into a fit of helpless giggles. I looked at Jess for an explanation.

'There was a car parked at the end of the bridle path.' she said grinning all over her face. 'The windows were all steamed up - I told him not to look!'

The weather throughout June wasn't much better than it had been during the previous two months. Beth, Mark, Jess and Sam spent a lot of time together over spring and summer. They regularly participated in Pony Club events and frequently either took part in or watched the show jumping at Birchinley Manor. One Saturday Beth drove the four of them to Bramham Horse Trials for the day. After they had set off

Alan suggested that he and I should go for a hack on Zulu and Jessie while Jess and Sam were out of the way. I was a bit surprised to say the least. I hadn't ridden very much but Alan had barely done any riding at all.

'OK' I said 'but no galloping!'

'I've got no intention of galloping.' Alan laughed 'I just mean a quiet hack. It's a lovely day and we can just take our time.'

Neither of us had jodhpurs so we dug out some track suit bottoms and borrowed the children's riding hats. We tacked up and set off down the lane hoping we looked as if we knew what we were doing. Approaching The Roebuck at a leisurely pace, we crossed the road into Green Lane heading towards the reservoir. As soon as we reached the trees the horses' ears pricked forward. I felt Jessie's pace quicken.

'No you don't!' I told her and tucked her in behind Zulu. We walked through the trees and continued round the reservoir walking and occasionally trotting. I watched with amusement as Alan bounced unsteadily in the saddle whenever we trotted and felt rather smug as my rising trot felt quite balanced and comfortable. We decided to take a short-cut and rode back towards the woods. We had enjoyed the ride and chatted as we rode around a bend in the path. There was a large puddle in front of us and Zulu stepped to the left to avoid walking through it. Taking that as an invitation to overtake Jessie took off like shit off a shovel! Completely taken by surprise I was thrown backwards, my feet shot up at the front and Sam's hat dropped down over my eyes. So much for 'balanced and comfortable'!

'Bloody hell! Slow down!' I heard Alan shout. I could hear Zulu's hooves pounding behind me. Jessie heard them too, evidently thought they were having a race and broke into a gallop.

'Stay on!' I told myself as we hurtled up the winding path through the trees. I managed to grab the front of the saddle and heave myself upright and taking a firm grasp of the reins I turned Jessie's head. She slowed down and much to my immense relief stopped at the top of the woodland path. Alan arrived with only slightly more control a few seconds later.

We were well aware that if some unfortunate soul had been walking down the path as Jessie had careered round the corner they would probably have been seriously hurt – or worse - and I knew that Sam would have been furious that I had allowed Jessie to gallop. We therefore rode home in a very controlled and sensible manner, turned the horses out in the field and confessed absolutely nothing!

The last day of June turned out to be a dreadful one. Although it started well enough, by early afternoon the weather had deteriorated. Sam had a lesson booked at 4pm. which was abandoned half way through due to thick mist and heavy drizzle. Jess and Mark came into the stable for a chat while Sam and I got Jessie untacked and rugged her up for the night. Beth arrived soon after and we all drifted into her stable while she mucked out. The weather was getting worse and Jess and Mark were arguing over which one of them should fetch Bliss from the field for Beth. To shut them up I said I would get her. Beth was laughing as she prepared Bliss's feed.

As soon as I reached the field gate I knew there was something wrong. Bliss was standing about ten yards away from the gate. I called her as I approached with her head collar but she didn't move. Thomas and James were messing about to the left of the gate half rearing and play fighting. I shouted at them to move away and put the head collar on Bliss. I set off but she was reluctant to follow, it was then that I noticed the damage to one of her front legs. Below the knee it was bleeding and she was holding it awkwardly. I unclipped the lead rope and ran to get Beth and the others. We moved Thomas and James away from the gate so that Beth could lead Bliss out of the field. With slow and agonisingly painful steps Bliss was led to her stable. On close inspection we could see splinters of bone protruding from the wound. Beth was inconsolable. I rang the vet.

Bliss was referred immediately to Leahurst at Liverpool. Memories came flooding back that I didn't want to think about.

Three days later I was in Bobbie's field mending one of the walls where the horses had dislodged some of the stone. I heard Jess calling me and walked down to meet her. She told me that Beth had come up to see me. When I got to her stable I could hear her sobbing; she was sitting in her tack room with her arms around Pete and her face buried in his neck. She looked up and told me that the bone in Bliss's leg had been completely shattered by a powerful kick. There had been nothing left to mend; the vets had no choice but to put Bliss to sleep. She asked me if she could borrow Pete for a few hours – I watched them walk along the concrete and get into her car. I felt so sorry. I knew how she was feeling.

Throughout July and August both Jess and Sam attended the Pony Club rallies and competed in the shows that were held despite the excessive rain which fell throughout the summer months. Jess enjoyed some success with Zulu in show jumping and working hunter classes and Sam had regular lessons on Jessie and also began to do well particularly in show jumping.

We borrowed Mark's trailer and took Zulu and Jessie to the 3rd Pony Club Points Show of the season. Alan drove onto the edge of the showground and spotted a parking space between a couple of vehicles at the right hand side of the field.

Shelley had plucked up the courage to enter Thomas in a novice dressage test and was practicing at the far end of the ground. In a collected trot she turned Thomas to face the open show ground just as Alan reversed the Land Rover and trailer into the parking space. Thomas caught sight of it and with a whinny of recognition he snatched the reins through Shelley's fingers and set off towards us at a full blown gallop across the show ground scattering children and ponies in all directions. An angry voice bellowed into the loud-speaker.

'Please do NOT gallop across the show ground!.. STOP GALLOPING!!'

'I'M TRYING TO STOP GALLOPING!' Shelley screamed back at the loud-speaker as bright red in the face she leant back in the saddle and tried in vain to stop Thomas. Jess and I got out of the Land Rover. Delighted to see us Thomas skidded to an abrupt halt inches from the Land Rover bumper. Almost immediately the voice on the loud-speaker requested the presence of the next dressage competitor – Shelley. All her concentration and nerves now in tatters Shelley rode Thomas back across the show ground to the dressage ring with considerably more control than before. She completed the test but lost several marks due to Thomas's exuberance every time he was ridden in our direction.

In the middle of August Jess and Mark competed at Charity Farm in a one day event. A horrendous traffic jam on the M62 made us late. We arrived with just 15 minutes to spare. Hurriedly they tacked up and took part in the dressage competition. Soon after the dressage they walked the cross-country course before riding it. Both of them completed it successfully – apart from Zulu losing a shoe. Fortunately we found the on-site farrier quite quickly and he replaced the shoe. Jess went clear in the show jumping as did Mark on James. Feeling pleased with their performances we loaded the horses into the trailer again and took them to Pony Club Camp in Osbaldeston where they stayed for the following week.

That summer had been dismal. Spells of consecutive fine sunny days were few and far between and whenever we did get a dry spell everyone who needed their grass cutting and baling all wanted it done at the same time. The likes of us who were completely dependent on the availability of man and machine had to be patient and wait until the farmers could fit us in between doing their own fields and other peoples. Consequently it was late August by the time Bill was able to cut the grass in the Five Acre field for us which was very late for a first cut.

Balers – particularly old ones – can be temperamental machines. Most of the farmers in the area had upgraded and started using machines which churned out big round bales of either hay or haylage in preference to those that produced the small rectangular ones like we had collected off the field the previous summer. On Bill's advice we decided to give haylage a go as it only needed three fine days to make it rather than the five or six required to make hay. Although it was more expensive to produce because it had to be wrapped, it was more nutritious, it could be stacked outside and the big bonus – bringing it in from the field was not labour intensive, all we had to do was watch. The machines cut, baled, carried, wrapped and stacked. By 6.30pm 38 bales of haylage wrapped in shiny black plastic were placed neatly in five rows of five and stacked two bales high in the far side of the garden beside the muck heap.

That evening we had a table booked at The Roebuck where we had arranged to meet Pat, John, Dianna, Matthew and Karen to celebrate our 25th wedding anniversary. After the men had finished the baling and the field gates had been secured it was a rush to get ready but we got there just in time. As a surprise Pat had brought a cake for us which a friend of hers had made. At the end of the meal it was carried ceremoniously to our table by a waitress accompanied by the exhuberant tones of Cliff Richard singing 'Congratulations!' at the top of his voice. The cake was decorated with an assortment of icing and marzipan livestock including a horse, a dog and a hen which were standing beside a chocolate muck heap. Brilliant!

Throughout the late summer our paddock continued to be well used particularly by the children. Jess practised her dressage tests and Sam, Gemma and sometimes Stephanie practised show jumping. Shelley's daughter Natasha began riding and looking after Ben with Gemma now that Sam had Jessie.

At the end of September Mark left the yard and began working at Shiloh Farm looking after Steve and Diane's horses. The arrangement included rent-free stabling for James so once again we had an empty stable. I was sorry to see Mark go but glad to see the back of James.

For sometime the Aga had not been working well. Most of the time it struggled to reach cooking temperature and once again had begun to give off fumes noticeable particularly first thing in the morning when the kitchen door had been closed for several hours. It got so bad that one evening I decided to put the dogs' beds in the dining room overnight. Next day I realised that the plants in the kitchen were wilting – it had to be something to do with the fumes so we let the Aga go out. When we moved into Jericho amongst all the clutter and rubbish that had been left in the shippon we had come across a flue brush. We rooted it out and when the Aga was cold Alan removed the little access plate in the flue and had a go at sweeping the chimney. After having taken out about a bucketful of soot he eased the brush back out of the flue, fastened the plate back on and re-lit the Aga. It seemed much better; there were no fumes thank goodness!

The weather throughout October continued to be wet and cold. At the beginning of November it snowed, not heavily, but it stayed for most of the day. I ordered 10 tons of crushed brick and stone to put into the winter field gateway, but when it was delivered the following week the wagon's tyres couldn't get enough grip on the wet mud to reverse right up to the gate so the driver had to tip it about 10 yards further down. I spent the next few days barrowing it up to the gateway and levelling it all with a rake.

The first weekend in December was cold and sunny. We took five loads of muck up to the muck heap in the top field. That weekend Bill had a visit from a fox which decimated his poultry leaving him with just two ducks. He asked me if I wanted them as the fox was sure to come back the moment he let them out. The foxes were so bold now that they came into his yard even when Bill was there during the day. He was sure that the reason I hadn't had any daytime visits from them was because of our dogs. Bill couldn't leave his own dog out in his yard during the day as it was as likely to kill the poultry as the fox was.

I persuaded Alan to make me a duck hut. He disappeared into the shippon during the evenings and the following weekend he proudly presented me with the result of his efforts. I was a bit disappointed because what he had made was the size of a small dog kennel. I had visualised something more along the lines of the hen hut. However it was very well made with a double door, the inner one of which was made with wire mesh so on misty days when they would have to be shut in, the outer door could be left open and they would be able to see out and have some fresh air.

'What's wrong?' he asked noting my lack of enthusiasm.

'It's a bit small.' I said.

'Just two ducks you said. It's plenty big enough for two ducks!'

'Not if they want to flap their wings.' I said.

'Oh, for goodness sake!'

'It's fine. It's fine.' I said hurriedly. Shaking his head with exasperation Alan picked up the duck 'kennel' and went out of the shippon.

'Where do you want it?' he asked. I showed him and he proceeded to set a concrete flag into the grass bank just off the concrete opposite the sixth stable and placed the duck kennel onto it. He then drove a couple of wooden stakes into the ground and fastened them to the duck kennel to anchor it down for when we had windy weather.

On the Sunday afternoon I collected the ducks from Bill. One of them was a big white Aylesbury. She was gorgeous and looked like Jemima Puddle Duck. The other was a very small, neat and extremely vocal Call duck with dark brown plumage. Needless to say neither of them had been given a name. After giving the matter some serious thought I decided to call the big duck 'Lily' and the little brown one 'Ruby'.

On Christmas Day Jess, Sam, Gemma, Samantha and Jane went for a hack together and managed to avoid the heavy rain which fell throughout much of the day.

The last few days of the year were predominated by torrential rain and high winds. As regards the weather 1998 had been an absolute wash-out!

1999

The New Year began in a similar vein to how the previous one had finished – wet! January continued to be a wet month and Jericho was a bleak and cold place to live. Jess took part in a Pony Club team show jumping competition at Osbaldeston. Riding Jessie she did well individually and the Saddleworth team was placed seventh out of twenty-five.

February, my least favourite month, was also wet and for much of the time Jericho was shrouded in mist. Everywhere was grey, the days were short and people on the yard came and went like shadows. The only people I spoke to regularly during the day were Norman and Margaret when they came up on alternate mornings to deliver our milk.

When Norman delivered milk in Uppermill and elsewhere on his round as a rule he was accompanied by Margaret, a family friend. She dealt with any payments that were made on the milk round leaving Norman free to get on with the delivery of the milk and eggs and so on. Norman always liked to have a plentiful supply of biscuits and snacks for himself in the milk float along with a few dog biscuits or treats for the various dogs that they came across regularly on their round. Often Kim had been given treats when they delivered milk to our house and always therefore had welcomed their arrival but at the time she was confined in our small back garden behind a large metal gate. Now of course she was on the loose along with Maggie and Pete. All three dogs watched for the milk float coming up the lane. On seeing it they invariably went to meet it, ran up the lane alongside it and then wagging their tails and licking their chops in anticipation of some tasty morsel they would surround the driver's door as Norman pulled up beside the house. Margaret loved the dogs and when Norman had struggled past them to see to our milk she would give them their treats. One morning however I heard a lot of angry shouting from Norman and I went outside to investigate.

'What's going on?' I asked.

Margaret was laughing 'It's his own fault' she said 'he'd eaten all the biscuits and there was nothing left for the dogs so I…'

'Nothing left!' interrupted Norman spluttering with indignation. 'I'll say there's nothing left! She's given them my pork pie!' I could still hear them arguing as they drove down the lane past the stables.

As the month progressed the damp clinging mists were blown away by strong winds which stayed with us until early March. That month after much deliberation Alan and I bought Zulu for Jess.

The next new arrivals on the yard were Joanne and Benson an eight year old 16.2hh American Standardbred bay gelding very similar in appearance to an English Thoroughbred, but bigger boned. Despite Joanne being about 10 years older than Jess the two of them hit it off right away. They hacked out together most weekends and Benson and Zulu became firm friends and allies in the field. Joanne looked after Benson and his stable meticulously and in that respect was a very good influence on Jess who appeared to regard mucking out as a necessary evil.

Last summer when Mark and Jess had competed in shows they generally took Zulu in Mark's trailer with James. Now however with the approach of the new show season and the prospect of both Jess and Sam competing regularly at Pony Club and Rochdale Riding Club

Life at Jericho

Kim and Maggie

Eric

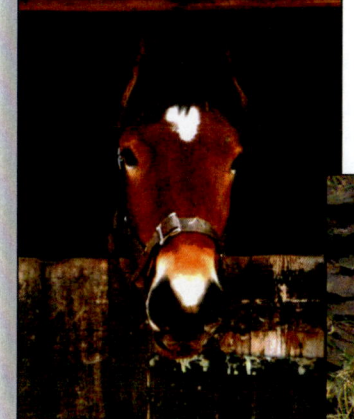

Mabel and Lucy

Reuben
10 months

Life at Jericho

Pete, Kim and Maggie

Billy Bull

Jess on Bobbie

Sam on Jessie

Life at Jericho

Jess on Zulu

Pete

Emily and Mary

Emily and Sam

129

Life at Jericho

Maggie and Jack

Emily and Mabel

Will

Joe and Jack

130

we decided that it was time we bought our own trailer to transport the horses. After having seen and rejected two or three which were advertised in the area we finally bought an old Sinclair trailer. It needed a new floor and we modified the rigid partition by exchanging the solid timber panel for a heavy but flexible rubber sheet. The bottom quarter hung loose allowing Jessie, who had been used to travelling alone without a partition, more room to balance herself. Zulu had amazing balance and travelled well in whatever space she left him. The two of them shared the trailer quite happily seeming to like each others company.

In April it was Sam's 11th birthday and he decided to get some more hens. To help him choose which breeds to buy he borrowed one of Bill Dawson's poultry books. After having poured over its contents for a few days he finally made up his mind. He asked Bill if he would try to find him either a couple of Speckled Sussex or two French Morans next time he went to Chelford market.

In the meantime Simon, one of Sam's friends who lived on a farm, sold him a large white Orpington hen which we named Simone after Simon.

At the beginning of the Easter break Shelley arrived on the yard just as I was bringing some bags of shavings down from the top barn where I stored them when there wasn't enough room in the barn down at the stable block. She broached the idea that perhaps we could build another lean-to stable at the car park end of the block next to Thomas. She could move Ben into that which would be much easier for her and the one he was in now could be used for storing bags of shavings which I had to admit would be easier for me. I mentioned her suggestion to Alan and as the area beside Thomas's stable was already concreted he said that he was quite happy to do it.

The following Saturday we made a start on Ben's new stable. Alan had already rummaged through the shippon and found some suitable timber out of which he had made three frames. We were attempting to get them into position ready to bolt together. A 12 foot length of 4"x 2"was laid horizontally linking the back panel to the one at the front temporarily while we positioned the side panel. At this point Shelley and Natasha arrived in the car park. Shelley enthused over our progress and as she peered into where we were working, she accidentally nudged the front panel. The heavy length of 4"x 2" was dislodged and before Alan could catch it, it landed on Shelley's head with a sickening thud making her knees buckle and almost knocking her to the ground.

'Ow! Ow! I think I'm going to cry' wailed Shelley clutching her head. Alan was horrified and removed the offending piece of wood. I helped Shelley walk to her car which she leaned against as she rubbed her head that now sported a lump the size of one of Simone's large eggs! Surprisingly the skin was not broken and after a cup of tea and much sympathy she said she was OK.

We resumed our work. Once the three sections had been bolted together Alan screwed the framework to the side of Thomas's stable then we clad the whole structure with larch lap - a large quantity of which had been stored in the shippon. Finally we lined the inside with sheets of marine ply and felted the roof.

Over the next week Alan made yet another stable door low enough for Ben to be able to put his head over and we partitioned off a narrow area at the back of the stable and put a door in it to create a narrow but useful storage area big enough to keep feed bins, buckets and grooming equipment etc. Shelley moved Ben into it straightaway.

A few days later Bill Dawson rang to say that he had two Speckled Sussex hens and one French Maran for Sam to look at, but he warned me that the two Sussex were in very poor condition and if Sam didn't want them he didn't have to have them as they could be returned to the market the following week. We went down to Bill's to have a look at them. The Sussex hens were huddled together in a small wire crate. Their burgundy coloured plumage speckled with white was dirty and dull, their claws were bent and their legs were calloused and they looked miserable. Having seen the neglected state of the poor wretched things we hadn't the heart to send them back to market so Sam said he would have them. The French Maran however was in beautiful condition. She was plump and alert and her charcoal grey plumage barred with black had a healthy shine. Sam bought all three of them with his birthday money and we took them home.

All three hens were put into the hen hut straightaway. The Maran confidently took her place amongst our Black Rock hens and after a couple of skirmishes with Eric and Blanche she was soon busily checking out her new accommodation. Sam called her Michelle and almost immediately she began to lay beautiful rich brown eggs and very quickly became his favourite. In contrast to Michelle the two Sussex hens were very subdued. There was no squabbling with the other hens they just stayed close together seeming to be unsure what to do.

After a few days when they plucked up the courage to venture outside we realised that they had no idea how to behave. They neither scratched with their claws nor pecked the ground with their beaks. They held their heads in the air and vaguely pecked at the seeds on the heads of long grasses. If food was given to them in a bowl they would eat it but had no idea how to forage for themselves. I thought it probable that their lives up to now had been spent in their cramped crate. It gave me immense pleasure as the days and weeks went by to watch the two of them begin to imitate the behaviour of the other hens and gradually learn what should have been instinctive behaviour.

The old faithful BMW which Alan loved so much was becoming expensive to maintain. More work needed to be done on it before it would pass its next MOT. I dare say Alan could have done some of it relatively cheaply but he had neither the time nor the inclination to do so. The fact that the car was also expensive to run forced the decision to let it go and replace it with one which was more economical. We advertised the BMW and sold it very quickly and almost as quickly bought a red Vauxhall Cavalier.

One of Shelley's friends had recently split up from her partner, leaving her in rented accommodation with a toddler and six cats. She had found homes for two of the cats and could get away with keeping one herself but desperately needed to find homes for the rest. Shelley had promised to ask me if I would have one. I saw no reason why we shouldn't have a stable cat so I agreed to go with Shelley to choose one. Needless to say when I saw them I couldn't make up my mind. I resisted the temptation to bring home an un-neutered tom called

Alan but couldn't decide between a three year old Tortoiseshell called Annie and a pretty two year old Tabby called Alice – so I took both of them. I brought them home and settled them in the barn with some food and a cardboard box to sleep in then left them to get used to their new surroundings.

The following day there was no sign of either cat. I called them repeatedly but it looked as if they might have run away. The next day however I heard a soft mewing I looked up to see Annie standing on the overhang looking down at me. I coaxed her down and gave her some food. She purred and rubbed against me. I hoped Alice was just keeping out of sight and would soon also pluck up the courage to come down and eat something. Next morning when I went into the barn both cats were standing on the hay bales together waiting for their breakfast.

The dogs soon accepted the new arrivals although Kim was a bit over enthusiastic which generally caused both cats to take refuge in the roof space whenever they heard the dogs come onto the yard. After a short time however Kim calmed down and treated them as if they were part of the fixtures and fittings. Joe cat also gave them some stick at first and used some appalling language if ever he met either of them face to face, but he soon mellowed and after a few weeks all three of them slept together curled up on the hay bales in the barn.

All the poultry settled in well. Lily and Ruby soon got into the routine of going back into their duck kennel each night, although getting through the small doorway was a tight fit for Lily so Alan had to make the hole a little bit bigger.

It wasn't until we had Lily that I heard a frog scream. On frequent occasions that spring and summer either me or Joanne would pursue Lily across the garden endeavouring to rescue some unfortunate frog whose legs were still frantically kicking for freedom outside of Lily's beak as she tried to swallow the screaming creature before one of us got hold of her and pulled it out before it was too late.

Billy Bull

In early May as usual Norman grazed his cows in the field next to our house. This year they were accompanied by an extremely large Friesian bull that frequently stood beside our wall accompanied by several cows watching our comings and goings with apparent interest. Sam was fascinated by him and regularly stroked him over the wall. I wasn't sure that stroking him was a good idea as he was bound to be protective of his cows. On one of these occasions I told Sam to leave the bull alone.

'But he's nice Mum. I think he likes me.'

I walked across to where Sam was stroking the bull's massive head. As soon as I arrived however the bull's demeanour changed. He began rolling his eyes and slavering.

'Come away Sam' I ordered.

'He was fine until you arrived.' Sam complained.

'Well maybe he doesn't like me, but whatever the reason I don't think a broken wall and two loose strands of barbed wire are going to stop him if he decides to chase us. Do you?'

'See you Billy!' Sam laughed as he raced me back to the house.

That evening I rang Norman and asked him to do something about the fencing.

'It's only Billy!' Norman said dismissively. 'He won't hurt you – as long as you don't turn your back on him!' he added chuckling.

'Norman! I've got two young children here. You must do something to strengthen that fence!' I insisted.

'Oh, alright' he sighed and put the phone down. I couldn't always tell whether or not Norman was joking so I left it at that for the time being.

A couple of days later I was relieved to see Norman and Jim arrive with a roll of barbed wire and about a dozen fence posts in the back of their pick up.

'You're so demanding!' Norman shouted at me when I looked out of the door.

'Demanding! So would you be if you had that bull leering at you every day! Just get that fence up!' I said and closed the door. Norman laughed and with Jim's help began to hammer in the posts alongside the wall.

For the first two weeks of June I had three horses on full livery. Alan was fitting a new plug socket in the kitchen and I was busy doing jobs on the yard. Alan shouted down to me from the house.
 'Have you seen the pliers?'
 'You left them in the dairy I think.' I shouted back.
 'Where in the dairy?' he bellowed a few minutes later. Refusing to keep shouting up the garden I walked up to the house and went into the dairy. After a quick look I soon found the pliers underneath the wash basket. 'Oh well, you didn't tell me you'd hidden them.' Alan muttered.
 'I didn't hide them!' I retorted crossly. 'You just don't look properly.' I went back outside. 'You can't expect everything to be right in front of you!' I called back at him as I walked down to the stables. About 10 minutes later I heard him shout again. I was running water into a bucket and couldn't hear what he was saying. Irritated to say the least I turned off the tap.
 'Why is it always me going up and down the ruddy garden?' I complained to myself as I strode up to the house. 'What have you lost now?' I asked when I reached the house.
 'Sorry!' he grinned not looking the least bit sorry. 'I didn't mean for you to come up the garden again. I just wondered if we had any insulating tape.'
 'Yes! It's in the kitchen drawer.' I said pushing past him and finding it straightaway. 'That's where we keep it!' I added slapping the roll of tape into his hand. Once more I returned to the stables to continue with my jobs.
 'Thanks Chuck!' Alan called after me.
 All I had left to do was to fill the hay nets – not my favourite job. A few minutes later I closed my eyes in disbelief when I heard Alan shouting me again. I ignored him at first but he kept on shouting. I stormed out of the barn.
 'What do you want?' I yelled angrily.

He beckoned me 'Come here.'
'You come here. I'm busy!' I replied turning back to the barn.
'Jan. No. Come here.' Alan insisted.

I was getting really mad by this time. I flung down the hay net that I had half filled and stormed back up the garden. Alan was standing beside the kitchen door with his arms folded.

'What now?' I demanded.
'Is that a cow or a bull?'
'What?!'
'Is that a cow or a bull?' he repeated
'Where?' I said turning round.
'Just coming into the car park I think – ah yes here it comes!'
'Oh my God! It's Billy Bull!' I exclaimed.

The massive bull walked slowly along the concrete pausing for a moment to look at Katie who was on box rest. We heard a thud as Katie evidently reversed into the back wall of her stable. The bull continued along the concrete and turned to look into the open barn. He disappeared inside.

'Oh my God!' I said again 'What would I have done?'

There was a new unopened haylage bale on the left side of the barn as well as the opened one at the front which I had been using. Maybe I could have clambered up onto the new one and from there climbed through into Soli's stable – I probably would have been so scared I'd have had a damn good try! Either that or I'd have hidden in the corner behind the new bale and hoped he didn't see me. Pallets covered the floor of the barn to keep the haylage off the concrete floor. As Billy disappeared from view inside the barn we could hear them snapping under his weight.

I went indoors and rang Norman. By the time he arrived about 15 minutes later Billy had wandered back into the car park and was investigating the muck heap.

'Come on Billy Boy let's be having you!' Norman called moving behind the bull and tapping him lightly with a white stick.

'Well look at that!' Alan said quietly. Billy placidly did as he was told and Norman guided him down the lane and back into the field.

During the last couple of weeks of June I had experienced a lot of painful twinges in my back. I assumed that it would sort itself out and carried on regardless but instead of getting easier it got worse. Sharp pains shot up my back if I walked across uneven ground. I struggled to muck out the horses and lifting bags of shavings and buckets of water became almost impossible. The problem came to a head when Alan and I replaced some fencing which enclosed a few hawthorn bushes in the summer field. Having finished the job we threw the tools onto the trailer and got into the tractor. Alan drove back across the field and I jumped out to open the gate. Immediately I was overwhelmed by intense pain. It was all I could do to struggle to the house. Alan helped me to get my coat and shoes off and shouting out with pain I laid on the sofa. A hot water bottle on my back gave me some relief as long as I lay still but the moment I tried to change position I was in agony. Walking was excruciating, getting up and down stairs took ages and lowering myself into a chair or getting into bed was incredibly painful.

Alan put a note up in the barn telling people on the yard that I would not be able to do any jobs for them until further notice. I gave myself complete rest for the next few days but my back got no better. Samantha advised me to go and see a retired reflexologist by the name of Ernest and I made an appointment to go and see him early in July. Sue took me and brought me back as there was no way that I could have driven. We found the small terraced house and I rang the bell. An elderly grey haired man quite short in stature and of medium build answered the door and we were greeted noisily by two small terriers. I introduced myself and Sue to Ernest. Samantha had warned me that he was 'a little unconventional'.

'Alright Jan, go upstairs strip off to your underwear and lay on the bed.' Ernest instructed as he closed the front door and waved vaguely in the direction of the staircase.

'But we've only just met!' I whispered to Sue as she helped me up the stairs. There were three doors on the upstairs landing one of which was open; we went through the doorway into a small dimly lit room. A narrow bed like those that you find in a doctor's surgery was in the middle of the room and a chest of drawers piled high with towels stood against one wall. The room was very warm and on the window sill were numerous scented oils and candles which filled the room with fragrance. Sue helped me to get undressed and trying not to shout out in pain I lay on the bed.

'Are you ready?' Ernest called.

'Yes.' Sue and I replied in unison.

Ernest came upstairs, covered me up – apart from my head and feet – with a large towel and put a drop of Rescue Remedy on my tongue he then began to massage my head.

'Try to relax' he instructed. I closed my eyes and tried to relax realising as I did so just how tense I was. After a while Ernest turned his attention to my feet and proceeded to spend several minutes massaging prodding and tweaking them. 'Turn over please' he said suddenly. It took me a long time to turn over and the pain which shot through my body made me cry out as I laboriously manoeuvred myself onto my front. 'Well done. Now try to relax again.' Ernest said quietly. He massaged my lower legs and feet then my neck and shoulders. As I felt my body relax in the warm room Ernest's hands moved to my lower back. He located the source of the pain and deftly worked on that area for several minutes. 'Right. That's all I can do for now.' he said brusquely. 'Come back on Monday at one o'clock. The majority of the pain that you are experiencing now will lift in about two hours; get dressed, go home and keep warm.'

Sue took me home. Alan was already there and made me a hot water bottle to put on my back. He covered me up with a blanket on the sofa and I kept warm as I had been told to do. Two hours later almost to the minute I felt the pain lift. I was able to stand up and walk about. I felt sore and my back ached but there were no shooting pains. My respect for Ernest was immense.

After the wet early spring the weather during May and June had settled and as the summer commenced it became very hot and very dry in fact July that year was the driest for thirty years! The beautiful weather caused feverish activity in the farming fraternity. The hum of tractors filled the air. Everywhere you looked fields were in the process of being cut or baled and large stacks of haylage bales tightly wrapped in black or green shiny plastic appeared to sprout up overnight in farm yards and fields all over the area.

That Saturday Bill cut the grass on the Five Acre field. By Monday 35 bales of haylage were wrapped and stacked beside the muck heap in the garden. I saw Ernest again that day and this time I drove there myself. After more head and foot massaging Ernest started to fire questions at me concerning my diet and life style, when I let it slip that I was a vegetarian Ernest rolled his eyes in despair. Having listened with obvious disdain to my replies he threw his arms up with frustration and told me how ridiculous it was that I drank semi-skimmed milk and didn't eat full fat cheese. In fact despite my protestations that I ate loads of fresh fruit and vegetables I apparently didn't eat properly at all.

'No wonder you've got a back problem!' he said. 'A woman of your age should consume full-fat milk, red meat, oily fish and plenty of cheese to maintain healthy bones and muscle tissue'. He sighed 'There's no need for you to come and see me again. I don't suppose there's any point in telling you to rest?'

'No.'

'I thought not, in that case if you have heavy things to lift then lift them properly. If things are too heavy for you to carry get someone else to carry them. Keep warm, and if you must be a ruddy vegetarian make sure you have a varied and nutritious diet!'

Feeling well and truly told off I thanked him and left. I gave our diet some serious thought and promised myself to make some changes.

Although I still get back pain from time to time depending on what I've been doing I have never had a reoccurrence of the pain which sent me to see Ernest that summer.

The dogs loved the hot sunny days and spent long lazy hours stretched out on the cool concrete in front of the stables or dozed in the shade of the Laburnum Tree. Late one evening I went into the kitchen, all the dogs were in their beds but I noticed that Pete was not relaxed he appeared to be staring at the cellar door. I crouched down and stroked him. He turned his head towards me but his eyes did not focus on me. The pupils were darting from side to side. I was worried but as he didn't seem to be distressed I decided to wait until morning to ring the vet. Next day the rapid eye movements were as bad as ever. I booked the first available appointment and took Pete down to the vet early that afternoon. The vet recognised immediately that he had suffered a stroke and prescribed medication which he was confident would enable Pete to make a good recovery over the next few weeks.

The end of July marked a change in the weather, August was a wet month.

Early one Saturday morning I fed the hens as usual and removed the concrete block from their doorway. Next I let the geese out and then opened the door of the duck kennel to let out Lily and Ruby. It was empty. My stomach turned over. I tried to recall what I had done the previous evening. I was so sure that I had shut them in - and then I remembered. I had been in the process of shutting up the ducks when Shelley had called me to look at a cut on Ben's leg. The ducks had been going into the kennel when I broke off to look at Ben. I must have returned to their kennel and locked their door without checking that they were still inside when in fact they must have wandered off out of sight. Immediately I searched for them in Misty's field, Norman's field and round the back of the house. Several times throughout the day Alan and I looked for the ducks and hoped they would reappear but they didn't. There was no sign of them and we guessed that a fox had taken them. I was angry with myself for being so careless.

Next day during the afternoon Jess took a short cut across Norman's field on her way home from the Sloanes. She went straight to Alan and told him that she thought she had seen Lily's body in the field. We searched and found Lily's decapitated body and a few minutes later I found her beautiful head some yards away. There was no sign of Ruby at all. I supposed the fox had taken her and intended to return later for Lily. We buried her under one of the oak trees near the bottom of the garden.

That summer both Jess and Sam went with their horses to Pony Club Camp at Osbaldeston. It was Sam's first time. Alan drove the Land Rover and towed the horses in the trailer. Sam travelled with him. All the tack and some of the equipment were crammed into the back. Jess and I followed in the car with the rest of the stable equipment and the children's clothes and bits and pieces.

Of the one hundred and one members of the Saddleworth Branch of the Pony Club that year only 17 were boys. Around 35 of those members attended Camp and only five of them were boys. At the tender age of 11years Sam was perfectly at ease in the company of girls but when it came to staying for the week at Camp it was good for him to have some male company. That year Dan Greenwood, one of Sam's school friends also attended Camp. The boys got on well together and Sam had been invited to go on holiday to Wales with Dan and his parents the day after they got home from Camp.

On the second day of their holiday Dan's mum rang to tell us that Dan and Sam had been riding their bikes at the caravan park where they were staying. Sam had hit a speed bump and been thrown over the handlebars. They had taken him to hospital his left wrist was broken and had been put in plaster but he was OK and wanted to stay with Dan's family in Wales until the end of the week as planned.

The first I knew about Norman's dire confrontation with Billy Bull was when Bill Dawson brought a delivery of small hay bales that morning and began unloading them from his trailer. As I helped him stack the bales inside the barn he frowned at me from beneath his bushy eyebrows.

'Its bad news about Norman isn't it?' he said looking at me quizzically.

'Why what's happened?' I stopped what I was doing.

Satisfied that yet again he was the first to impart the latest piece of local news he settled himself comfortably on a bale of hay. Realizing that this was going to be a lengthy chat I sat down and gave him my full attention.

It transpired that three days earlier Norman and his wife Beryl had driven up to the field next to Jericho in their pick-up towing a livestock trailer intending to collect a young heifer that was in need of some medical attention. Over the years Norman had performed similar tasks on countless occasions and as usual he had driven through the gateway into the field. While Beryl closed the gate Norman reversed the pick-up for a few yards so that the back of the trailer was facing into the field before he dropped the loading ramp. Standing beside the pick-up he cast his eyes over the grazing cows that were scattered over the field. He soon located the sick heifer lying close to our wall where she had been the previous day. Next he noted with some satisfaction that Billy Bull was at the top end of the field. Norman confidently expected to be able to load the heifer into the trailer with very little fuss and without arousing the attention of the other cows. However, the young heifer was unwilling to be separated from her companions and apparently dodged and evaded Norman numerous times before he finally managed with Beryl's help to separate her from the others and drive her across the field towards the trailer. Concentrating on outwitting the heifer Norman broke his golden rule and as they approached the loading ramp he not only took his eyes off Billy as he tapped the heifer's rump with his stick but he turned his back on him as well.

The activity lower down the field had not gone unnoticed by the bull who's first instinct was to protect his cows and as Norman focused all his attention on dealing with the heifer Billy set off down the field towards him. Having successfully loaded the heifer into the trailer Norman lifted the ramp and fastened it shut while Beryl went to open the gate. Norman was about to get into the pick-up when he heard pounding hooves. He turned to find himself facing the angry bull. Beryl had just reached the gate when she too heard the hooves and became aware of the situation. She watched with horror as the huge beast approached Norman, knocked him to the ground and repeatedly mauled him with his massive head. The bull was fired up and attacked Norman again as he lay on the ground. Terrified, Beryl ran back to the pick-up and slipped into the passenger side without the bull noticing her. She held down the horn hoping to scare the bull and attract somebody's attention while with her other hand she frantically searched for Norman's mobile phone in the glove compartment amongst the old receipts and papers. On finding it she first rang Jim Taylor and then dialled 999 to call for an ambulance. Beryl remained in the cab of the pick-up knowing that any attempt to intervene between the bull and her husband would be futile and probably inflame the situation.

The first to arrive was Jim in his milk float. Quickly he opened the gate and drove across the field stopping a few yards past the pick-up close to our wall hoping to lure the bull away from Norman. He beeped the horn repeatedly to attract the bull's attention then hurriedly he got out of the milk float, climbed over the wall and ran down the lane opposite to where the pick-up was parked. As Jim had hoped Billy Bull turned his attention to this latest intruder. He charged the milk float lifting its front wheels off the ground then backed off slowly and stopped; with his head swaying from side to side and his eyes rolling he faced the vehicle and prepared to charge again. Jim took his chance and climbed back over the wall into the field and then ran to Norman who was barely conscious and obviously badly injured.

The ambulance arrived and Beryl ran to explain the situation to the driver. Billy was concentrating on attacking the milk float. The gate was still open so the ambulance driver drove into the field and reversed as close as he could to Norman and then he and his associate got out of the ambulance and opened the rear doors. Keeping a watchful eye on the bull they proceeded with Jim and Beryl's help to manhandle Norman onto a stretcher and lift him safely into the back of the ambulance.

The feverish activity and urgency in the voices over by the pick-up attracted the bull's attention once more and having vented his anger on the milk float he turned to face the ambulance. Beryl quickly got back into the pick-up and drove out of the gateway. Jim stood by the gate. The slavering bull charged the ambulance and one of his short horns penetrated the passenger door. The bull caused a lot of damage to the ambulance in his attempts to upturn the vehicle as it made its steady progress across the field. It was with enormous relief that Beryl watched the ambulance emerge from the field and drive through the gateway battered but intact. Hurriedly Jim closed the field gate securely behind it and once more Billy Bull was left alone in the field with his cows.

Sam came home on Sunday. Because he had attended a hospital in

Wales as a tourist, a follow-up appointment had been made for him to attend his local hospital in Oldham as a matter of course when he got home. Dan's mum had been concerned about Sam's arm as he was still in a lot of pain. I took him to Oldham Royal the next day to have his wrist checked. It turned out that the fracture was more serious than was first thought. There was some misalignment of the broken bone and because it had been set in plaster he had to be admitted to hospital the following Wednesday to have the bone re-aligned. The timing was unfortunate as this meant that Sam's wrist would be in plaster for his first week at Saddleworth Comprehensive School.

Sam was discharged from the hospital the day after his operation. Before we went home I made some enquiries to find out which ward Norman was in and briefly we called to see him. I was shocked when I saw him. His face and upper body were badly bruised and he looked weak and frail. He was surprised to see us and got upset when he told us that Billy Bull had to be put down. He asked me if I would send him a copy of the photo I'd shown him some weeks earlier of Billy looking over our wall – he wanted it by his bed while he was in hospital! He was clearly upset about the whole business and apologised for not taking my fears about the bull's escape more seriously. He said he felt guilty for putting our lives in danger. He was a kind man and I felt sorry for him.

With Joanne's help Jess and Sam had arranged for Bill Dawson to buy a pair of young white Call Ducks from Chelford market. He had kept them at his farm until the first of September when he brought them up to Jericho in a small cardboard box which he handed over to Jess and Sam. The children gave them to us as a present for our wedding anniversary. The ducks were very small and very neat with bright orange feet and beaks. Their plumage was white with traces of adolescent yellow down. The female in particular was very vocal and they were both absolutely beautiful. We called them 'Billy' and 'Lottie'.

The next day was Sam's first day at Saddleworth School. As I had done with Jess on her first day I insisted on taking a photo of him. He didn't mind though as he could show off his broken arm in the sling.

It was just over a month since Pete had suffered the stroke and thankfully he had made a good recovery. His eyes and his balance were pretty much back to normal and he had resumed his routine circuits of the farm and stables. Three or four times each day he would make his way down the lane turn right through the car park and along the concrete in front of the stables where he would spend time with anybody who was on the yard. Before long he would continue up past Misty's field, turn right to come in front of the hay barn and arrive once more beside the kitchen. Wagging his tail he would potter inside to check that all was well before going back outside to lay down for another sleep next to the house wall or on the grass under the Laburnum Tree.

The convenience of being able to use the lean-to stable at the end of the block as a shavings store was short lived. Samantha's brother bought a 14hh leggy black Dales pony for his wife and Gemma to ride. They asked if there was any chance we could make room for him on our yard. We gave it some thought. The lean-to would only just be big enough for a 14hh pony and another on the yard meant that there would be 10 horses grazing on our fields which was really too many – that is if we could seriously count Ben as a horse! Also in summer we did have the use of the Five Acre field which rested our summer turn-out and Samantha agreed to give the pony only limited winter turn-out. So because it was for Samantha and Gemma we agreed and I prepared the stable once more for its new occupant.

That weekend they brought Max to the yard. Now that Gemma had Max to ride Natasha had Ben all to herself; but as had been the case for both Sam and Gemma, Ben was fine to ride when out on a hack but was difficult and lazy if required to do any work on the paddock. Natasha lacked confidence and was making very little progress. Shelley worried that Ben's stubbornness might put her off riding altogether and she decided to look out for a different pony. If Natasha had a pony that had been properly schooled she would be able to concentrate on actually learning to ride it rather than spend all her time fighting with it as she was doing at the moment with Ben. Having made up her mind Shelley loaned Ben to a local riding school as a lead rein pony – something for which he was ideally suited. Before long she saw an advert for a 15year old 13.2hh chestnut gelding which apparently had been a reliable equitation and show jumping pony for his previous owners.

In the middle of October 'Pride' arrived on the yard. Shelley had arranged to have the pony for a short trial period and she put him into Ben's tiny stable. Pride was a beautiful pony but he lacked manners. His worst fault was that he would barge out of his stable the moment the door was unbolted. He was strong and lively and for the first week or so he was difficult to handle; when he was tacked up however he behaved quite differently, he became calm and sensible and because of this Shelley bought him. With time and patience he settled well on the yard and became easier to handle, he was a nice pony which excelled at equitation and enabled Natasha to succeed in Pony Club competitions.

Towards the end of October Jess and Zulu took part in a working hunter class at the Wythenshawe Show which they had qualified for earlier in the season. Having walked the course Jess, not only being the youngest but also the smallest competitor, was completely overawed by the size of the jumps and very nearly bottled it. To her credit as a representative of the Greater Manchester region she gritted her teeth and took part in the class along with over 50 other entrants. The jumps were the highest she had ever attempted on Zulu. She completed the course only picking up four faults which took her through to the second round after which she was placed seventh overall.

The following Saturday afternoon Joanne went for a hack on Benson and returned to the yard at about four o'clock. As soon as she got back she put Benson in his stable and then came to find me. She told me that as she had ridden along Two Acre Lane she had noticed two small white hens at the side of the road. As it would soon be dropping dark she was concerned that they would be caught by a fox so we decided to try and catch them. We borrowed a crate from Bill then Jo drove back to where she had last seen them. We were relieved to find that the hens were still there pottering about at the side of the road. Jo parked up and we got out of the car. There was no empty box nearby to suggest that they had literally fallen off the back of a lorry, so how they had got there was a bit puzzling as the nearest place that kept poultry was about half a mile away. The hens did not appear to be unduly concerned by our arrival. They were white Leghorn Bantams and I imagined that they could move pretty damn quick if they wanted to!

'How are we going to catch them?' Jo asked quietly. The larger of the two hens was scratching at the ground just by my feet.

'Like this!' I said and snatched up the startled hen. Squawking frantically it flapped its wings but there was no escape. I held it in a vice-like grip and unceremoniously stuffed it into the crate which Jo was holding. Almost as surprised as the hen had been Jo collapsed into uncontrollable giggles. Panic stricken the other hen legged it. Screeching hysterically she fluttered over the low wire fence beside the road and landed in a boggy area full of reeds. I pursued her at once. I jumped over the fence and sank up to my ankles in the clay bog. The reeds hampered the progress of the hen so I threw myself on top of her to prevent her escape.

A car drove past slowly. The occupants were watching my behaviour suspiciously which caused Joanne, who was already doubled up with laughter, to become completely helpless. Somewhat dishevelled I climbed back over the fence with the traumatised bird and put it into the crate with its friend.

'Thanks for your help!' I said to Joanne as I took the crate from her and put it into the car. Having composed herself to some extent Jo drove back to Jericho. We took the crate up to the hen hut. Our hens were already roosting so I put the unopened crate on the floor inside the hut until morning.

Next day I let the Leghorns out of the crate, took the concrete block out of the hut doorway but left the safety run door shut so the birds could socialise but not escape. There was very little aggression from our hens and none at all from the Leghorns. Later that day I called at two or three places to enquire if anyone had lost any hens, but nobody had so I kept them. Jo christened the larger one 'Foggy' the other one was just known as 'the little Leghorn'.

As winter approached the evenings became shorter and colder. The kitchen and dining room were reasonably well heated but upstairs condensation was a problem. The outside wall on the upstairs landing ran with condensation as did the two outside walls in Sam's bedroom which made his room feel terribly cold and made his bedding feel damp. The outside walls in Jess's room and ours too felt damp when the weather was very cold. We decided that central heating was essential for the good of the house as well as an overdue luxury for ourselves.

Throughout half-term that October we made a start and hung radiators in every upstairs room, one on the landing and one in each of the two downstairs rooms. Once again we lifted floorboards and spent several hours drilling holes through joists to accommodate the new pipes. Alan struggled to drill and bash a hole through the thick stone wall between the toilet and the shippon which would be big enough for the central heating pipes to pass from the new boiler in the dairy to the circuit of radiators and back again. We prepared an area on the grass bank behind the house to position the large plastic oil tank which had been delivered and then we laid a copper pipe from the tank to the central heating boiler which Alan had plumbed into the dairy.

Having decided on oil fired central heating we decided also to convert the solid fuel Aga to oil. I loved the warmth of the Aga and preferred it to any other sort of oven but I had to admit that this one was very dirty. The Aga had to be topped-up regularly with fuel and because of this the kitchen surfaces always seemed to be coated with a fine covering of coal dust no matter how often I wiped them. We arranged for the conversion to be done by a local man called Ziggy who had worked on Agas for years and was about to retire. He not only agreed to convert the Aga but he also found us two reconditioned lids and a black enamel top to replace the old cracked and battered one.

Before the conversion could be done the chimney had to be swept and a flue liner put inside it. As Ziggy swept the chimney he became more and more agitated and annoyed. Before he could insert the flue liner he had to extricate half a brush head which despite repeated attempts to dislodge it remained firmly wedged in the bend in the chimney. It was no wonder that we had experienced such problems with fumes and fluctuating cooking temperatures! Once converted the Aga was a lot cleaner the temperature more constant and my cooking more successful.

At the beginning of November we changed over to winter turn-out and a busier daily routine for me with horses to turn out and bring in at different times of the day, hay nets to replace and water to top up. Once Alan and the children had left the house in the mornings I lived a solitary existence during the short misty damp days. Socialising, as far as the stable yard was concerned, was confined to weekends.

It was well into November before we finally filled the finished central heating system with water and sorted out any leaks. Having lit the boiler and bled the radiators we felt pleasant warmth permeate the house for the first winter in six years. The warmth transformed the house. The condensation on the walls completely dried up and Jericho that winter became a much more pleasant place in which to live.

It had taken me quite a while to get to know Jane even though she was one of the first to rent one of the stables. A small woman in her thirties with short strawberry blonde hair Jane got on with looking after her horse and left everyone else to look after theirs. She rarely bothered with idle chit-chat, she was blunt to the point of rudeness and if asked for her opinion she gave it sparing nobody's feelings. However if anybody's horse was sick or injured she was the first to offer help or advice. She was extremely knowledgeable and I liked her a lot.

One day while I was tidying the barn I heard her calling me and I went outside to see what she wanted. She was standing outside her stable with her feet together, knees slightly bent and her hands clasped to her ample bosom giggling nervously.

'What on earth's wrong with you?' I asked.

'There's a mouse in my wellie.' she said 'Will you get it out?'

This irrational fear of small rodents shared by so many people who happily ride and handle big, often temperamental or badly behaved horses has always baffled me. I walked over to her stable.

'It's in there' she whispered pointing to the offending wellie which had been hurriedly discarded on the floor. I picked up the wellie brought it outside and looked inside it. I couldn't see anything. Jane never took her eyes off the boot 'It's hiding' she said assertively.

I tapped the heel of the boot hard on the concrete then tipped it up expecting the mouse to drop out – but it didn't.

'It must have a vice-like grip!' I laughed looking at Jane who was watching closely.

'It's in there I tell you. I'd have seen it if it had come out!'

Jess and Shelley came out of Thomas's stable to see what was going on. I smacked the heel of the boot two or three times sharply against the stable wall and then shook it upside down – still nothing came out.

'Well it's not in there now.' I said handing her the wellie.

'Well it was.' said Jane sounding less confident. She tilted the leg of the boot towards her and peered down it. The mouse chose that precise moment to make its escape, fled up the leg of the wellie and leapt straight down Jane's cleavage. Jane screamed, hurled the wellie in the air and frantically scooped at the mouse which was nestling in her bosom. Finally the terrified creature made its last leap for freedom and landed back in her stable where it quickly disappeared beneath the horse's bedding.

'Oh bloody great!' Jane snapped, zipped her jacket up to her chin and strode off down the concrete.

This year my family was coming to Jericho for Boxing Day. Pat rang me on Christmas Eve to warn me that Karen had acquired a kitten. Pat had told her that she couldn't keep it so it was more than likely that before long Karen would ask me if I would have it. Sure enough within a few hours Karen rang me with some cock and bull story about having found a tiny black kitten in a gutter. She told me that her mean mother wouldn't let her keep the poor little thing which desperately needed a good home and she pleaded with me to have it. I was a complete push over of course but told her that Alan might object. However I agreed with her that there was no way that we could leave the little mite homeless. So if she hadn't found a home for it by

Boxing Day I told her that she had better bring it with her when they came over. We would keep it hidden from Alan until I'd had a chance to work on him.

By the time Pat, John and Karen arrived, the rest of the family were already gathered in the dining room with a drink having deposited their gifts under the Christmas tree. I met Karen as she came into the kitchen. Hurriedly she passed me a miaowing cardboard box which I put into the dairy out of the way. When all the Christmas presents had been opened I took the hot food from the Aga to the table in the dining room and everyone tucked into the buffet. After a while Karen checked on the kitten and asked me if she could move her into the kitchen as it was a bit cold in the dairy. The atmosphere was relaxed and comfortable and everyone was chatting happily. Alan went into the kitchen to top up some drinks.

'What was that?' he demanded loudly. Everyone fell silent and looked at me. We could hear the kitten's plaintive cries emanating from behind the kitchen waste bin. Karen grinned and pulled a face at me. 'I can hear an animal!' Alan announced.

A few stifled giggles confirmed his suspicion that he was the only one who was unaware of the situation. I went into the kitchen and lifted the kitten out of the box.

'Oh look what I've found!' I said showing him the tiny ball of black fluff with its two big amber eyes

'Yes, well it's not staying here!' Alan stated with futile firmness. Ignoring his remark I deposited the kitten on Mum's lap knowing that she would be suitably gooey and affectionate with it and just to clarify the situation Karen mumbled something about finding it in a gutter. Before long a succession of Christmassy names were being bandied about for the newest arrival. Ultimately Karen's suggestion of 'Mary Christmas' was decided upon and despite Alan's initial grumblings Mary became a permanent member of our expanding family and settled in very quickly.

Looking through the dining room window as we ate our evening meal on New Year's Eve we had an excellent view of the firework celebrations in Manchester and all round the region which welcomed in the Millennium New Year.

2000

The first week of January was cold. I busied myself trying to build up my stock of shavings after the Christmas and New Year holiday breaks. Alan strengthened the flimsy door which led from the kitchen into the dairy by cladding it with lengths of pine. It looked much better and was much more substantial. I spent time with Sam helping him to pull Jessie's mane and generally tidy her up.

At the weekend Alan came with me to get shavings. We took the horse trailer and filled sixteen bags. On the Saturday afternoon Benson appeared to stumble as he went into his stable; after which he would not put any weight on his back right leg. Jo examined his leg and foot carefully but couldn't see anything wrong so she left him on a thick bed of shavings and hoped he would be OK in the morning. Next morning however Benson was as lame as ever so Jo called the vet. The vet was full of gloom and doom and said it was either a fracture or tendon damage. Needless to say Jo was very upset. He made arrangements to X-ray Benson's leg the following day.

The X-ray showed up no fracture. The vet seemed a bit at a loss, gave him two injections and advised two weeks box rest. Jo decided to poultice the foot as it felt very hot.

Early the following Thursday evening Benson began with colic. We had no idea what had brought it on as he'd been fine all day. We wondered if it was due to the pain in his foot or the stress of having to stay in. Whatever the reason he had it very badly. He groaned, arched his neck, tried to lie down and kicked out violently with both back legs making some massive holes in the stable walls. Once again Jo had to call the vet who made several visits during the night. Benson became so distressed that the vet finally decided to refer him to Leahurst. Alan agreed to transport him in our trailer. By this time it was snowing and the prospect of Benson kicking out in a trailer on the M62 in the middle of the night in snowy conditions was not a pleasant one. The vet made a phone call only to be told that Leahurst was full to capacity and to ring back in the morning if Benson was no better. In the meantime we were to walk him out and not let him lie down – which is what we'd been doing for the last two hours. Jo stayed with

Benson all night. We stayed up with her until 2am. By about 3am Benson began to relax and by 4.15 he had improved enough for Jo to risk going home to warm herself up for an hour or so.

We got up early in the morning and were relieved to find Benson much happier and more his old self. We were so glad that we hadn't trailed him over to Liverpool. Samantha and Gemma arrived a few minutes later to find Max very agitated. They soon discovered that their saddle was missing from their tack room. Further investigation revealed footprints in the snow leading from Max's stable to Steve Foster's fence. We called round there and found that he too had been burgled as had the Sloanes. Some of their tack had been taken from a locked tack room which had been smashed open in their barn. The police came up and plodded about nodding wisely at the footprints in the snow but didn't really do anything constructive.

Our unwelcome visitors must have been disturbed by Jo when she returned to check on Benson at 5.30am and consequently they only managed to get away with Max's saddle. Despite their visit Benson was surprisingly quiet and content with no apparent further damage to his bad leg despite the hammering he had given it against his stable walls!

On Monday night we hadn't been in bed long when we heard a horse squeal. We listened intently. It sounded like Thomas. We peered out of the bedroom windows into the darkness but couldn't see anything. It was unusual for any of the horses to make a noise at night so we suspected something was wrong. Alan went downstairs, let Kim out and went down to the stables to investigate. Kim began to bark. Alan almost bumped into Thomas who was standing in the garden; his stable door was wide open. We think the burglars must have come back to finish what they had started in the early hours of Friday morning. However Thomas was very possessive of his stable and if somebody he didn't know had come into his stable at night he would *not* be happy. His tack room door was locked and he would not just stand there while they forced it open. Evidently the intruders had decided to turf him out so that they could get on with breaking in. When Kim started barking they must have made a quick getaway. Alan returned Thomas to his stable and came back to bed.

Next morning we found out that Highmoor Stables and Blunder

Hall, both within a couple of miles of us, had been burgled that night and lost a substantial amount of tack from some well secured buildings.

Four weeks later Benson was given the all clear by the vet – we were still none the wiser as to what had been wrong with his leg in the first place!

Trader was now nearly four years old and despite Sue's efforts there was little or no improvement in his behaviour. He was excitable and difficult at the field-gate when people were trying to bring in their horses and being 16hh this was causing problems. Over the past few weeks his behaviour had been worse than usual resulting in all the horses being wound up and anxious when it was time to bring them in. It culminated in Pride being kicked – fortunately not seriously as according to the vet he had been kicked 'by an unshod hoof '. Due to the fact that Trader was the only one that was unshod the finger of blame inevitably pointed at him. So because of the recent tragedy with Bliss I asked Sue to turn out Misty and Trader separately from the other horses until we moved into the summer grazing in May when the horses would have more room to get out of each others way. I had a responsibility towards everybody's horses and their safety was my prime consideration. However, a few days later Sue gave a weeks notice and said she was going to another yard. In her opinion I was treating her horses unfairly.

The next weekend we managed to shift three loads of muck from the muck heap on the yard to the one in the field. Alan harrowed the paddock and the summer field gateway and we mended the broken fencing in Misty's field. On Sunday Sue left the yard with Misty and Trader. A day or so later Samantha moved Max out of the lean-to stable and put him into Trader's.

The Lambs

I had often thought that it would be a nice idea and good for the land to have a couple of sheep grazing at Jericho. Earlier in the year I had mentioned my idea to Simon, Sam's friend who lived on a sheep farm across the valley in Diggle. That spring the number of orphaned or rejected lambs on their farm was rising so Simon contacted me and asked if I could take two. I said I could and Sam and I went up to his farm and collected two three day old lambs. One was a Cheviot, all white with small pricked up ears. The other was a cross bred Suffolk with dappled face and legs. Sam chose the white Cheviot and called her Emily. Jess called the other one Molly. They were very cute and fed well on their bottles which we gave them every four hours.

Sam and Joanne had already prepared one of the back stables with some straw which Bill had brought up for us. They had opened up one bale and spread it thickly over the floor then put another five bales around the front of the stable to make it cosier and less draughty.

The following day was very cold and when we fed the lambs early in the morning they were both shivering. Their bodies felt cold and their pink skin showed through what little wool they had on their backs. I hated the thought of them being cold and knew they wouldn't thrive if they were using up their energy just to keep warm. Joanne brought up a couple of little jumpers which her niece had outgrown and we put them on the lambs temporarily until I could sort out something which was a bit more hard wearing. I remembered a small rug which Jess used to have in her bedroom when she was younger. I found it and cut it into two pieces. I lay one across Emily's back and pulled it round her chest and under her belly. I trimmed it to fit then made some holes through which I threaded a piece of baling twine so I could tie it in place. It fitted remarkably well so I did the same for Molly. They wore them night and day until the weather improved. Both lambs seemed much happier they were more active and their bodies felt warm when I put my hand under their rugs. By the time they had grown out of them they had enough wool of their own to keep themselves warm.

March continued to be a cold month. The temperature plummeted during the last week of the month and Wednesday in particular had been a bitterly cold day. Early in the evening the wind picked up making it feel even colder. I hurried to get the evening chores done and get back indoors. Alan woke in the middle of the night.

'What's that noise?'

All I could hear was the wind. 'What noise?' I said hutching myself up on one elbow.

'Ssh listen, a moaning noise.'

'I can hear it… I don't know…Oh Christ, did Sam put the hen's block in?'

'I don't know.' Alan said getting out of bed quickly. He dragged on some clothes and ran downstairs grabbed a torch and went outside with the dogs. I followed him down the stairs and rifled through the kitchen drawer. I found the other torch then put a waterproof jacket on over my nightie, pushed my bare feet into cold clammy wellies and followed Alan outside into the bitter wind. The awful wailing noise was coming from the hen hut. Alan came out of it as I got there.

'A fox has been in.' he said. 'There are only two hens in there and they're terrified. I'll go and look for the others.' he said and left. I shone my torch inside the hut. The two big Sussex hens were perched on the roosts wailing in distress with their heads against the side of the hut. The block was laid beside the entrance. Evidently a fox had been right inside the hut, there were feathers everywhere but apart from the two Sussex there were no other hens to be seen.

I also went outside hoping to find some survivors. I searched in the garden but I couldn't see any. Alan found Eric dead on the paddock, he'd obviously put up a good fight. I walked round to the summer field and shone my torch around near the gateway. I found Foggy and about twelve feet away from her I found Peggy. They were both still alive laying still and silent completely traumatised. I picked them up and carried them straight back to the hen hut and put them on the perches next to the two terrified Sussex hens. I shouted to Alan to help me look again in the field. He came with me but we didn't find any more of them. We returned to the hen hut put the block in and shut the door. If any of the missing five hens were still alive they would be too traumatised to make their way back in the dark and hopefully would stay hidden. Anyway we couldn't risk leaving the hen hut unsecured in case the fox came back. We were both shivering. The wind was cutting through me like a knife. We walked down the garden and returned to the house from opposite directions for one last look. The whole episode was horrible and made me sad.

Next morning we decided not to tell Sam until he got home from school in the hope that by then some of the missing hens might have turned up. About 10 o'clock much to my relief Cilla, Simone and Michelle appeared out of the shrubbery and stood together nervously in the garden. I called them to the hen hut gave them some corn and shut them inside with the others. Peggy died later in the day Blanche and the little Leghorn never came back. Foggy was very quiet and barely moved all day. The two Sussex calmed down but none of them ate anything or attempted to move from the hen hut.

When he came home from school I told Sam about the fox. He was very upset particularly about Eric and said he was sorry for not putting the block in. I said I was sorry too for not checking. We decided to write a permanent note on the blackboard in the kitchen to remind us both to make sure that the block had been put in each night.

The first weekend in April was spent making a pen for the lambs. Emily was thriving but Molly was not feeding well and had become very lethargic.

I told Bill about the visit from the fox and asked him if he would try and get a Rhode Island Red cockerel for Sam.

Early on Monday morning it began to snow heavily. I took everyone to school. The sticky snow had settled thickly making driving very difficult. I came off the road and skidded down a bank near Highmoor Stables on the way home. I managed to reverse out and got home OK.

Next day Bill came up in his tractor and handed me a small cardboard box. Inside it was a very large Rhode Island Red cockerel. I lifted him out and apart from his tail feathers being a bit bent he was very handsome and I put him in the hen hut straightaway with the hens. Sam decided to call him 'Henry'. Foggy and the two Sussex hens in particular were much happier as soon as Henry joined them. He was a young bird with a nice temperament and all the hens stayed close to him as they had done with Eric.

Young cockerels cannot crow properly immediately, it comes with time and practice. All through that spring and summer Henry practised hard from sunrise to sunset until he could crow in a respectable manner.

It was Sam's 12th birthday on the 6th April and Bill brought up some hens for him to buy with his birthday money if he liked them. Sam chose two Rhode Island Reds and a Black Rock. Joanne bought him a sandy coloured Game Bird too which he called Sarah. All the hens got on well and Foggy and the two Sussex gradually regained their confidence.

All that week Molly lamb deteriorated. She seemed uncomfortable, was reluctant to feed and barely moved around at all. She died on the Friday. Alan buried her near Lily duck. I decided to move Emily out of the stable at the back of the house and install her in the lean-to at the end of the stable block now that it was no longer occupied. It was the first time she had been on her own and she cried all night.

That weekend Jess competed on Zulu at the first show of the new season at Rochdale Riding Club. She came sixth in the working hunter class and Zulu chucked her off at the first fence in the show jumping class!

The following Saturday Sam competed on Jessie in a Pony Club team show jumping competition at Wood Nook Equestrian Centre in Meltham. He completed two clear rounds and his team was placed fifth out of eighteen teams.

Alan found time during the weekend to finish the lamb pen.

After Molly died I pestered Simon repeatedly to let us have another lamb. Exceptionally heavy rain the following week caused terrible problems for pregnant ewes giving birth out in the fields. Many lambs and some ewes died and Simon rang to say we could choose a lamb from four weak little orphans which had been put in a pen. Sam and I went to the farm and came home with a very small, very frail two day old Suffolk lamb. She was gorgeous with her black face and big black ears which stuck out at each side of her head like handlebars. 'Molly 2' was a sweet little soul who loved human contact. In fact she would only take her bottle when I cuddled her up close. Emily seemed pleased to have a new companion but was rough with her. She head butted and body slammed her several times before I risked leaving them together in the stable! I got up at 3am to feed them and to my relief found them cuddled up together. They quickly became close friends and Molly soon got stronger.

During March Ann loaned Soli out again but this time stipulated to the woman who loaned her that Soli was to be kept on our yard.

At the end of April Ann agreed to sell Soli to the woman hoping that she would continue to keep her here but almost immediately the new owner gave notice and took Soli to a yard several miles away. We were all sorry to see her go.

The excessively wet weather had prevented us from getting on the fields with the tractor. It was the beginning of May before Bill was able to spread fertilizer on the summer fields which delayed the start of the summer grazing.

The first Saturday in May was a hive of activity on the yard. Sam washed Jessie's mane and tail and generally tidied her up. Shelley and Natasha gave Pride a bath and Samantha and Gemma spent hours grooming Max. They were all preparing their ponies for the show the following day. It was the Pony Club Novice Show and Sam competed in equitation, mounted games, show jumping and working hunter and he won the Championship for his age group. We were really chuffed for him.

On the following Wednesday I took the lambs up to Simon's farm. Emily was to be wormed and Molly was to have a docking ring put on her tail. The farmer wormed Emily and to my dismay wormed Molly too.

'She'll be fine.' he said noticing my concern. He then proceeded to place the docking ring on her tail. I took the lambs back home and put them in their run.

First thing on the Saturday morning I found little Molly dead in her stable. That really upset me. Molly was almost four weeks old she was happy and lively and had been literally skipping along the concrete with Emily before I'd shut them up the night before.

Lambing was pretty much over now so Emily would have to be on her own from now on. She was seven weeks old and for the first few days she stayed close to me if I was working outside and close to the house if I was indoors, but as time went by she became content to potter about with the poultry or lay down on the concrete beside the barn.

The old window frames in the dairy and shippon were rotten. Alan made new ones and by the middle of May all the old window frames had been taken out and replaced. It was now down to me to treat and paint them. On the Thursday I made a start and sanded and primed the new window frames. Monica, one of the new Rhode Island Red hens disappeared and was nowhere to be seen when it was time to put the block in. We left it as late as possible then reluctantly secured the hen hut without her. Next day I continued to work on the windows and in the afternoon Monica turned up alive and well. Zulu however came in from the field on three legs. On close inspection we found a nail embedded in his foot. Alan managed to pull it out and then we cleaned and poulticed the wound. By Sunday evening I'd finished all the windows.

It was the last weekend in May before we were able to turn out the horses into the summer fields for the start of summer grazing by which time Zulu's foot had healed well. Rochdale Riding Club One Day Event took place on that Sunday – Jess did really well on Zulu, they were placed second and she won £15.

Bill lent Sam a broody Silky bantam hen and gave him half a dozen duck eggs for her to sit on for the next four weeks. She arrived already comfortably installed on top of the eggs in a nest of hay inside a cut down oil drum. We put the oil drum complete with hen inside Emily's tack room with the door left open for the next four weeks and hoped for the best.

Early in June as I drove down Shiloh Lane Bill stopped me in his tractor. He asked me if I wanted any ex-battery hens. Someone had asked him to get them some and had then changed their mind. Our hen hut was already pretty full now with 11 birds but I said I would take one to make it up to a dozen. The new addition was a Warren – ginger and white – with scruffy broken feathers and a beak which had been cut short. She was surprisingly tame and quite happy to be picked up and stroked. I called her 'Betty' and she soon became my favourite. She was always the first on the scene if I did any digging in the garden and when we dug back the muck heap she quickly appeared and watched closely ready to snatch up any unfortunate worms that were uncovered – her shortened beak seemed not to hamper her in the slightest.

Jessica

As a young child Jessica was amusing, as a young teenager she was hilarious and very good company. Having turned 15 however, a few black clouds had begun to darken her sunny personality. She could be considerate but also selfish, sensitive but also cold. She could lighten up a room when she walked into it or ruin a pleasant atmosphere with a scowl or a slammed door. She teased Sam mercilessly, left clothes, make-up and plates with half eaten snacks all over her bedroom floor and wet towels in ridiculous numbers all over the bathroom or on her bed after one of her frequent long steamy showers.

When she was a little girl she never grasped the true meaning of the word 'no'. Now well aware of what it meant she resisted it vehemently with pleas and protestations and ultimate sullen silences.

Time spent socialising with her friends was of prime importance to her but living where we did left her somewhat out on a limb. Unlike her peers she could not just flounce out of the house and meet up with her friends – she had to ask for a lift – no doubt a source of intense irritation! Her desire to be with her friends, quite natural though it was, began to clash with her responsibilities toward Zulu. Although she still thoroughly enjoyed competing on him the mundane chores involved in looking after him evidently were becoming even less attractive to her than they had done previously and on school days particularly they tended to be done with more than a little reluctance.

Despite all this Jess and I remained close but confrontations between Jess and her dad were becoming frequent. At the end of a school day the last thing Alan needed was yet another stand off with a belligerent teenager – particularly if that teenager was his own daughter. Jess always liked to have the last word in any disagreement but was yet to learn the wisdom of keeping her thoughts to herself and her mouth shut when Alan was close to losing it. Being sent to her room or choosing to go up there rather than spend time with the rest of us was becoming common place. On reflection Jess compared pretty well to many teenagers but at the time she tried my patience.

Over that summer season Jess and Sam enjoyed their riding. At the beginning of the season they both enrolled on an eight week cross-country course held on Monday evenings at Rochdale Riding Club which increased their confidence and improved their riding a great deal. As the season progressed they competed in all the Pony Club shows many of the Pony Club team show jumping competitions and most of the Rochdale Riding Club shows as well.

Pete had another stroke at the end of June and once again I had to take our gentle old dog to the vet who gave him the same medication as he had given him last time – but warned me that this time it would probably take him longer to recover.

Bill's broody hen hatched four beautiful ducklings. One of them was very frail and I put it in a shoe box on top of the Aga overnight. By morning the duckling was much stronger so I took it back down to the broody hen removed the unhatched eggs and renewed the bedding. The hen seemed much happier and was very watchful of her new offspring.

Our regular involvement with Pony Club introduced us to people who had similar equine interests. That summer we were approached by members of two families who had become aware that I ran a livery yard. The first was Emily a 14 year old competent rider who regularly competed against Sam in show jumping and working hunter classes. Sam had told her that there was an empty stable and she came up to Jericho with her mum Ann to look at the stable and the yard. One week later they brought Ben onto the yard. He was a chunky black 13.2hh Fell pony with the glossiest mane and tail I'd ever seen. He was well mannered both inside and outside the stable and Emily looked after him conscientiously. From that day we referred to our Emily as 'Emily Sheep' to avoid any possible confusion!

The second family to approach us was Paula and Graham with their young daughters Sophie and Bethany. Sophie had just joined Pony Club with Lucky their 12hh lead rein pony. They were anxious to move off their present yard. The only available stable we had was the little lean-to next to Thomas but as the pony was so small we agreed to rent it out once again.

By mid July Bill had cut the grass on the Five Acre Field. Two days later by 11pm there were 32 bales of haylage wrapped and stacked in the usual place beside the muck heap.

During the summer Alan and I had taken numerous trailer loads of muck up the fields in an attempt to keep the muck heap as empty as possible. We had come to the conclusion that the existing muck heap area was not big enough for the yard. It had lasted nearly six years and some of the original fencing was now rotten and needed to be replaced. Rather than mend or replace it we decided to make a new, much larger more permanent muck heap out of concrete kerbs. When we had taken the last of the muck up the field we laid two planks up against the back of the trailer so that wheel barrows could be emptied directly into it.

Having decided on the size of the area needed to accommodate the new muck heap we removed the old fencing and flags and cut back some of the small trees and bushes to make room for it. Early in August we hired someone to dig out the area. Then we ordered 10 tons of crushed brick which was tipped in the middle of it. After having levelled that up as best we could we shuttered up the area with long pieces of sturdy timber to make it ready for the delivery of concrete.

The annual Saddleworth Pony Club Camp week took place

during August. On the Sunday afternoon Jess, Sam, Emily, Shelley and Natasha all left for Osbaldeston with their horses leaving the yard unusually quiet. The following Tuesday evening Jess rang from Camp to tell us that she had come off Zulu during a jumping lesson. She had been thrown head first at the jump and hit her face on a jumping pole. Her teeth had gone through her top lip. She had been taken to hospital for treatment where her lip had been glued together - thankfully her teeth were OK. She said she was being well looked after and wanted to stay at Camp.

Thursday dawned warm and bright and the concrete for the prepared muck heap base arrived at probably the hottest part of the day. It was an awful job. More water should have been added to the mix to make it more manageable for us on such a hot day. It was far too dry and consequently very difficult to move around and get level.

On Saturday morning we fetched Jess and Sam from Camp. As usual various competitions took place followed by a presentation of prizes and rosettes which were awarded to the children for various achievements and for participation in classes held throughout the week. Jessica's mouth had begun to heal and the combination of the glued staples and the healing cut gave her the appearance of having a small moustache. Throughout the week and during the presentation she was referred to as Hitler.

After some persuasion Alan agreed to make a new poultry hut. We prepared an area and mixed our own concrete to make a base for it to stand on. It took a lot more concrete than we had expected and seemed to take forever to mix enough of it but we persevered. The hut was constructed in sections like the hen hut. It was big – about seven feet by five feet -with a pitched roof and two doors at the front. Inside it was divided into two halves by a three foot fence. One half was for the geese the other half was for the ducks. A coat of creosote bolts and handles completed the job but not before I fell heavily on the concrete cutting both my knees, bruising my hip and hurting my wrist!

We received our first delivery of massive concrete kerbs during the last week of August and with them we made a start building the three walls of the new muck heap. The kerbs were terribly heavy.

The more courses we built the higher we had to lift them and the more we struggled.

We made carrying straps out of some webbing that Steve Sloane had given us which made it a bit easier but by the time we had completed four courses we both found the kerbs were just too heavy and I couldn't lift them high enough for us to continue. Graham arranged for us to borrow a mini-digger to help us to lift them.

In September Sam began working for Norman Taylor on a weekend milk round. Every Saturday he got up at 4am. Also that month Samantha and Gemma left the yard with Max.

By mid October the new muck heap was finished apart from the pointing. Alan showed Sam how to do it and he helped us to finish it – remarkably well.

The first boyfriend that Jess plucked up the courage to introduce us to arrived at Jericho early one evening towards the end of October. He was a lanky youth with fair hair and a pale complexion dressed in light coloured clothes. Jess took him straight down to the stables to show him Zulu. I peered out of the kitchen window at him. My first impression was that he looked a bit feeble as he wouldn't go near the horses but when Jess brought him up to the house and introduced him I found him to be amusing and chatty and actually quite likeable. However their relationship was short lived lasting barely a month. It foundered one evening when they went out together and met up with some of Jess's friends. The young man in question apparently became more and more inebriated and objectionable as the evening progressed having consumed an indeterminable quantity of alcohol and was despatched into a taxi and sent home by Jess who was more than a little tired of his company! When the taxi arrived at his home his horrified father saw his wayward son covered in what he believed to be blood and rang me for an explanation as there was no sign of Jessica. Equally horrified I rang Jess and demanded to know what had been going on. Fed up with the whole episode Jess assured me that it was not blood that he was covered in but watermelon flavoured Bacardi Breezer that he had thrown up in the taxi! A little later his father confirmed that this was indeed the case and not surprisingly Jess decided to have no more to do with him.

The next indoor project we tackled was the dairy. We cleared the room discarding anything we didn't need and things we wanted to keep we stored in the shippon. The ceiling was clad with grimy water stained sheets of cellotex. We pulled them down to reveal the asbestos roof. It was dirty and full of cobwebs and had a couple of cracks in it. Previously the rain had seeped into the cellotex but now it dripped directly onto the dairy floor. I tried to mend the cracked asbestos with a fibreglass paste to make it waterproof but despite my efforts the roof continued to leak badly. It was too dangerous to get onto the roof when it was wet so I had to wait for a dry spell before I could attempt another repair. I had a long wait!

I loved the old Land Rover and always chose to drive that in preference to the car. The rest of the family however did not share my affection for it. Admittedly it was and always had been unreliable. Jess and Sam were taking part in more and more equestrian competitions and so we had to use the Land Rover frequently to tow the two horses in the trailer. When the competitions were held at Birchinley Manor or Rochdale Riding Club the Land Rover coped perfectly well because the journeys were on the flat. However when the competitions were held at Meltham the journey involved a lot of hills which it struggled with. In fact it practically expired when it pulled the trailer up the last steep hill to the Wood Nook Equestrian Centre. If we were at the back of a line of horse boxes and trailers making our way up to Wood Nook we chugged along quite inconspicuously. If however we found ourselves at the front of the traffic it became embarrassing. Alan had to put the Land Rover into low ratio and even then it only just managed to drag itself over the brow of the hill; because we were moving so slowly we prevented everybody behind us from keeping up their momentum so everyone else struggled too.

Alan found this extremely frustrating and began to browse through various auto sales magazines to see if he could find something which we could afford that had a bit more power. Before too long he saw an advertisement for a Nissan Patrol which was for sale in Glossop so we went to look at it. We went to see it a second time, took it for a test drive and decided to buy it. The Nissan proved to be a good buy and towed the trailer and two horses with absolutely no problem at all.

By mid-November the worst of the rough walls in the dairy had been either re-plastered or filled depending on how large the holes were, and it was ready to be painted.

October and November had been exceptionally wet with frequent storms and torrential rain. York and Shrewsbury and many other towns suffered from horrendous flooding; our fields were desperately wet.

To help fund her desire to possess such luxuries as make up, jewellery and music CDs Jess began to look for some kind of part-time employment. The Cross Keys pub in Delph, a couple of miles away, incorporated a restaurant which enjoyed a reputation for providing excellent food and service. A vacancy existed for a part-time waitress to work there on Saturday evenings and Jess applied for the job. After a formal interview she was offered the job subject to a preliminary trial the following week. Having completed the trial successfully she commenced work as junior waitress at the end of November.

The same weekend Alan took Sam and Jessie to Croft Top a few miles along the M62 to take part in a Pony Club team show jumping competition. A lady who was helping to run the competition recognised Jessie and remarked how good she looked for a 22 year old. Alan told her that she was only 17 but the woman was adamant that this was the pony that she had known several years ago and disappeared into her office. She emerged a few minutes later with some photographs of her son sitting on his pony next to a young girl sitting on a chestnut pony which was unmistakeably Jessie. The lady told Alan that the children had often competed together and their ponies were the same age.

Sam was very upset and we were annoyed that Jessie's previous owners had lied about how old she was. We would not have looked at her had we known that she was 20 years old let alone pay what we did for her – which of course they knew. However as it turned out it would have been our loss if we had not bought her. We have no regrets and although they were dishonest about her age they in no way exaggerated what a good pony she was.

By the end of the month we had finished the dairy. Alan had taken some of the cupboards and work surfaces out of the kitchen and fitted them in the dairy instead and had plumbed in a new sink. No doubt sometime in the not too distant future we would make more radical alterations to it but for the time being it was a big improvement. We intended to start work on the kitchen soon after Christmas.

Whenever we completed a job successfully I felt that all the hard work had been worthwhile and I was filled with a sense of achievement that we had done it ourselves. Between jobs I know Alan would have liked to have taken more days off than he did do to play golf and such like whereas I was always anxious to get straight on with the next project. In retrospect I think I probably became a little obsessed with Jericho. My life existed within its boundaries. I was quite content for it to be that way but I expected Alan to feel the same. When he didn't it annoyed me. I felt frustrated when he sat and watched the telly when we could have been beginning the next job. Probably he was shattered and just needed a break but I couldn't see that at the time – I just wanted to get things done. Oh well, what do they say about hindsight?

During the Christmas break Alan and Sam took two loads of well-rotted muck in the tractor trailer to spread on Bobbie's field. Sam stood in the trailer and chucked it out with a pitch fork while Alan drove slowly over the field. The odd forkful of muck which flew past Alan's head every now and again was of course entirely accidental.

2001

As planned during the first week in January we made a start on the kitchen. We decided to make a feature of the Aga and built a pier at each side of it out of reclaimed bricks. Each pier had a stone seat built into it after which it continued up above head height. Both piers were then topped off by an eight foot length of chunky pitch pine which we bought from a reclamation yard.

The weather throughout January was exceptionally cold and the ground in the winter field was rock hard. Unfortunately the tractor refused to start so we couldn't take advantage of the hard ground and shift any muck from the new muck heap which was filling up quickly.

Over the previous two winters Alan had taken trailer loads of muck from the muck heap on the yard up to the one in the top field. That muck was now well-rotted and ready to be spread on the fields. We contacted the Longdens and arranged for them to spread it for us on the lower half of Bobbie's field and on the summer field. Despite the fact that it had been snowing on and off all weekend the Longdens still came and managed to spread most of the contents of the old muck heap before their tractors started to slide sideways in the snow at which point they had to stop.

Sam and I went up to Simon's and bought two white Indian Runner Ducks. I called one Slim and the other one Olive. About ten days later Olive went missing. One minute both Runner ducks were together with the rest of the poultry the next Slim was on her own. I searched for Olive as soon as I noticed she was missing but there was no sign of her anywhere. Slim was distressed at first but eventually settled with the other ducks. Amongst the numerous ducks belonging to Simon there was one particularly large one with unusual cream and light brown plumage that Sam had taken a fancy to and which he persuaded Simon to part with. Sam called her 'Debbie' and during the time that we had her she made it her business to decimate the frog population as Lily had done before her.

Throughout January and February I collected shavings from two or three different places each week to keep up a steady supply for the yard. At the beginning of February I started to feel ill. Ten days later I still ached and felt shivery and could barely do the stable jobs. I probably had a touch of flu.

Work in the kitchen continued. Alan plastered the wall above the Aga to level it up with the length of pitch pine. We measured the walls and worked out the sizes and number of cupboards that would be needed and then we bought some new kitchen cupboards and work surfaces from Ikea.

The headlines in the national newspapers and on television were dominated by reports of Foot and Mouth Disease which was spreading menacingly from Devon to Carlisle.

During the last week of February it snowed heavily. On the

Wednesday there was a blizzard so I kept Jess and Sam off school. By this time Foot and Mouth Disease had spread all over the country – there were terrible, unforgettable images on TV.

By the end of the week much of the snow had gone. The weather was cold and bright. I gave the horses some turn-out but the ground was still very hard.

We decided that if we didn't have a family holiday this summer we might miss the opportunity to do so. At the end of January Jess had turned 16 and probably would not want to go with us as she got older. We all discussed where to go and it appeared that Greece was the favourite destination. We also discussed our plans with Joanne who readily agreed to live at Jericho while we were away to house, dog, cat, horse, sheep and poultry sit!

Early in March we went to a Holiday Hypermarket in Huddersfield. For some reason there was a shortage of flights to Greece in high season that year and consequently booking two weeks in Greece and getting flights to match was a problem. We ended up booking two weeks in Turkey instead for the last week in July and the first week in August. I could hardly wait!

At the beginning of the month I had started to decorate the kitchen and we continued to work on it whenever we had the time. As soon as I had finished painting the walls Alan began to put up the wall cupboards.

By the middle of March the spread of Foot and Mouth Disease had become critical – it had reached Halifax – and was much too close for comfort.

More snow fell. The roads were very slippery. An Ikea delivery lorry arrived with our kitchen work surfaces and the fridge but the lorry couldn't get up our lane to the house. Fortunately we had an empty stable so I helped the delivery man unload all the stuff into that. By the end of the month Alan had fitted the rest of the kitchen cupboards and work surfaces.

It was Mum's 85th birthday at the end of March and we all went over to Pat's for a family party to celebrate.

Emily and Ann had sold Ben as Emily felt that competitively she had achieved as much as she could on him. As his replacement they bought a 17hh chestnut Thoroughbred called Marco. Marco was very handsome but very big – too big in my opinion but time would tell.

Just one week after they had bought him Marco chucked Emily off in Sloane's paddock during a lesson. It soon became apparent that not only was he dangerous when being ridden but he was also dominant and unpredictable in the stable. I told Ann that I did not want to handle him. Ann told me that she didn't either!

It was Sam's 13th birthday that April. For the last two years he had been saving up to buy himself a 4 x 4 quad bike. The gifts of money which he received this year for his birthday added to the money that he'd already saved was enough to enable him to buy one.

The last to survive of the original five Black Rock hens was Cilla. I don't know exactly how old she was but she must have been quite a geriatric! One afternoon as I walked down the garden Cilla appeared to suffer some sort of attack and collapsed on the grass gasping for breath. I picked her up and rubbed her scrawny breast. She rallied, shook her head and after a few minutes set off walking up the garden like the poultry equivalent of the Hunchback of Notre Dame! Cilla recovered in all respects apart from her posture which remained crooked and disfigured. For some reason she had taken a liking for Jane. If the poultry were out when Jane arrived on the yard Cilla would totter along to meet her. She would follow her into Katie's stable and in an ungainly and awkward fashion would hop into the tack room or scratch around the feed bucket looking for spilt corn. The affection was not mutual however in fact Jane disliked the poor bird intensely referring to her as 'Ugly bird'. When poor Cilla finally fell off her perch later in the year Jane's reaction was of relief rather than regret.

The large muck heap that we had built last summer was already pretty full by the end of December 2000 with the result that by the end of spring 2001 we had our very own Millennium Dome! It was massive and there were only so many times we could keep digging it back.

The long spell of torrential rain throughout October and November had prevented us from emptying the muck heap for the start of winter and now the situation was serious. We were in imminent danger of the muck heap taking over the car park! We decided to make an overflow area between the existing muck heap and the road. Hurriedly we levelled the ground and lay a dozen or so flags next to the muck heap wall. We then fenced it on two sides. It wasn't fantastic but it gave us a breathing space until we had some drier weather.

The following weekend Alan took Sam to look at a quad bike in Littleborough. It was in good condition and looked as if it would be a good buy. Sam really liked it so they came home, fetched the horse trailer, went back to Littleborough bought the quad and brought it home.

The previous spring Shelley had part-loaned Thomas to a veterinary nurse called Karen. Several months later Karen acquired a horse of her own called Giggs and moved him up to Jericho. Giggs was young and very green and Karen, herself inexperienced, struggled to bring him on. Hacking out on her own was difficult as Giggs lacked confidence and was reluctant to go forward and so whenever possible Karen rode out in company, usually with either Jessica or Joanne. One Sunday afternoon in April Karen and Joanne hacked out together. On their return they untacked their horses and Karen lead Giggs to the winter field and turned him out after which she got into her car to go home. Jo decided to ride Benson bareback to the field as she had done on countless occasions. She took Benson to the far end of the yard climbed onto the mounting block and prepared to mount him but somehow missed her footing fell and landed heavily between the mounting block and Benson's feet. Karen reversed her car out of the car park into the road and glanced along the yard expecting to see Jo riding Benson and was going to wave goodbye to her as she left. Instead she saw Benson standing quite still at the far end of the yard with Jo at his feet. Unable to see clearly what was going on she got out of her car and walked along the concrete to check that all was well. It was obvious immediately that Jo was badly hurt. To avoid her being trodden on by Benson's huge feet Karen took him to his stable while she tried to ring for an ambulance – but there was no signal on her mobile phone. She took off her coat and covered Jo up with it then ran up to the house to use our phone.

I went down to the yard with Karen and found Jo lying in probably the only puddle left on the concrete. She was a ghastly grey colour and was obviously in terrible pain. Before long the ambulance arrived and Jo was taken to hospital. It was no wonder that she was in so much pain – she had dislocated her ankle and her lower leg was broken in three places. It needed to be pinned and plated permanently.

The following week the water pump in the cellar stopped working. Alan spent a couple of hours unsuccessfully trying to fix it. Before we realised how serious the problem was the water storage tank in the loft had been emptied by the people on the yard who had filled numerous buckets of water for the horses. We were too late to turn off the stop tap in the kitchen and were left completely without water. Next day Alan managed to get a new part for the water pump and got it working again.

Now that he was in possession of a quad bike Sam's popularity reached an all time high not only with the girls on our yard but also with the Sloane girls – all of whom he gave rides to. At weekends he divided his time between driving his quad with or without a passenger, and riding and looking after his pony.

Jess and I had visited Joanne twice in hospital since her fall. Each time she had been in a lot of pain and was feeling depressed and unhappy. The third time we went to see her we were relieved to find her much more cheerful and looking forward to going home.

By the middle of April Emily had finally accepted that she couldn't handle Marco – he was far too strong for her and in my opinion had more than one screw loose! They returned him to his previous owner and resumed their search for another horse. Eventually they found Henry, a beautiful Dales x Shire 15.2hh bay gelding with a pleasant temperament. They brought him up to the yard at the end of the month and he settled in well.

Early in May several loads of muck were taken up to a new heap at the top of the summer field, fences were mended and fields were harrowed. Sam competed at the Rochdale Show in a show jumping class and was placed second. He rode very well.

It was the middle of May before we were able to turn out the horses into the summer fields. That week I borrowed some hand shears from Simon so I could have a go at shearing Emily. Over the next two weeks Jess began revising in earnest for her GCSE exams.

Towards the end of the month Alan rang me at lunch time to say that he would be late home from work. It wasn't until one of his work colleagues rang me an hour or so later that I found out that he had been admitted to hospital. Feeling unwell he had walked from school to the Health Centre in Uppermill and had arrived there somewhat disorientated and in obvious discomfort. He complained of chest pains and was given an emergency appointment. The doctor could find no pulse whatsoever and despite Alan's protestations he sent for an ambulance and admitted him to hospital immediately.

After an overnight stay involving ECGs and blood tests the doctors were satisfied that there was nothing wrong with his heart and allowed him home, but because they could not explain the low heart rate he was to have a number of follow-up appointments. I fetched him in the afternoon relieved that he was OK.

Before long he got on with tiling the kitchen and by the end of the month the room was finished.

Emily Sheep

Anybody who believes that sheep are stupid could not be more wrong. Emily was certainly far from stupid. It didn't take her long to learn that if she took hold of the kitchen door handle in her mouth and pulled it down she could open the door and let herself into the kitchen. The outside porch door closed with a latch rather than a lever which Emily was unable to get hold of. If the latch was not properly fastened however she could ram the door open with her massive head and let herself into the porch and from there into the kitchen. We all had to make sure therefore that the outside door was closed securely whenever we went out.

One morning after letting Emily out of her stable I turned out the horses into the field and got on with the usual jobs on the yard. It occurred to me after about an hour that I hadn't seen Emily for some time. With a sinking feeling I hurried to the house. The outside door was ajar. I opened it fully and on the porch floor there was unmistakeable evidence that Emily had been there. The kitchen door was wide open and Emily was standing on the mat in the middle of the kitchen. Startled by my sudden arrival she spun round leaving an unwelcome brown smear across the fridge door and promptly weed on the floor.

'Emily. Get out!' I ordered. She barged past me into the porch then hurtled outside pausing briefly to butt Pete who had followed me up the garden.

Emily was just over 12 months old now and was a very large animal. She had a huge head, stocky legs and an extremely broad girth. Sam played with her regularly. Dropping his head and shoulders he would square up to her. Emily would stand and face him slowly moving her head from side to side before lifting both front feet off the ground, dipping her head and throwing herself at him. They would make contact shoulder to shoulder and push until one or other of them backed off – usually Sam. Although these battles were amusing to watch there were repercussions. If Emily was in a buoyant mood and Sam was not around anyone could become a target – particularly if they were bending over in the barn filling a hay-net!

The fact that a plentiful stock of hay and haylage was stored in the barn did not escape Emily's notice; she would lay on the grass opposite the barn or on the concrete against the stable wall and as soon as anyone approached the barn door she would get up and rush towards it with surprising speed. If you were too slow to get inside and close the door before she arrived you were in danger of being propelled into the barn by Emily as she launched herself past you through the doorway. Torrents of abuse could be heard emanating from inside the barn on such occasions.

Shelley and Natasha struggled to control Emily who made a bee-line for them whenever she saw them arrive in the car park. Delighted to see them she would make a nuisance of herself jumping into their tack rooms to try and steal a few hasty mouthfuls of horse feed or she would wait until they had finished mucking out when she would do a large wee on newly prepared shavings in the stable. Probably her most unpopular misdemeanour as far as Shelley and Natasha were concerned occurred when Shelley returned from the corn merchant one morning having stocked up with several sacks of horse feed and extra bales of shavings. Shelley drove onto the concrete in front of Thomas's stable so she didn't have as far to carry everything. She lifted up the rear door of the car and began to unload the shavings calling to Natasha as she did so to help her by unloading Pride's feed sacks which were inside the car. Natasha opened one of the car doors, pulled out a sack and carried it into her tack room. Screams of rage attracted my attention. I came out of the duck hut to see Shelley angrily grabbing Emily who was leaning into the back of the car biting holes into the remaining bale of shavings and spilling the contents all over the carpet. Shelley managed to remove Emily with a swift but accurate kick to her rear end, and then heaved the burst bag of shavings out of the car and muttering something I couldn't quite catch carried it into Thomas's stable. Drama over I resumed what I had been doing. Having been somewhat violently removed from the rear of the car Emily turned her attention to the open side door and began to climb inside the car biting chunks out of the feed sacks as she did so. Natasha returned for the next feed sack only to find that Emily had beaten her to it. Screaming for her mum to help her Natasha ran round to the driver's side to try and stop Emily from climbing any further inside the car.

'Jan! Will you get your bloody sheep out of my car?' Shelley demanded angrily pulling frantically at Emily as the determined sheep clambered over the feed sacks toward Natasha. Trying not to look amused I pushed in beside Natasha and chastised Emily firmly. To my relief she slithered backwards out of the car and bolted down the concrete leaving a scene of total devastation behind her.

On one occasion I came back from doing some shopping at the super market to find Emily lying comfortably on the doormat enjoying the sunshine. She was facing down the garden and unusually didn't bother to get up and greet me. I lifted the bulging plastic carrier bags out of the Land Rover and threaded them onto each arm so that I could take them all into the kitchen in one go. Struggling with the heavy weight of all the bags on my arms I approached Emily with the door key in my hand.

'Move Emily' I said nudging her with my foot. Apart from tearing a chunk off one of the bags she stayed exactly where she was. 'Emily. Move!' I shouted, but she was evidently perfectly happy where she was and resumed her steady gaze down the garden. With a sigh I stepped over the irritating sheep with my left foot and with the carrier bags hanging uncomfortably from my wrists I put the key into the lock. As I turned the key I must have leant against Emily which evidently startled her because she stood up quickly. The width of her body pushed my legs apart and lifted my feet off the ground. I fell forward dropping the bags which landed on the ground behind her with a crash. That together with my weight on her back caused her to panic and she set off at great speed with me on her back clinging to her rear end.

Fortunately the little garden gate was shut forcing her to change direction at which point I fell off, which was just as well otherwise we could have both ended up at The Roebuck!
At the beginning of June Jess sat her first GCSE exam – the first of 10 over the next couple of weeks.

A polo-cross practice was held on the Pony Club field in preparation for a charity event which was to take place at Birchinley Manor later in the month. Sam rode Jessie but Jess doubted that Zulu would be able to cope with long sticks being waved in the air. Not wishing to end up on the floor she borrowed Pride.

The day before the actual event another polo-cross practice was held, this time at Birchinley. Sam didn't want to take part in the match and said that Jess could ride Jessie if she wanted to. We decided to give Zulu the benefit of the doubt and took both him and Jessie to Birchinley so that Jess could try out both of them. However Zulu confirmed Jessica's suspicions almost immediately and was indeed panic stricken when the sticks were flailed about.

On Sunday several Pony Club members including Jess took part in the charity show which was held in aid of 'Animals in Distress' at Birchinley Manor. As well as the Polo Cross match there were other displays including a fashion show and 'The Full Monty' which was performed by a group of farriers.

The staircase and landing were beginning to look decidedly scruffy – largely due to Sam's mucky hand and finger marks which were evident all down the staircase and around the light switches! I could hardly believe that six years had passed since I had last painted it and the following week I painted it all again.

We enjoyed a spell of glorious sunny weather towards the end of June, the downside of which was that we completely ran out of water. The level of the water in the well was too low for the pump to draw from. So once again we lifted the 1000 litre water tank onto the tractor trailer and filled it at the hydrant near The Roebuck. We had to make numerous trips that week as we needed water for the field bath and the stables as well as for our own use.

After having sat her final exam at the end of the month Jess celebrated by going out with her new boyfriend. I got a brief glimpse of him when he picked her up in his car.

The time for our holiday was fast approaching and Joanne was still hobbling about with her leg in plaster. We were concerned about how she was going to manage but she assured us that she would cope alright living at Jericho while we were away and if she did have any problems there were plenty of people on the yard who could help her.

I wanted to make a secure run for the ducks so that Jo could let them out and be sure to get them back in again if she was short of time or if the weather was bad. We decided how big it was going to be and made a start on it early in July. We hammered posts in the ground next to the duck hut and worked out how much chicken wire would be needed to cover it all.

To complicate matters further, in the middle of May one of the hens had become broody. I had installed her and her eggs in the now unoccupied old goose hut where early in June she hatched just one fluffy yellow chick. As the end of July and our holiday approached the little chick was still much too small to live in the hen hut with the other hens which meant that they would have to remain in the old goose hut for a few more weeks. So in addition to making the run for the duck hut we also made a small outdoor area for the broody and her chick accessible by means of a sliding door on the side of their hut which could be opened or closed by manoeuvring a lever which protruded outside the run – very ingenious!

A new wine-bar/restaurant/night club was about to be opened in Saddleworth. 'The Mill Experience' occupied the entire top floor of an old stone built mill situated between Delph and Dobcross. The conversion was modern and tasteful and the floor space was large. Prior to opening in July the owners recruited bar staff and waitresses the majority of who were friends of their eldest son and daughter – as was Jess. She worked her notice at The Cross Keys and joined the new staff at The Mill two nights a week. The hours were long and it was very late when she finished but taxis were provided for the staff and Jess thoroughly enjoyed the work and the camaraderie of the young staff and the buzzing atmosphere of the place.

The second Saturday in July we did more work on the duck run. We managed to get half the chicken wire fastened on and Alan made the door. Betty hen went missing that weekend and there was a change in the weather.

    Torrential rain and gales throughout the week prevented us from doing any more work on the duck run. We had to wait until the following Saturday to finish fastening on the wire netting. We completed the job towards the end of the afternoon and then Alan gave me a hand to dig back the muck heap. We'd been working for about 20 minutes when Alan noticed a hen huddled up against the muck heap wall. It was Betty. She was wet and dirty, her feathers were dishevelled and stuck to her body. A full week had gone by since she had gone missing and I had given up hope of ever seeing her again so I was delighted at her re-appearance and amazed that she had survived the appalling weather let alone managed to evade the foxes.

    Betty remained calm and quiet as I picked her up and checked her over to find out if she was hurt. Her head was tucked in against her breast and her body felt cold and clammy and strangely heavy but there were no obvious injuries.

I carried her up to the house and put her into a small cardboard box which I placed on the floor in front of the Aga. Each of the three dogs got out of their beds and inspected the exhausted hen with interest. They then returned to their beds accepting with resignation this latest casualty with as much canine humility as I could have hoped for. I offered Betty some corn but she made no attempt to eat so I left her in the box in front of the Aga until it was time to shut up the rest of the hens for the night. By then she had warmed up considerably so I carried her out to the hen hut and put her onto the roosts with the others. On Sunday morning Betty bore no resemblance to the miserable bird which had appeared beside the muck heap the previous day. She had preened herself; her breast feathers were fluffed up and her wing feathers once more lay straight and tidy. She was alert and her bright eyes watched with interest as I put a bowl of corn onto the floor of the hut. As soon as I saw her tucking into the corn with the rest of the hens I was confident that she would make a full recovery.

That evening Jess went out with her boyfriend again – a few hours later she rang to ask for a lift home. Alan set off to fetch her in the Land Rover. As soon as he had gone out of the door I remembered that I'd left my hand bag in the Land Rover and I hurried to fetch it before he set off. It was a very dark night and I ran across the grass beside the kitchen to where the Land Rover was parked on the concrete. It was so dark I didn't see the large stone on the edge of the grass and tripped over it landing heavily on the tow ball bracket of Sam's quad trailer – which I hadn't seen either. I put my hands down to break my fall and ripped my left hand open on the rough ground. Fortunately Alan heard me shout out and came to see if I was alright. My leg hurt terribly but I could move it so he helped me walk back to the kitchen. My hand was a mess and badly cut. It hurt so much I thought it might be broken so after Alan had fetched Jess he took me to the A and E department at Oldham Royal Hospital where we spent most of the night. I was in a lot of pain but after an X-ray it turned out that there were no broken bones. My hand was just badly cut and bruised. I was given pain killers and a dressing was put on the palm of my hand. The doctor told me to keep it dry and return to the hospital in two days time to have the dressing changed. I explained that I was going on holiday to Turkey the next day and that I was hoping to be able to swim; so they gave me a supply of dressings, bandages and latex gloves to try and keep the hand as clean and dry as possible while I was away.

Next morning any outstanding jobs had to be finished. Alan laid some concrete flags around the edge of the duck run to prevent foxes from digging under the wire. He also placed a couple of heavy kerb stones along the front edge of the run. As he positioned the last one and dropped it in place he misjudged the space between them trapping his finger and splitting the nail from top to bottom. He was in agony. We dressed the finger as best we could and cut a finger off a glove to try and protect it a bit. Fortunately by the time this latest catastrophe occurred all the stable jobs had been done and the suitcases had been packed. Both children had packed their own cases. Jess no doubt had packed more than she would need and Sam more than likely had packed barely enough despite my efforts to supervise what went into his case.

Steve Sloane arrived about five-o-clock to take us to Manchester Airport. While he and Alan put the suitcases into the boot I called the dogs into the kitchen. I hugged them all, checked that they had water and gave each of them a biscuit. Three pairs of worried brown eyes watched me close the door. It was only going to be two weeks but I hated leaving them.

We arrived at the apartment in Marmaris at about 4am and went straight to bed absolutely shattered. Later that morning as we unpacked Alan and I overheard Jess exclaim

'What on earth have you brought that for?!' I peered round their bedroom door. Beside Sam's bed stood his rusty red metal warning lantern that he'd 'lifted' from some road works one day when out on his bike. How on earth that had got through the detectors at Manchester Airport I'll never know!

Marmaris

We all loved Marmaris but the atmosphere of the place completely intoxicated me. I adored everything about it and soaked up the whole experience: the blazing sunshine, the bright blue sky, the palm trees, the colourful umbrellas and basket weave sun-shades which sheltered the sun-beds that were set out in rows along the silver sand. The massive hotels in their beautiful grounds, the countless restaurants and bars each with their own Turkish front man who hassled the passers-by to come in and try their menu, the sexy waiters with their slim hips and dark eyes who did their very best to keep everyone happy – I loved them all.

We swam in the pool, lay on the beach and dived off anchored rafts into the sea. We went on a boat trip, had a ride on a banana boat and all got ditched in the sea – so much for keeping my hand dry! In the evenings we ate and drank in numerous bars and restaurants. It all seemed a million miles away from the continuous hard work that we'd left behind at Jericho. Alan and I must have looked an odd couple with our bandaged hands and the massive bruise on my thigh but after a day or so our wounds began to heal and became less painful.

On the third day Jessica's boyfriend dumped her by text – the rat – but her misery was soon forgotten mainly due to a brief dalliance with a handsome Turkish waiter who worked at a restaurant close to our apartment. We ate there often as the food was very good and it was always busy with a good atmosphere.

On the Thursday of the second week around midday Jess left us on the beach and wandered off to have a cool drink and a chat with her favourite waiter. Sam was messing about in the sea with a snorkel and having enjoyed a light lunch and a cold drink the only important decision that Alan and I had to make was whether to read another chapter or have another swim.

'I'll bet that's followed us here from Manchester.' Alan commented gravely.

'What has?' I asked looking up from my book.

'That cloud.' Alan said screwing his face up and pointing at a small fluffy cloud in an otherwise perfect blue sky.

'Don't worry it never rains in Turkey in July or August.' I replied confidently having glanced at the insignificant little cloud.

'What never?'

'Hardly ever.' I carried on reading my book.

Half an hour later Alan said 'It's getting closer.'

'So it is.' I replied dismissively. We went in the sea for a dip and then came back to the sun-beds and dried off in the sun.

'I'm sorry, but that looks like a rain cloud to me.' Alan persisted 'Why don't we go back to the apartments. If it does rain we can go indoors if it doesn't we can stay by the pool.'

'OK if it'll make you happy!'

We called Sam, gathered up our stuff and made our way back collecting Jess on route. As we approached the apartment block we felt a few spots of rain.

'I told you!' said Alan smugly. 'Look!'

The insignificant little cloud was now big and black and right overhead. As we reached the steps which lead to our apartment the heavens opened. Rain came down like stair rods and within a matter of seconds Turkish hotel workers at all the neighbouring hotels and apartments were scurrying around moving electrical equipment and upholstered furniture and anything else that would be spoilt by the rain.

Safe and dry on our balcony Sam and I watched people less fortunate running up and down the street seeking shelter from the torrential downpour. Within minutes the large drainage channel at the side of the street that had been bone dry all week became a fast flowing stream. The large sun canopies which sheltered the holiday makers from the hot sun were sagging under the weight of the unseasonal rainfall and everywhere was awash with water. Jess joined us on the balcony.

'Mum, there's a message from Joanne on my phone.'

'I asked her not to contact us unless there was a serious problem – what does it say?'

'*Please ring me as soon as possible.*' But I haven't got enough credit to ring home.' Immediately I imagined the worst.

'It'll be Pete, I'll bet he's had another stroke…if he's died I'll never forgive myself for being away…or maybe Zulu's been kicked…'

'What about Jessie?' said Sam looking as worried as I was.

'If it was anything to do with the animals Joanne would have sorted it out' Alan interrupted. 'It's more likely that we've run out of water. Stop worrying. I'll ring her.' Alan was always calm in these situations. He and Jess left the apartment immediately to find a phone.

After about 20 minutes the rain stopped but the volume of water which had fallen so quickly had wreaked havoc in Marmaris that day. All the previously dry and dusty drainage channels which ran along the edge of many of the side roads filled up with fast flowing water making its way from the steep hills above the town down to the sea. Drain covers in the roads were lifted, open-air bars and restaurants were flooded out and upholstered furnishings were saturated. No doubt the latter problem would soon be sorted out by the reappearance of the scorching sunshine but other damage took a little longer – the phones for example!

Alan could not use the phone in Reception as it was not working due to the heavy rain. Neither were the ones in the three or four public telephone boxes which they tried to use. Eventually Jess asked the owner of the restaurant which we went to regularly if he could help them. Obligingly he marched them down to the taxi rank and gabbled something in Turkish after which Jess and Alan were ushered into the office and allowed to use their telephone. Quite why that should be working when the others were not I have no idea, but work it did and they got through to Joanne.

While they were gone I paced about the apartment imagining endless calamities and accidents which might have happened at home. After what seemed like hours they returned.

'All the animals are fine Mum.' Jess said as soon as she came through the door. I was so relieved I could cope with anything else.

'What is it then? Have they run out of water?' Alan and Jess smiled ruefully.

'No not exactly' Alan replied. 'Just the opposite in fact. The hot water cylinder has burst – it's taken down part of the dining room ceiling and ruined the sofa and one of the armchairs.' He paused giving me time to take in this information before continuing. 'I've told Jo how to turn everything off properly and she's moved back home with her mum and dad. She'll see to the dogs each morning and evening until we come home.'

They both looked at me waiting I suppose for me to react in some sort of distraught fashion.

'Well there's nothing we can do about it now that it's happened. We'll just have to sort it out when we get back. Right, I'm off to the pool. Are you coming?' I picked up my towel and left the apartment with Sam. I think Alan and Jess were a bit taken aback at how calmly I had accepted this latest catastrophe. As far as I was concerned there wasn't any point in letting a fallen ceiling and a wet sofa ruin the rest of the holiday.

After a good flight home we finally arrived back at Jericho around 9pm on Tuesday evening. We opened the door to three very excited dogs. The Aga was turned off of course and so the house was cold and unwelcoming and smelt damp. The sofa and one of the armchairs were both completely saturated; as was the carpet that had been taken up and draped over the Vauxhall which we had left in the barn. There were water marks down the wall next to the fireplace and down the chimney breast. Much of the ceiling plaster beneath Jessica's bedroom had fallen off and had been shovelled into black plastic bags.

The hot water cylinder was in the airing cupboard in the corner of Jess's bedroom. When the cylinder had split the water must have spurted out like a fountain. The carpet was ruined as were all her clothes which she had kept on the shelves above the cylinder. All her bits and pieces which were at that side of the room were marked with water and spoilt. The room smelt damp and when I went in to look at it Jess was already there crouched on her bed with tears running down her face. We took down her bed and put it up temporarily in the back room downstairs along with her chest of drawers, bedside cupboard and various bits and pieces.

Alan and I worked hard all the next day. While I cleaned up the mess and emptied the room Alan took out the old hot water cylinder and went out and bought a new one. He managed to fit the new cylinder, refill the system and turn the Aga on again before we went to bed.

We contacted the insurance company, filled in and sent off the claim form promptly and while Jess and Sam were at Pony Club Camp later in the month we worked on Jessica's room. Alan fitted new doors on the airing cupboard while I re-decorated. We bought and laid a new bedroom carpet and before the end of the month the dining room ceiling had been re-plastered as well.

It was late August before Bill cut the grass on the Five Acre field. Unexpectedly it rained the following day. The weather was sunny and warm over the next two or three days and Bill turned our hay twice hoping to dry it out as much as possible before it was baled – this time we got 38 bales. It would be six weeks before we could unwrap one and see if it was OK.

The broody hen's chick had grown quite large by this time and the two of them joined the rest of the hens in the hen hut with Henry. Now that its yellow baby feathers had been replaced by bright orange plumage we began to suspect that it was a cockerel.

This was confirmed when a splendid green sickle feather emerged from amongst its tail feathers. He wasn't as colourful as Henry, being predominantly orange, but he definitely had a look of Olivia – a particularly nice Leghorn who was most likely his mother - so I called him Oliver.

At the beginning of September Jess enrolled at the Sixth Form College and Alan and Sam returned to school.

On September 11th there was a horrific terrorist attack in America. Two hi-jacked passenger planes were flown into the Twin Towers – thousands were killed.

Evenings and weekends throughout September and October were spent working on the dining room. The water damage to the chimney breast could be put right with a couple of coats of paint but before we got a new carpet we decided to build a fireplace instead of just re-painting the wall. We made a visit to a reclamation yard bought some re-claimed bricks and found an old stone mantle and a big slab of stone which was suitable for a hearth. Alan built the fireplace and I made a template of the inside of the chimney and had a metal plate made with a hole in it for the flue to pass through. Alan fastened some angle iron to the inside walls of the chimney and screwed the metal plate to it. After we had sealed up any gaps I painted it black. When the wood burner was put into position the fireplace looked really nice and it was a more striking focal point for the room than the recess had been.

Having given the newly plastered dining room ceiling plenty of time to dry I repainted the whole room. We were now ready for the new carpet. Two days after the carpet had been fitted the new three piece suite arrived. The delivery men struggled to get it in through the small front porch. Once the new carpet had been fitted and the new suite had arrived the circumstances behind the repairing and repainting were soon forgotten. The hard work was all worthwhile and we were able to sit back and enjoy our new room.

That evening Jess went out on a date. The following morning at about a quarter to eight I heard Sam go downstairs to see to Jessie. I followed a few minutes later. When I opened the door at the bottom of the stairs and walked into the dining room I couldn't believe my eyes. A large youth lay fast asleep on our lovely new sofa! I turned, ran back up the stairs and stormed into Jessica's bedroom.

'Who's that boy?' I demanded. Jess awoke with a start and peered at me from beneath her duvet.

'What?'

'There's a boy asleep on the new sofa! Who is he? Why is he there?'

'Boy?' For a moment she looked blank. 'Oh, him! He brought me home in a taxi last night and I told him he could stay. Is that OK?'

'It'll have to be won't it!' I snapped.

The fact that she'd let, who ever he was, stay overnight didn't bother me - at least he'd seen her home. What annoyed me was that he had spent the night on the new sofa! I went back downstairs. Half covered with a spare duvet the boy was still dead to the world sprawled untidily across the sofa squashing the big cushions. I went through to the kitchen, made him a brew and put it down on the coffee table beside the sofa. Then with a flourish I opened the curtains.

'Wakey! Wakey! Rise and shine. I've made you a brew – it's time to go home!' I said cheerily. The boy jumped, sat bolt upright then froze like a startled rabbit. Wide eyed he stared at me then looked around the room with a look of utter bewilderment on his face. Finding it hard not to laugh I left him and went down to the stables knowing that Jess would soon come downstairs. Sam had already broadcast to the yard with great glee that Jess had 'brought a boy home last night!' So I was met with broad grins and intrigued questions from Joanne and Jane. Soon afterwards the poor lad was collected by somebody in a car. We didn't see him again.

Monday the 5th of November – the day began well enough. I made an early start and got on with my usual jobs before taking Jess to college. I had already turned out three horses when the dogs caught sight of Norman's milk float as he drove back along Shiloh Lane after delivering to the Sloanes. Kim was in Taylor's field. I called her but she just looked at me, wagged her tail then continued to watch the progress of the milk float. Maggie was standing in the lane with Pete. I should have made Kim come to me but I didn't I continued walking down to the yard and went into Pride's stable. I was taking off Pride's stable rug when the milk float drove up the lane. Moments later I heard the dreadful yelping. I ran out of the stable. Norman was standing in the lane with his head in his hands looking at the milk float. When he saw me he shouted in anguish.

'I didn't see her! I'm so sorry. I didn't see her.'

Kim was laid in the lane behind the milk float writhing and moaning. Maggie was snapping at her. I pushed Maggie away and tried to calm Kim. I knew she was dying – the milk float had driven right over her. Confused by the noise that Kim was making Maggie attacked her again. In her agony Kim snapped back mistaking my hand for Maggie and bit me quite badly. Norman kicked Maggie away and she ran off up the lane. I stroked Kim's head and talked to her reassuringly until she became calm then I gathered her up in my arms and carried her up to the house. The undamaged armchair had been put outside the kitchen when the new three piece suite was delivered and was yet to be removed. I lay Kim in it then opened the kitchen door and shouted to Jess telling her what had happened and asking her to bring a cover for Kim. Jess hurried outside with a large towel and burst into tears when she saw Kim in the chair. I covered my dear brave dog with the towel stroked her head and talked to her quietly. I was aware of Norman standing behind me desperately upset about what had happened.

He said that as he had driven up our lane Maggie had run to meet the milk float as usual. He could see her and Pete trotting along beside the passenger side of the float but had not seen Kim jump over the wall on the driver's side. Kim's front leg had been troubling her recently and she had been limping for several days. The small bank beside the wall was steep and the grass was wet. She must have slipped off the bank and as Norman avoided Maggie and Pete on his left Kim must have slid between the front and back wheels on his right and he ran over her.

As Norman apologised yet again I watched Kim's life slip away and she died in my arms. Norman pleaded with me to do something about my hand. I looked at it and was surprised at the severity of the wound – until that moment I had felt nothing. I hugged Norman and assured him that I knew it was a complete accident and that I didn't blame him for what had happened. I promised that I would go to the hospital and still distraught Norman drove away. Jess and I stroked Kim and cried together for a few moments before I covered her completely with the towel. I told Jess that I would drop her off at college on my way to the hospital.

In a daze I returned to the stables rugged up Pride and Jessie and turned them out into the field. I then went upstairs washed my face and managed to get changed. By this time my hand was throbbing painfully. Jess was upset and wanted to ring Alan so he could take me to hospital but I wouldn't hear of it. I dropped her off at college then drove to A and E at Oldham Royal Hospital where in due course my hand was seen to. My fingers had swollen by this time and the nurses had to cut off my eternity ring. All I could think about was Kim – my loyal protector. I generally made the dogs do as they were told – why had I let her stay in the field? I should have made her come to me. I knew she would chase the milk float. Poor Kim, she was 11 years old a bit stiff but otherwise healthy and strong. She shouldn't have died like that.

By the time I got home I was in a lot of pain and felt very emotional. Jess had rung her dad and he came home at lunch time arriving soon after I did and he buried Kim. Next day my hand was very painful and swollen. It was strange without Kim and Maggie was very subdued.

Throughout the rest of November I carried on running the yard as usual. Things took longer to do and I had to be careful with my hand but I managed and by early December it was pretty much healed. The memory of that day and the extent to which I missed Kim took much longer to fade.

On Christmas Eve Alan went over to Ilkley to fetch my mum so she could spend Christmas with us. On Boxing Day it was our turn once again to have the family over and the weather was beautiful.

A substantial amount of snow fell during the last couple of days of 2001.

2002

The first week of January continued to be cold and icy. Our next major project was to convert the shippon into living accommodation. We moved Alan's work bench and tools into the back stable which became his workroom. Anything that we wanted to keep was either brought into the house or stored in the hay barn. Everything else was taken to the tip.

Sam demolished two of the three stalls in the shippon with a sledgehammer. Since the holiday in Turkey last summer Sam had grown taller and filled out. He had strong shoulders and demolished the stalls without any problem.

Work in the shippon continued throughout January and February. Once the stalls were down we made a start on breaking up the entire floor with the sledgehammer. All the broken concrete was barrowed out and either spread on the road or in the field gateways.

Over the last three or four years the weather had changed noticeably. The heavy snow which we had experienced over previous winters had been replaced by rain often torrential and prolonged. On those occasions there was only so much water that the ground could absorb before it became completely water logged resulting in surface water flowing down the fields and flooding over the Foster's wall like a waterfall or down the road breaking up the surface into sizeable pot holes which were practically impossible to avoid in the car. The lie of the land was such that all the surface water from the summer field and the paddock and any underground springs in that area flowed down in the Fosters' direction. The only way we could prevent their garden and outbuildings from being flooded after heavy rain was to divert the water by digging trenches which would carry it away to a stream which flowed beyond the bottom corner of Misty's field. Having decided what to do we began to dig two trenches. The first was a long one which started at the end of the stable block and continued to the bottom corner of Misty's field. The second was much shorter and ran parallel to the first one along the lower side of the paddock at the bottom of the steep bank. We dug through the track which led to the summer field and laid a drainage pipe to link the two.

The last week of January and the first week of February were cold with gales and heavy rain. Each weekend we persevered digging the trenches. At the point where the trench below the paddock joined the drainage pipe beneath the track it was almost three feet deep. To be able to get at the loosened clay soil and shovel it out I had to get right inside the trench. I got so cold that day I didn't warm up until I went to bed.

At the end of January Jessica turned 17 and told us that she had decided to give up riding. Sam was fed up of getting up at four in the morning every Saturday so he stopped working on the milk round. Instead he began working at Highmoor Riding Stables mucking out some of the horses which were kept there on full livery.

Now that he had grown so much taller Sam had practically outgrown his beloved pony. We had to make the decision, if he continued with his riding whether to get him a different horse or move him onto Zulu. Sam had never really taken to Zulu but agreed to give him a go. He had a few lessons on him and hacked him out but the two did not bond at all. He really wanted a bigger version of Jessie, and Zulu was nothing like her in any respect.

Early in spring Sam bought himself a small metal trailer to tow behind his quad. It proved very useful for transporting various items such as bags of shavings or bales of hay or taking tools up the field when fences needed mending. It also enabled him to spread muck in Misty's field. He made numerous trips from the muck heap to the field with the loaded trailer and worked his way methodically across the field flinging the muck over the grass with a small pitch fork.

As far as Alan and I were concerned the majority of the Easter break was spent making two new doors for the hay barn. The old yellow ones were falling apart and got worse every time they were opened or closed. Maintenance work was done on the stable block and Alan managed to get three fields harrowed before he returned to school.

Work in the shippon continued whenever we had the time. We carried on breaking up the old concrete floor and regularly shifted barrow loads of rubble out onto the road. It was several weeks however before we were ready to put down a new concrete floor.

Back in 1995 one of Alan's friends had offered him a garage which he wanted to get rid of. It was made of concrete sections and had already been dismantled. Although we hadn't needed it at the time Alan thought it might come in useful and had collected it and stacked it at the bottom of the stables car park where it had remained until now. Sam needed somewhere to keep his quad. Since he had bought it last year he had kept it in the bottom of the hay barn but that wasn't ideal. Alan suggested we made use of the garage. We decided to erect it against the side of the back stable at the gable end of the house where much of it could be concealed by plants and a water butt. We prepared the ground and made a base with some concrete flags then spent time over the last two weekends of April positioning the heavy concrete sections and bolting them together.

Frequently during that spring we advertised Zulu in local newspapers and put up For Sale posters in corn merchants and equestrian shops. Although various people came to see him none of them wanted to buy.

Jess was completely besotted with her latest boyfriend and spent more and more of her free time with him and less and less time at home. The majority of Zulu's stable care therefore fell on me and inevitably this led to friction. She continued to ride Zulu when she could find the time – but as far as I was concerned she didn't find enough of it and so there were frequent arguments. The more we argued the less time she wanted to spend at home and instead she spent even more time with the boyfriend - a situation which led to even more friction ...and so it went on.

Sam bought two Guinea Fowl and put them into the hen hut with the hens. They were very nervous and flighty and the following day when I went into the hen hut to give them all some corn the Guinea Fowl cock flew into my face bruising my eye and cutting my nose.

At the end of April another lady came to see Zulu. She was very interested in him and took him on a two week loan. We kept in touch with her regularly as the two weeks progressed. Although she was happy with how he behaved when she rode him she was concerned by his refusal to eat. Before the end of the second week she brought him back saying that she felt she could not keep him any longer as he would not settle and had barely eaten in all the time that he had been with her. We unloaded him from the trailer and led him to his stable – immediately he tucked into the haylage in his hay net!

Sam's Guinea Fowl cock flew away and didn't come back so a week later Bill brought him another Guinea hen to keep the first one company. This one had pretty speckled blue grey plumage and the most irritating repetitive cry we had ever heard. She sounded as if she was calling for 'Lisa...Lisa...Lisa...' which is what we decided to call her and within twenty four hours Alan had threatened to ring her neck.

Oliver the young cockerel was now a big strong bird and had already been involved in several skirmishes with Henry so before either of them got hurt I decided to separate them. I had acquired an old play house which after a few modifications became a new home for Oliver along with two black hens.

Over the next couple of weeks two more people came to look at Zulu and I bought another white Indian Runner duck from Simon and called him 'Linford'. Slim and Linford became inseparable and pottered about together as if they were attached to each other by a piece of elastic.

Alan and I spent the last weekend in May finishing off Sam's quad garage. On the Sunday Sam cycled down to the Pony Club field to help run a Mounted Games competition. During the afternoon there was a horrendous storm followed by a torrential downpour which lasted for three hours. The field by this time was under several inches of water and the competition had to be abandoned. Sam cycled back home wet through and freezing cold.

This time last year I had spent several hours over a three day period endeavouring to shear Emily for the first time. I had shut myself in the stable with her and after following her round in several circles clutching the shears I managed to pull her feet from under her and cut off most of the wool on one side of her body before she decided that enough was enough got to her feet and began hurtling round the stable stopping frequently to butt me. I let her out and we repeated the performance on her other side the next day. On the third day when I finished her off her fleece looked as if it had been chewed off rather than sheared and I decided that I needed a bit of guidance before I tried again. So this spring I arranged for a local sheep farmer to shear Emily using hand shears so that I could watch him and see how it should be done. He did the job in about 30 minutes and removed the fleece in one piece but he admitted that it had not been easy as Emily was one of the largest, heaviest sheep he'd ever sheared.

At the end of May we prepared the shippon floor for concreting and over the first weekend in June we managed to get it all done.

Pat and John had moved to a smaller house. Their snooker table which had been in a purpose built room over the garage in their previous house was now in storage costing them a fortune. Nobody in the family had room for it apart from ourselves so John offered it to us at a price that Alan could not refuse. Our efforts to convert the shippon into part of the living accommodation were stepped up a gear and the new accommodation looked like it was going to accommodate the snooker table!

In June I spent most of my time working in the shippon sanding the big beams and painting the walls and the window frames.

Pete was now a very old dog. His eyesight was failing and he was also going deaf. We had to clap our hands loudly to attract his attention. He had lost weight and was very frail.

In the middle of June there was an incredibly heavy downpour. The ditches that Alan and I had dug worked well and prevented the Fosters' land from flooding but the surface water which was pouring down the track from the summer field flowed onto the concrete and threatened to flood the two end stables. Sam and I brushed the water away as best we could but we were fighting a losing battle until Jo and Paula grabbed a brush each and came to help us. Sam ran up the track and started to build a dam to divert the water to the lower ditch. I went to help him and before long we had made a ridge across the track like a sleeping policeman which considerably lessened the amount of water that reached the concrete.

By this time all four of us were soaked through to the skin our hair was plastered to our heads and our clothes were completely saturated and stuck to our bodies – we looked as if we were taking part in a wet tee-shirt competition!

Next day Alan enlisted some help and took the horse trailer to Pat and John's to collect the dismantled snooker table. While he was gone I decided to get on with some gardening. Looking for some gardening tools in the bottom of the hay barn I hadn't noticed the heavy steel rake which we had used to level out the concrete in the shippon. As I stepped forward to look over the wall of the pig sty I stood on the head of the rake and the steel handle smacked me in the face cutting my eyebrow badly. It was very painful. Later Alan removed the rake and put it out of the way.

The close relationship which Jess and I had always enjoyed continued the slow and steady deterioration which had started when she began seeing her current boyfriend. He was older than her by several years and filled her head with his ideas and opinions and uncharacteristically she hung onto his every word. As time went by she continued to see more and more of him and seemed to come home as little as possible. She stopped waitressing at The Mill and instead worked with him in his small restaurant. After work or an evening out with him when she needed to come home he always had an excuse for being unable to bring her, and she almost always had to ring us for a lift. Jess resented my criticism that he was selfish, inconsiderate and manipulative and defended him unreservedly. Most of our conversations ended in harsh words or stony silences and there was a growing distance between us. I felt hurt and angry.

Life at Jericho

Early in July Cath and Jim called up to see how we were progressing with the shippon. It had been several months since their last visit and Cath was shocked and upset when she saw how old and frail Pete had become.

Every summer one or more of the hens became broody. This summer the first to show reluctance to leave the nesting box was the grey Game Bird which, partly because it had no comb on its head, resembled a large crow. Three weeks earlier I had put her on half a dozen eggs on a nest of straw in the old duck kennel where she had just hatched three chicks.

I checked on them during the morning and noticed that one of the remaining three eggs was cracked and about to hatch. When I had finished my jobs I checked again. A black and yellow chick was partially out of its shell. I left them alone and checked again about an hour later expecting to see the fourth chick peeping out from between Crow's feathers with the others but instead Crow was settled on one side of the duck kennel with her three chicks and the little black and yellow apparently lifeless chick was left abandoned on the other side. Wishing I'd checked sooner I picked up the limp, cold little body and set off up the garden towards the house to dispose of it. Suddenly a massive sigh shook its tiny frame. Taken by surprise I held it close to my face and breathed my warm breath onto it. I hurried into the kitchen and laid it on a towel on the lid of the Aga simmering plate then gently massaged the fragile little body. It soon responded to the warmth and began to show more signs of life so I plugged in the hair drier, put it onto a warm setting, cupped the chick in my hand and directed the warm air at it. Within a couple of minutes it had lifted its head opened its eyes and begun to move its wings. A few minutes later it began cheeping. I foraged in one of the cupboards and found a large margarine tub which I lined with a few sheets of paper towel then I sat the chicken inside it and put the tub back on the towel on the Aga lid to keep it warm. Half an hour later I carried the little chicken - now cheeping loudly – back to the duck kennel. I could hear Crow clucking as I walked down the garden so I knew she had heard it. I opened the door and placed the now lively little chicken in front of her. Crow looked at me with her black beady eyes then she extended one leg and with her long clawed foot she scooped the chicken under her feathers to join the rest of her brood. I felt extremely pleased with myself as I returned to the house.

After Cath's visit a couple of weeks ago I thought about Pete constantly. He was so old now and although he was eating well he continued to lose weight. Sometimes his back legs gave way when he was coming up the garden and he would struggle pathetically to get to his feet or just lay there until one of us noticed and rescued him. Reluctantly I told myself that it was time to let him go.

Next day I helped dear old Pete get into the car and set off to the vet to have him put to sleep. As usual when he was in the car he laid his head in my lap and I stroked him as I drove. I wanted to take him back home and keep him for just a little longer. I turned on the radio. Westlife were singing a mournful song which made the situation even more poignant. I made myself continue into Uppermill and took him to the vet. Afterwards feeling numb and empty I carried his body to the car and gently laid him on the back seat then somehow I drove back home. Alan buried him next to Kim. The first thing I saw when I went into the kitchen was Pete's empty bed. I stroked Maggie whose eyes were boring into my skull. I told her Pete had gone and I knew she understood. I picked up Pete's bed and took it into Alan's workroom in the back stable and just when I thought my day couldn't possibly get any worse I stood on the wretched rake head again and this time the steel handle whacked me on the side of my head. It hurt so much it made me cry.

If the people at Pike View had been right about Pete's age back in 1995 when they said that he was 15 then he had lived until he was 22 years old! Even if they had been wrong and he had only been 10 he would still have lived until he was about 17 – a good age whichever it was. I knew he had been happy while he lived with us at Jericho and we would all miss him terribly.

Sam

Sam had always been a straightforward sort of child. He had a strong sense of what he considered to be right or wrong, fair or unfair. He enjoyed the security of his own room and the familiarity of his own possessions and he disliked change. He hated arguments or raised voices whether or not they involved him and would take himself off to Jessie's stable or up the fields if there was any friction in the house. He was very single minded and could be aggravatingly stubborn. If his mind was set on having something, doing something or going somewhere it was extremely difficult to change it.

Right from the start Sam had liked living at Jericho. He loved the open space of the fields and stayed outside for hours. Although he enjoyed having friends to come up and play he had been quite happy to amuse himself if he was on his own.

As a small boy in Uppermill he played constantly with toy tractors and diggers in the back street. He had been able to reverse his sit 'n' ride tractor and trailer with commendable accuracy for one so young! Now that he was older he had moved onto the real thing. When Sam was eleven Alan taught him how to steer the tractor and harrow the paddock; now that he was fourteen he drove the tractor confidently around the farm and could reverse the trailer with precision into the muck heap to within an inch of the sidewall.

He developed a keen interest in the land and as he grew up spent a lot of time chatting with Bill Dawson about the best way to care for it. He wanted me to drastically reduce the amount of winter turn-out in order to make the winter field recoverable through summer. He was keen that we continue to spread and harrow the fields and insistent that we also had Bill spread them with fertilizer. We gave him Misty's field to do with what he wanted – and told him that if he significantly improved the condition of that field over the next twelve months he could also be responsible for the top back field on which the grass had never grown well.

A physically capable boy Sam was helpful and hardworking, inventive and creative but academic he was not and he continued at best to endure school. It was with much relief therefore that he broke up for the summer break at the end of July.

One afternoon towards the end of July Sam wandered into the kitchen and watched me prepare the vegetables for our evening meal.

'Why has Dad dug that hole in front of my garage?' he asked, crunching a carrot noisily.

'What hole?'

'The one by my garage – only it's really big and it's in the way when I get the quad in and out.'

'He hasn't dug a hole as far as I know.'

'Well there's a big hole there. Come and look.' Curious I followed Sam to the quad garage. Sure enough in front and just to the left of the garage doors was a hole about two feet across and at least a foot deep.

'It hasn't been dug out.' I said. 'The ground has sunk!' Until we sorted out the problem Sam had to put his quad back in the barn.

Two years ago in front of where we had just erected the garage we had dug out a large area of nettles at the gable end of the house. Whilst clearing the ground we had uncovered four massive stone flags, beneath which was a chamber full of water. We believed that the water which collected in the chamber originated from underground springs before seeping away underground. Many years ago it had probably been used to provide water for livestock. After our investigations we had covered the flags over again with soil and left well alone. The four massive flag stones were all supported at one corner by a stone pier which stood in the centre of the chamber. The excessive rain which we had experienced during June must have filled the chamber with such force that the old stone pier became unstable and then collapsed resulting in the now unsupported corner of all four flags having dipped which created the hole.

Throughout the following day the hole became bigger and bigger. The massive flag stones fell into it one by one and sank out of sight beneath the water. This left the front corner of the garage precariously unsupported and the hole was now about six feet square and about four feet deep! There was no possibility of our being able to lift the flags out again so we decided to lay four reinforced concrete lintels across the hole and cover it all up with a dozen concrete flags – a job which we would have to get on with as soon as possible during the summer break.

Annie cat went missing. She didn't come home for her evening feed. Three days later she was still missing and that afternoon there was another prolonged torrential downpour. The next couple of days continued to be wet but by Friday the weather had improved and after having collected some bags of shavings Alan and I sat outside in the sun with a brew. I heard a faint miaowing. At the top of the garden close to the hen hut Annie appeared out of the long grass slowly dragging herself towards us trailing her hind legs. I ran over to her wondering if she had been hit by a car. Carefully I picked her up. She began to purr loudly and stared intensely into my face. I carried her into the house and offered her some food which she devoured hungrily, and then I rang the vet. I explained the situation and took Annie at the end of his surgery that afternoon. The vet was of the opinion that Annie had finally succumbed to some sort of genetic problem which had caused the paralysis rather than her having been hit by a car. He gave her two large steroid injections and told me that unless there was a significant improvement in the mobility of her legs in the next 24 hours she was unlikely to recover and I should have her put to sleep. Next morning Annie was bright eyed and perky. She ate hungrily and continued to gaze into my eyes and purr loudly whenever I touched her, but her legs remained limp and completely paralysed. In the afternoon I returned to the vet and had her put to sleep. The loss of both a dog and a cat in the space of 10 days I found very hard.

Alice, the remaining stable cat, had never liked living in the stable block and now that Annie had gone and she found herself on her own she plucked up the courage to come up to the house. The Aga drew her into the kitchen like a magnet. Before long she was cuddled up with Joe on one or other of the cushions beside the Aga. Mary wasn't impressed by Alice's arrival and remained aloof for a while but ultimately accepted her and would fall asleep curled up with either Joe or Alice – or both of them! Finding available seating next to the Aga for ourselves invariably involved a struggle to remove one or more of them.

Alice wasn't the only one who had felt lonely. Maggie had never been on her own before and she was miserable. Most of the time she stayed curled up in her bed only coming outside to lie in the sun or go for a walk after a lot of gentle persuasion.

 Before Pete died Sam had asked on numerous occasions if he could have a dog of his own. He wanted a Jack Russell Terrier that he could take with him in the tractor or on his quad. I told him he could have one but not while Pete was still with us. Now that Pete had gone Sam started to ask again. I contacted the Oldham Branch of the RSPCA but they had no small dogs at all. We looked in the local papers and at adverts in pet shop windows but we couldn't find any Jack Russells. Disappointed Sam told Jo who said she would ask a relative of hers who had something to do with the RSPCA and Manchester Dogs Home.

Early in August a new pony moved onto the yard. A local florist Alyson and her daughter Holly brought their 13hh bay pony 'Feathers' onto the yard and settled him into the sixth stable.

Jack

Jo put us in touch with her relative who was presently fostering a small puppy that had been run over and was recovering from its injuries. Jo had told him about our situation and when we rang him he invited us round to see the puppy that was apparently part Jack Russell.

 The tiny puppy was eight weeks old. His rough coat was caramel coloured with some white on his face and chest and his nose was light brown and reminded me of a Werther's Original. He was very cute and very lively but looked absolutely nothing like a Jack Russell in fact when his large pointed ears were pricked up he resembled a fox cub. He was feisty and playful with the two dogs that lived there and his two broken legs one of which had been pinned appeared to have healed well. Apart from a slight limp you wouldn't have known that he had suffered such serious injuries. Our offer to give him a home was readily accepted and we brought him back with us immediately. Sam named him Jack.

Little Jack's arrival had an immediate and positive effect on Maggie. Jack regarded her as his new mum and brought out her maternal instincts. They played together and slept together. Maggie was unbelievably patient and gentle with him and she enjoyed a new lease of life.

Sam was delighted with Jack and the little pup became a favourite with everyone on the yard. He adored people particularly children and loved to be picked up and cuddled which was just as well as Jess carried him everywhere.

For a long time we had been anxious to get rid of the asbestos sheets which covered the shippon and dairy. We decided to replace them with insulated metal roofing sheets. Alan spent some time looking for a good deal and came across a firm which was selling off a number of sheets at a reduced price. He ordered 17 of them which would be enough to cover the entire length of all three outbuildings. Delivery was arranged for the middle of August.

While Sam was away at Pony Club camp with Jessie we stripped off the dairy and shippon roof. The sheets had to be unbolted and removed very carefully. We wore masks and put on different work clothes each day to keep any movement of asbestos dust and fibres down to a minimum. As soon as the sheets were off the roof we wrapped them in black plastic put them in the trailer and took them to the council tip where there was a collection point for asbestos. I was relieved when we'd got rid of it all.

The new metal roof sheets measured 15 feet long and 3 feet wide. They were very heavy and because of their size were difficult and cumbersome for the two of us to manoeuvre. Positioning them onto the roof timbers was not easy. We heaved up one end of the first sheet and leant it against the top edge of the front wall of the dairy. Then we lifted the other end and while I pushed it as hard as I could and slid it over the roof timbers Alan guided it into position and lined it up against the side wall of the dairy. We carried on in this way with each successive sheet until the room beneath was covered. The following day we continued to lift more roof sheets onto the roof timbers and covered the shippon with the sheets. By 7 o'clock that evening we had put two bolts in each sheet over the two rooms to secure them while we worked on the stable roof.

The following day we lifted off the Yorkshire slates and stacked them carefully against the wall at the back of the house. The stable roof had always been lower than the roof over the shippon and dairy and the roof timbers had sagged under the weight of the stone. Over the next few days we discarded the old rafters and replaced them with some new timber purlins which we adjusted to be the same height as the purlins on the dairy and shippon. It was heavy work and time consuming but essential if the new roof was going to look straight along its entire length. Once the new timbers were in position and all the old ones were levelled up we were ready to continue. By the end of August we had laid the rest of the roof sheets over the stable. The whole roof looked level and was a vast improvement. We secured all the sheets with plenty of bolts then mortared lead flashing into a seam in the house wall just above the sheets to make it watertight. Each of the three rooms needed pointing up against the roof on the inside and once that was done all the rooms were much warmer and we were pleased with the job.

Ever since we had moved into Jericho back in 1994 we had harboured a distant dream to convert the hay barn into living accommodation and replace the big barn doors which covered the arch with a big window. Now in 2002 some eight years later we decided that the time was right to re mortgage the farm and make that dream a reality. Drawing up plans for a barn conversion involved technical information which I was unfamiliar with so at the beginning of September we employed somebody to do it for us. About ten days later we received the plans and submitted them for planning permission and building regulations.

Two weeks after we had submitted them the plans were rejected by the Planning Department because they needed more technical information. We re-submitted them as soon as we had obtained the required data.

That month I began repainting all the outside windows on the farmhouse starting with the toilet window and Jessica's bedroom windows all of which I could reach from the new roof over the dairy.

At the end of September Sam packed in his job at Highmoor stables and began to work on a private yard instead.

One of the most successful and popular ponies in the Saddleworth branch of the Pony Club was 'Charlie' a 14hh chestnut gelding. He was about 16 years old and had recently come up for sale. Alyson had been on the lookout for a larger pony for Holly. She sold Feathers and decided to buy Charlie who turned out to be one of the nicest ponies we'd ever had on the yard.

The chicken which I had revived with my hair dryer earlier in the summer turned out to be yet another cockerel! He was very handsome with bright colourful plumage and I thought he deserved a colourful sort of name so I called him Worthington after the hair dryer.

At the beginning of October I started working on the windows at the front of the house. The upstairs windows particularly were in desperate need of attention but not being too good with heights I was reluctant to use our wooden ladder which was old and springy and in any case was barely long enough. Alan noticed an advertisement for a lightweight tower scaffold which was for sale in the Manchester Evening News – we decided to buy it.

When erected the tower was tall but not very wide and would have to be repositioned three times to enable me to reach all the windows. As soon as Alan had set up the scaffold with planks I began preparing and repainting the first three of our bedroom windows. Protruding from the house wall here and there were steel pins. Alan tied the scaffold to one of them with a strong blue rope whenever he repositioned the tower beneath a new set of windows. He also braced it with some timbers.

I much preferred working on the scaffold platform to clinging nervously onto the old rickety ladder and I got on with the job without the height worrying me at all. I had finished all but Sam's bedroom windows when there was a change in the weather. It became very windy and despite the safety precautions which Alan had taken it was too precarious and too cold to work on the scaffold and I decided to wait for the wind to die down before attempting to continue.

Over the summer months Sam and Emily had spent a lot of time together on the yard riding, chatting and scheming. One of their bright ideas involved the old armchair which had been stored in the hay barn since last November. They thought it would be a great idea if Sam were to tow it down Shiloh Lane behind his quad with Emily sitting in it. When Sam mentioned their plan to me – much as I could see the appeal – I told him it was much too dangerous and they were not to do it. A few days later he casually asked me if I knew where the old blue rope was. I told him I had no idea.

In the middle of October – unexpectedly - we completely ran out of water. Once again the water level in the well had dropped so low that the pump was unable to draw up any water. The following day the situation remained the same; no showers, no brews and no toilet flushing!

The wind remained as strong as ever so I was unable to continue painting the windows. As usual I worked down on the yard in the morning and my last job was to go into the hen hut at the top of the garden to clean the roosts and collect any eggs. As I bent down to unscrew the feed barrel to give the hens some corn there was an almighty crash. Something landed heavily on the roof of the hen hut making it shake violently. The hens squawked with fright. Cautiously I opened the door. It would only open a few inches – I pushed hard and peered out of the gap. I could see a steel pole across the doorway blocking the door and realised with horror that the scaffold tower had blown over. I put my arm through the gap and managed to push the pole up a couple of inches and force the door open wide enough for me to squeeze through. Having emerged through the doorway I stopped in my tracks. Before landing on the hen hut roof the scaffold tower had hit the roof of the Vauxhall which unusually had been parked in front of the house. Suddenly it dawned on me.

'SAM!!' I exclaimed. Evidently he had noticed that the rope he had been looking for a day or so previously was tied to the scaffolding and had helped himself. He had also more than likely already whizzed Emily down the lane in the old armchair behind the quad! Having examined the badly dinted car roof I made a mental note to tackle Sam on both counts as soon as he got home from school.

The relationship between Jess and her boyfriend had become decidedly rocky over the past few weeks. She stopped working at his restaurant and made enquiries to see if there were any jobs going at The Mill. On Friday 25th October – a truly momentous day as far as I was concerned - she finished with him. Despite my genuine attempts to be supportive and sympathetic I could barely conceal my delight that the relationship was over. Jess had seen the light at last and admitted as much.

That night became exceptionally windy.

The Roofing Sheet Incident

On Sunday the weather deteriorated as the day progressed with torrential rain and gale force winds. Around lunchtime I dropped Sam off at Simon's for a couple of hours. When I returned Alan and I cleared out rubble and debris from between the rafters in the kitchen roof space in preparation for insulating it – a job which was long over due. Later in the afternoon I went down to the yard and got on with the stable jobs. I'd almost finished when I saw Alan go out in the car to pick up Sam.

The rain stung my face as I walked back up the garden to the house. It was starting to get dark and there was an icy chill to the wind. I put up my collar and tucked my chin into my coat promising myself a hot drink when I got inside. As I approached the kitchen door I heard a loud thudding sound. I stopped and listened. The wind was howling and the electricity was fizzing in the damp atmosphere as it was carried along the cables between the massive pylons. There it was again – a heavy thud. It seemed to be coming from the back of the house. I went round to investigate. The thudding noise was intermittent. I had just reached the gable end of the house when there was another powerful gust of wind. To my horror I saw the lower third of the end roofing sheet over the old stable lift up about six inches in the wind and then drop down again on top of the back wall with a thud. I ran round to the back of the house and climbed onto the old rabbit hutch which Emily had given me when her rabbit had died. Pulling down on the bottom edge of the roofing sheet as hard as I could I fought against the next strong gust of wind which was trying its best to rip it off the roof. If it were to succeed it would probably take all the others with it one by one. Desperately I clung to the edge of the roofing sheet and as I waited for Alan and Sam to come home memories of our life at Jericho over the last eight years came flooding back... ...as my recollections came full circle I was jolted back to the present by the welcome sight of car headlights shining onto the grey brick wall at the back of the concrete where we parked the cars. From my uncomfortable position on top of the rabbit hutch at the far end of the stable I could now see the car bonnet as Alan drove up to the brick wall. Sam opened the passenger door and got out of the car.

'Sam! The roof's blowing off!' I shrieked. 'Do something!'

Sam shouted something to Alan then ran towards me pausing for a moment to assess the situation before disappearing inside the old stable. Alan hurried over to me. I was about to explain what had been happening when there was another strong gust of wind which saved me the trouble. I was so cold and wet I could hardly hold onto the roofing sheet let alone pull it down.

'Do something!' I shouted at him. I could hear Sam hammering inside the stable.

'I'll try to weigh the roof down.' Alan shouted over the noise of the wind. I nodded and continued to pull down on the edge of the roof. All I wanted to do was get indoors out of the rain and rest my aching arms. Frantically Alan searched for something heavy to put onto the bottom corner of the roof. 'This should do it' he said pulling at an old plastic bag full of building sand which had been discarded and left against the stone wall months ago. He staggered towards me carrying the heavy bag then stepped up onto a stone beside the rabbit hutch to give himself some extra height. Grunting with the effort he heaved the bag of sand over the top of me and dropped it heavily onto the roofing sheet. On impact the brittle bag split open and spewed its contents over my head. Icy cold sandy water dribbled down the back of my neck inside the collar of my coat and the filthy bag of sand slid down the roof and rested on my shoulders. There are no words to describe my feelings for Alan at that precise moment.

'Dad! Come here and hold this while I nail it!' Sam shouted from inside the stable. Lost for words Alan ran to help him. A few minutes later the frantic hammering stopped and they came out of the stable. 'OK Mum you can let go now. We've fastened...' Sam's words trailed away when he saw me crouching miserably on the hutch with the now half filled bag of sand draped round my shoulders and wet sand covering my hair and face. 'What the...?'

'Ask your father.' I seethed between clenched teeth. Rigid with cold I persuaded my cramped hands to let go of the roof then because my legs were so stiff I practically fell off the rabbit hutch. Shivering uncontrollably I trudged miserably into the house dumped my saturated coat on the kitchen floor and hugged the Aga.

'I'll run you a hot bath.' Alan said and went upstairs. If there had been even the faintest glimmer of amusement on his face I would have summoned up enough energy from somewhere deep within me to flatten him!

Submerged in the steaming hot bath my body gradually warmed through and slowly my aching limbs started to relax. I began to imagine how funny I must have looked and suspected that downstairs Alan and Sam were probably having a good laugh at my expense.

The following day I bought some metal roof stays and that evening Alan screwed them to the walls and roof timbers of both the stable and the shippon to secure the roof and hopefully prevent it from lifting in future gale force winds.

It was around this time that one of Alan's golfing pals mentioned that his Border collie was expecting puppies due to an uninvited visit from his neighbour's Belgian Shepherd – and he would need to find homes for them. I missed Kim and Pete and wanted another big dog. The prospect of a Border collie crossed with a Belgian Shepherd was an attractive one and Alan spoke to his friend and offered to give a home to one of the pups.

Early one evening Henry Cockerel was nowhere to be seen when I put the poultry in. I hoped he would be there in the morning. But Henry didn't re appear the next morning or the next so we had to assume even though there were no feathers to be seen anywhere, and despite his size that a fox had taken him.

Since he had out grown Jessie Sam had ridden various horses for other people. That November we heard about a young Irish Sports Horse which was being sold by a local horse dealer. After several visits when he rode and spent time with the horse Sam decided he would like to have him and we made an arrangement whereby the dealer would take Zulu in part exchange.

The following week 'Will' arrived on the yard and Zulu left. I felt awful letting Zulu go like that but the dealer had found him a good home not far away from us – where he still is as far as I know. Will was a four year old 15hh chestnut gelding. He was very gentle and in many respects was as much like Jessie as we could have hoped to find. However he was young and inexperienced and it would require a lot of work and commitment on Sam's part to bring him on.

In the middle of November the pregnant Border collie produced just two offspring – a dog and a bitch.

As winter closed in I began hacking out on Jessie to give her some exercise when the winter field was too wet for turn out. I enjoyed riding her as she was sensible and safe. I often rode her round the reservoir but when pushed for time I would ride a shorter circuit which took me past Bill's farm up the hill and back along the bridle path which came out at Shiloh Farm.

One morning after heavy overnight rain I took Jessie round the bridle path. We had a short canter on the last stretch before reaching Shiloh Farm. There were a couple of large shallow puddles ahead of us. Jessie cantered straight through the first one so understandably I expected her to canter through the next one as well. However Jessie must have disliked being splashed with the cold water – she swerved to avoid the second puddle and I landed in it! Immediately she stopped, turned and looked at me then waited patiently while I picked myself up and remounted. Wet, muddy and feeling rather foolish I hoped I could get home without being seen. I told Jessie to walk on. A few moments later I cringed when Steve Sloane come out of his barn and approached me for a chat. Before long I continued on my way hoping that he didn't turn to watch me go as he would see that my back and my hat were covered with mud.

A few days later Bill Dawson rang and asked me if I would go down to see three cockerels that were on death row. He hoped I might give one of them a reprieve – which of course I did – I brought home a massive white Brahma that was so big he got wedged in the entrance to the hen hut and Alan had to enlarge it! I called him Edward. He was very placid and settled in well. Fortunately there was no animosity between him and Worthington who was the only cockerel in the hen hut at the time. Oliver was a bit stroppy with Edward if he approached his hut at the bottom of the garden or showed any interest in his two hens but I don't think Edward was that way inclined. Most of the time he pottered about at the top of the garden rooting around under the oak trees or he would stand with his feathers fluffed out watching the comings and goings of the rest of the poultry. On the occasions when he decided to join them he reminded me of an Edwardian gentleman wearing plus fours holding his hands behind his back as he swaggered down the garden.

By December Will was happily settled on the yard. He was full of character loved company and was inquisitive and mischievous. Mucking out his stable tended to take rather a long time if Will was in it at the time. It got to the point where even in bad weather Sam chose to tie him up outside while he mucked out to prevent him from getting hold of the shavings fork or the sweeping brush or knocking over the wheelbarrow with a well timed nudge. Not to be outdone Will would watch Sam through the stable window and several times I saw him deliberately knock the light switch with his nose and turn off the light just to have Sam come out and scold him – it seemed any attention was better than none!

Initially when hacking out Will was sometimes difficult and headstrong but several lessons and continued perseverance from Sam eventually eliminated these early problems. By and large Will was very well behaved and a pleasure to look after. He stood still while he was groomed or tacked up. He put up with the farrier and tolerated being clipped. He walked quietly when being taken to and from the field and when in the field he was sociable and playful and tended to be submissive rather than dominant with the other horses and therefore caused no problems.

PART THREE

From a Vision Emerged a Reality

In the years that have passed since the episode with the roofing sheets animals have come and gone as have owners with their horses on the yard. Hard work has continued both inside and outside at Jericho and with every project that we have completed and every problem that we have solved our lives have continued to become a little easier.

2003

Early in January when he was eight weeks old we collected our new chunky puppy which with his dense black coat resembled a bear cub. He was big and beautiful and I called him Mikey. Jack now six months old was delighted with his new play mate. The two puppies got on very well and apart from when they flung themselves down with exhaustion they played together constantly. Maggie was happy to excuse herself from their games and watched over them like a proud parent.

In February I noticed an advertisement for a part-time support assistant required to work in a comprehensive school in Tameside. I attended an interview but instead of being offered the post that was advertised they offered me a six week stint from the second week in March working in their Art Department covering for a member of the teaching staff who was off sick – a much more lucrative position. The extra income was very welcome - and I earned every penny! With the numerous animals I had to see to before and after work I found the whole experience completely exhausting and was relieved that it was only a temporary position. After I had completed the six week block however, I returned to the school regularly to do odd days of supply throughout the summer term.

In the middle of March we received planning permission for the barn conversion. We contacted a builder who Alan knew by reputation in the hope that he might be available to do the conversion for us. He had done some exceptional work at the golf club in Huddersfield where Alan was a member and had also worked on his neighbour's house – the neighbour with the Border collie bitch.

That month we sold the old David Brown tractor and replaced it with a smaller Universal tractor which had a loader. Now we had a tractor with a loading shovel we no longer had to use pitch forks to transfer muck from the muck heap into the tractor trailer and the job could be done in a fraction of the time.

Muck spreading also had always been a laborious task for us. Whether we used the tractor and trailer or the quad and trailer it still had to be done by hand. We had been looking out for a muck spreader for some time and at the end of January a friend of Bill's told us that a flat bed muck spreader was for sale at Strines Farm just down the road from us. On his recommendation we bought it and Sam was able then to spread all the fields properly.

The water level in the well had dropped very low by the beginning of April, a situation which continued throughout the spring and summer making life very difficult at times.

As we moved into May the weather began to get much warmer. I decided to have another go at shearing Emily. Early one Saturday morning Alan and I went down to her stable. I took with me a plastic bucket to sit on and after a struggle Alan manhandled the reluctant and somewhat alarmed sheep into a sitting position. Quickly I put the bucket down behind her and sat on it, then with one knee either side of her body I clasped Emily to me. After an initial struggle she became calm as if in a daze just as she had done when the shepherd had sheared her. Alan passed me the hand shears and tentatively I began to clip away the wool from around her face and neck. Now that she had become calm and quiet Alan left me and went back up to the house. I continued clipping and cut away the wool from her chest. As I slid the blades close to her pink skin I pushed my left hand through her fleece in front of the blades to ensure that I didn't cut her. The lanolin felt smooth and oily and the blades cut cleanly through the wool. By this time I was using the shears more confidently and started to clip down her right side when without warning she threw her head back hard against my shoulder and thrust her front legs out before her like wheelbarrow handles. Taken by surprise I was knocked off balance. The weight of her body pushed me down onto the bucket which crushed beneath me. I fell backwards and Emily landed heavily on top of me winding me. Lying upside down Emily made harsh rasping noises as if she was struggling to breathe – I wasn't doing too well in that respect myself! After a few desperately uncomfortable minutes I managed to push her over onto her side and we both scrambled to our feet. Emily soon calmed down and allowed me to continue shearing her as she stood by the stable door – definitely a less traumatic option for both of us!

An hour and a half later I opened the door and let a cleaner and considerably slimmer Emily out of her stable. She looked very good even though I say so myself and she must have felt much better. I on the other hand looked and smelt disgusting and my right hand was stinging due to a large red blister which had appeared between my thumb and first finger. I swept up the wool on the stable floor and picked up the bucket which now resembled a frisbee before returning to the house for a long hot shower.

Jo left the yard with Benson on the first weekend in June and his stable was taken almost immediately by Nicola who had originally come to the yard with Soli back in 1995. This time she brought with her a beautiful black Thoroughbred mare called Star.

July was a hot dry month. Tractors and balers were busy for days on end and with every field that was harvested the colours of the fields changed the landscape.

We set to work preparing the hay barn for the forthcoming conversion. The first job was to remove the joists and timbers which we had put in when we made the floor for the hay barn upstairs. That done Alan managed to rive out the old goat chewed steps which we had always intended to replace but had never got around to doing. The next job was to demolish the pig sties in the bottom of the barn. They were built of brick which was rendered over and were incredibly solid and difficult to knock down. In desperation Sam invited Simon up to give us a hand. Simon was now big and powerful and with his help the two sties were soon reduced to a heap of rubble which we smashed up as small as we could before barrowing it laboriously down the lane to fill the numerous pot holes.

The following day Simon rang me as he had forgotten to mention that there was a duckling at his farm which apparently had my name written all over it!

'Why, what's wrong with it?' I had asked suspiciously.

'It's got a bit of a bent neck but other than that it's fine.' he laughed. He went on to tell me that I could have another duckling to keep it company which had nothing wrong with it at all!

I collected the ducklings which were about three months old. I couldn't tell for sure if the one with the bent neck was male or female but I guessed it was female. She was a dark brown Indian Runner and was pathetically cute and hopelessly devoted to a much larger Mallard drake who's head seemed a little too large and his feet were definitely a size too small – apart from those minor defects he was a handsome chap. I named the bent-necked Runner 'Quasimodo' – Quasi for short and her Mallard friend I called Big Eddie. I didn't hold out a lot of hope for Quasi's survival as her plumage was sparse to say the least but I put the two of them in the duck hut with the other ducks and they seemed quite happy. Quasi stayed close to Big Eddie at all times. They often lay together under the oak trees in the long grass enjoying the summer sunshine; Quasi rested her neck across Eddie's back as if it was more comfortable that way.

Early in August Paul the builder arrived to begin the barn conversion. An irascible man in his early thirties Paul was tall and lanky with an unruly mop of dark wavy hair. He had an arrogant air about him and an abrupt manner both of which took a bit of getting used to. He brought with him a labourer called Steven who was of a similar age but in contrast to Paul, Steven was cheerful and friendly and very easy to get on with – and his head was completely shaved. Accompanying them each day was Paul's Belgian Shepherd – Mikey's father.

Soon after the commencement of the building work Sam took Will to Pony Club camp where good progress was made with his schooling.

In the course of the next few months the two builders became practically part of the family. At first they ate their dinners in their pick-up or in the barn but before long they made themselves at home in the kitchen instead where each day they perched on the seats at either side of the Aga like a pair of book ends.

Rapid progress was made with the conversion. The stone roof slates over the barn were taken off and stacked on scaffolding. The massive roof trusses were taken out and replaced by hefty new steel beams which were swung into position by a huge crane. When the mullions had been built into the walls at the front and the back of the house to create the new upstairs windows the roof slates were put back on again. The barn roof looked so good it made the roof over the rest of the house look uneven so we decided to get that done too while we had the scaffolding on site. The heavy roof slates were taken off the other half of the building and stacked as before. The existing trusses and purlins were treated and the spars were either mended or replaced and discrepancies of height were adjusted so that when the stone slates were put back on the entire roof was straight and looked better than it had done in years.

Sam's riding instructor recommended Jessie to a couple who wanted to loan a pony for their little boy. A couple of days later they came to see her and by the end of the week arrangements had been made for them to take Jessie on loan from September subject to a week's trial.

By this time Jess had taken her A-level exams and left the Sixth Form College. She had secured a place at Leeds University but was unsure whether or not to take up the place. Finally she decided to take a year out and applied to join the Police Force – a prospect which had appealed to her for quite some time. The application procedure was a long drawn out affair so in the meantime she took a job at Saddleworth Golf Club as a member of the bar staff and earned herself some money until she knew whether or not her application had been successful.

Before the end of October Paul had rebuilt both chimneys and put on the chimney pots and Steven had prepared the front of the house for re-pointing. Early in November we discussed with Paul the layout of the new upstairs rooms in the hay barn.

Unusually at that time of year we ran out of water yet again and had to trail down to the hydrant by The Roebuck more than once to fill the water tank on the tractor trailer – not a pleasant job in winter.

The enthusiasm with which Sam began riding and working with Will had waned noticeably by the end of the year. I was not surprised therefore when Sam told me after much soul searching that he had lost interest in riding and much as he loved Will he no longer wanted to keep him.

That Christmas it was our turn once again to have my mum stay with us for a few days. But away from the familiarity of her own home she became confused and anxious. On Boxing Day all the family met at Pat's and although Mum was pleased to see everyone she was overwhelmed by so many of us being there all at the same time. Instead of just seeing her as my mum I also saw her as a confused and vulnerable old lady.

2004

The weather was cold and damp when Paul decided to knock through from our upstairs landing into the hay barn. The new landing area was spacious and had two mullioned windows which allowed natural light to flood into the old upstairs landing for the first time. Unfortunately it wasn't just the light that flooded in – so did an icy cold draught. For the first few weeks of the year nocturnal visits to the bathroom were uncomfortably cold for all of us!

That winter was a bad time for the poultry. Foxes were seen from time to time during the day making me feel uneasy about leaving them out if I wasn't at home. Frequently I kept them shut in when the weather was damp and misty. Despite plenty of straw bedding in the duck house little Quasi was unable to withstand the cold and died during the night early in January. Big Eddie finding himself on his own tagged along behind the other ducks trying his best to keep up with them.

Jess began riding Will regularly and we had a new addition to the yard. Nancy had moved on with Molly a three year old coloured Cob with a gentle disposition and an unnerving adolescent immaturity which manifested itself in causing the hock on one or other of her hind legs to lock after she had been in her stable overnight. The joint would stay locked often for several hours during which time the affected leg would remain absolutely rigid and Molly would drag it about her stable quite unconcerned. Suddenly it would free itself and she would then be fine for several days or even weeks before it happened again. Will adored Molly and followed her around the field playfully nibbling at her rug or attempting to share the same blade of grass.

In February Slim went missing. Linford spent several days after her disappearance quacking pathetically as he searched for her all over the garden and round the house. Later the same month Edward cockerel was caught and killed by a fox in front of the last stable traumatising Merlin the 17hh grey horse that occupied it at the time.

By the end of March the barn conversion was complete and the builders left. Upstairs in what used to be the hay barn Alan and I had a new bedroom with ensuite and there was also a spare bedroom above the big arch. Downstairs where the pig sties had been there was now a massive sitting room with a stone flagged floor. The arched doorway had been replaced by a window which was divided into three vertical panes. The view at night with the lights over Oldham and Manchester and many miles beyond was spectacular. We installed a tall Italian wood burning stove which produced more than enough warmth to heat the big room.

I was kept busy for several weeks painting seemingly endless walls, ceilings, doors and skirting boards in the new rooms. One chilly evening I was tired out after having come to the end of yet another day of continuous painting and we decided to light the new stove. After enjoying a couple of glasses of wine with our meal I relaxed on the sofa in front of the stove with a cup of coffee – promptly fell asleep and spilt it all over myself!

Jess was learning to drive. She had a number of lessons with a driving instructor between the winter of 2003 and the autumn of 2004 during which time either myself or Alan accompanied her while she practised.

Alan was methodical and discussed with her the workings of the car or the weather conditions which might affect her driving before allowing her to even turn on the ignition. I tended to just get in the car and we would set off. Undoubtedly Alan's method was the most instructive but I was available more often than he was and so invariably it was me that had the dubious pleasure of going out with her. Her driving improved as her confidence increased but as with anyone who learns to drive there were some aspects of it which needed more work than others. At one point she developed an unnerving habit of depressing the clutch as she approached a corner and would then coast round rather than drive round it – which caused a few hair raising moments!

It was Mum's birthday at the end of March and Pat arranged a family party for her. She fetched her from Ilkley and during the afternoon most of the family met up at Pat's to celebrate. It was obvious right away that Mum was unwell. Back in Ilkley the following day Pat sent for the doctor who admitted Mum to hospital immediately. By the time Jess and I met them at the Airedale General Hospital in Keighley Mum was weak, confused and quite belligerent!

Over the next few weeks one or other of us managed to visit her on most days. It was an upsetting and worrying time. The frequent journeys to and from the hospital were tiring. Often Jess came with me taking the opportunity to drive the eighty mile round trip which provided her with some valuable driving practice. On one occasion we were running low on fuel. I pointed out a petrol station some distance in front of us and asked Jess to look in her rear view mirror, indicate, slow down and when the road was clear to drive into the petrol station. Jess did precisely what I had asked her to do until we got to the slowing down part. There was no oncoming traffic and she flew across the road into the entrance of the petrol station like Lewis Hamilton. Without slowing down at all she took a sharp left turn between a grass verge and a startled woman who was re-fuelling her car and despite my calm and precise instructions 'F…! SH..! SLOW DOWN! F…ING H…!' or words to that effect she tore past the petrol pumps in the centre of the forecourt and with surprising accuracy and laughing like a woman possessed - which was due either to her nerves or my vocabulary - she slammed on her brakes beside a petrol pump at the far side of the garage and stalled the car. The man behind the counter in the garage stared at us in alarm as did the other customers on the forecourt. Relieved to be still in one piece and not wishing to put myself through any more traumas I refuelled the car and drove the rest of the journey to the hospital myself.

During her seven week stay in hospital Mum had good days and bad days. One week she would improve and the next she would regress. Arrangements for her to come home were made and ultimately abandoned and on the 18th of May at 88 years old she passed away. The fact that she had reached such a good age with so little ill health gave us some comfort but having been such a strong and important figure in our lives her loss inevitably hit us hard.

On a more positive note her hospitalization and death drew myself and Pat even closer. It also re united us with Jude a very good friend of mine who I first met when I was five years old and with whom I spent almost every day of my childhood until we left school after which we went our separate ways and drifted apart. One day when she visited Mum at the hospital we met again briefly. We arranged to meet up later and have continued to do so regularly ever since.

It was time once again to shear Emily. Last year's attempt to shear her correctly resulted in me ending up on my back with her on top of me – a situation which I had no desire to repeat. This year therefore I decided to see if I could shear her while she was standing up. Whether Emily actually remembered last year's traumatic experience or whether she was just too hot to care I don't know but whatever the reason she stood quietly by her stable door and allowed me to clip off the wool all around her neck, down her chest, half way along her back and under her belly at which point she had evidently had enough and proceeded to let me know by butting my knees. As she had been so well behaved I decided not to argue with her and I let her out of the stable intending to finish the job the next day. With the front half of her body clipped short and her rear half left untouched she emerged from her stable as if from a pencil sharpener.

I continued to look after Will each day and had become very fond of him. Jess rode quite regularly but her time was divided between working at the golf club, practising her driving and spending time with her latest boyfriend which meant unfortunately that Will often was left un-ridden. Jess and I decided that I should get on him and exercise him myself. Because Will was so much bigger than Jessie he had a much longer stride than she had and so was a very different ride. In fact I fell off him twice in the paddock! After a few lessons however I soon got used to him and became more competent. Encouraged by Nancy I began to hack out with her and Molly.

By the middle of June Sam had finished the two year day-release bricklaying course that he had taken at Oldham College and had also finished his GCSE exams and left school. In July through college he began an apprenticeship with a local stonemason.

Jessica's application to join the Police Force had been rejected – their loss - so she decided to take up her place on the Events Management course at Leeds University commencing that September. We bought an old VW Golf from Pat and John. It had been Karen's and we gave it to Jess so that she could practice her driving and take it with her to Leeds when she passed her test.

Our existing central heating system had to be modified to accommodate the extra radiators in the converted barn. Once this had been done and I had finished decorating all the new rooms we turned our attention back to the original part of the farm house and made a start on the alterations which we had planned for it.

First we tackled our old bedroom. The ceiling had always been a mess. We had been unsure what to do with it until in the course of the re-roofing Steven had put his foot through it which pretty much made the decision for us and we had it re plastered. Alan replaced the old tiles on the window sill, many of which were loose or broken, and I re-decorated the room for Jess. Early in August she moved into it which freed up her old bedroom for conversion into a good sized modern bathroom: a complicated and tricky project which took us a long time to complete due to the fact that none of the walls were straight and the floor sloped down towards the middle of the house.

Later that month we lost Alice to an unidentified and virulent infection. Within a 48 hour period it took every ounce of her strength and left her fighting in vain for her life.

Early in September we bought various items of bedding, crockery, toiletries and food which together with clothes, stationary and electrical bits and pieces we crammed into two cars and took with Jess to Leeds. She had been allocated a room in one of the student flat complexes opposite the University which was to be her home for the first year of her course. Jericho was strangely quiet without her and I missed her a lot. She returned home on alternate weekends for a while to practice her driving or to have a driving lesson until she passed her test at the end of October after which she came home less frequently.

A one year, part time evening course in Interior Design was about to commence at the end of September at Oldham College. Before moving to Jericho I had done a lot of water colour painting and design work. Now 10 years later I had reached the stage of having to hold text at a distance and screw up my eyes in order to make out small print and I seriously wondered if I would be able to see well enough to do any art work at all! Nevertheless I decided to enrol. The course work took up a lot of my time in the evenings over the next few months but having invested in a pair of cheap reading glasses I found that I could indeed do the work and thoroughly enjoyed it.

At the end of October Pat and John threw a fancy dress Halloween party to celebrate their Ruby wedding anniversary. Wearing a long red dress and clutching a red trident I went as a sorceress with a pair of red horns on my head. Jess went as Medusa with serpents flowing from her hair. Dan – the current boyfriend – went as Count Dracula, Sam was a ghoul and Alan was an extremely reluctant and grumpy monk. Alan had bought a different car that week and we travelled across to Bradford in that. Unsure of just where the venue was Alan stopped the car and I asked a passer-by for directions. By mistake I opened the car door instead of the window and as I was shutting the door Alan set off again and my trident dropped through the gap and fell onto the road.

'Stop! I've dropped my trident!' I shouted much to Jess and Dan's amusement and grudgingly Alan stopped the car. I didn't want to get out because of my long dress so we volunteered Sam who ran back up the road looking extremely ghoulish as he retrieved my trident from the gutter.

That Christmas Mum's absence was felt keenly by all of us particularly on Boxing Day when all the family descended on Jericho for the usual get together. Boxing Day that year was memorable also for the catastrophic tsunami which hit Thailand and claimed the lives of over two hundred and thirty thousand people.

2005

Extreme weather conditions continued to dominate the early days of January. Gales and heavy rain wreaked havoc in various parts of the world. In Britain it was Scotland that bore the brunt of the dreadful weather with Carlisle experiencing terrible floods. In the United States Florida was battered by appalling storms.

During the cold winter evenings throughout January and February I concentrated on producing work for my college course. In February my favourite hen - Betty the ex-battery hen - died in her sleep on a thick bed of straw in the hen hut. February and March were very cold months with ice and heavy snow frequently causing treacherous driving conditions.

Although we had every intention of commencing work on our new bathroom at the beginning of the year the cold weather and dark evenings were not conducive to tackling the required plumbing jobs. We decided to leave it until Alan had broken up for the Easter break before making a start. In the meantime I gathered up glossy brochures from bathroom showrooms and we spent our time instead choosing which bathroom furnishings we were going to have.

Around this time Jess began seeing a new boyfriend – Malc – an electrician. How useful! We hoped this relationship would last for a few months as before long we would need some new wiring in both the new bathroom and Sam's new bedroom.

In February I advertised Will for sale but every time anyone came to see him or ride him I found myself hoping that they wouldn't want him. I needed some sort of recommendation that whoever took him would treat him right and spoil him rotten and advertising him was too impersonal. I asked our farrier if he knew of anybody amongst his customers who was looking for a horse like Will. Coincidentally a lady had asked him to look out for a nice horse for her and he gave me her phone number. I rang her and described Will. She was very interested and came over to see him early in March. I liked her immediately. Will behaved impeccably when she rode him and nudged and nuzzled her in the stable which won her over completely. After a return visit the following weekend she decided to have him. A few days later we took Will to his new home in Glossop. Although I would miss him I was quite confident that he would be well loved and cared for properly.

Sam turned 17 early in April and straightaway began learning to drive. Having driven the tractor for quite some time he quickly mastered the mechanics of driving a car. The practice he needed was doing so on the roads. The experience of sitting in the passenger seat with Sam driving the car was not as hair-raising as it had been at times with Jessica and Sam soon became relaxed and confident behind the wheel.

My Interior Design course came in useful enabling me to plan different layouts for the new bathroom. Having decided which one was the best we moved the radiator onto a different wall, worked out the required layout for the plumbing and changed the existing hot water cylinder for one with a greater capacity.

Once again by the middle of April we had completely run out of water. The frequency with which we had to put up with this situation was driving me up the wall. When it happened again early in May we decided to investigate. Even though there was water in the well the pump struggled to draw up enough water to fill the tank. We suspected that we might need to buy a new pump but before replacing it we decided to check to see if anything was blocking the filter at the end of the pipe that was submerged in the water down the well. We lifted off the well head cover and I lowered a broom handle with a wire hook on the end of it down inside the well. Before long I had managed to catch the pipe with the hook and drag it up high enough for Alan to be able to reach down and grab it. The filter was a kind of wire basket - a very basic affair. Alan unscrewed it from the pipe and on close inspection found that a small section of it had broken leaving a hole in it the size of a golf ball. There appeared to be a blockage inside the pipe which he hooked out with a piece of wire. It was a frog long since deceased that must have been close to the damaged filter when the pump came on and got sucked through the hole and into the pipe blocking it almost completely. We bought a new filter and fitted it to the end of the pipe which we then dropped back down the well. We turned the pump back on. This time it drew up the water quickly and so for the time being the problem was solved. We were aware however that there was not much depth of water from which the pump could draw so unless we had a prolonged spell of heavy rain before long we would run out of water again. Due to a long spell of warm dry weather this happened sooner than expected and so at the end of the month we made enquiries about having our own bore hole drilled.

Sue rang and asked if I had any available stables. Now that Will had gone there were two and she wanted both of them. One was for Trader and the other for Pike, a young 14hh coloured gelding. I repainted the insides and creosoted the outsides of both stables in preparation for the arrival of the two horses the following weekend.

It soon became apparent that Trader was still every bit as badly behaved as he had been when Sue had left the yard with him and Misty five years before. Now standing at 16.2hh he was a handsome and powerful horse but he was unpredictable and was as likely to walk quietly to the field with either Sue or myself as he was to barge past and pull free from us after which he would canter away into the paddock, car park or garden. In the stable he was a nightmare nipping at sleeves and collars, getting hold of the shavings fork or brush or leaning into the tack room where he would try to raid his feed bin or drag his rugs onto the floor. In short he was a complete pain in the arse. His only saving grace was that he was pleasant with the other horses in the field. Pike was a nice pony - a little nervous and jumpy but not badly behaved. He was more dominant in the field than Trader was but he wasn't a problem.

Work continued on and off in the bathroom. Before the end of June the new bath, shower and washbasin had all been plumbed in. After an evening which had been fraught with problems Alan and I had fallen out about something and he had stomped off downstairs leaving me endeavouring to strip off the last remaining area of old wallpaper. I had positioned the step-ladder carefully to avoid a hole in the floorboards where the radiator plumbing had been. Pieces of wallpaper fell stickily to the floor at the bottom of the step-ladder. I scraped the last piece of paper off the wall and stepped off the ladder. My foot went straight through the hole in the floorboards and continued through the dining room ceiling showering Alan's head and shoulders with plaster as he sat in the armchair watching TV. I cannot remember his exact words but I got the distinct impression that he was not amused.

By the end of June my college course had finished and all my project work had been handed in. Jess too had completed her first year at University and the two of us booked a late deal in Marmaris for the first week in July – much to Sam's indignation. Just before we left for Turkey my lovely Linford was taken by a fox. The only consolation being that he had left behind a duckling recently hatched by Crow.

When Crow had gone broody six weeks earlier I was unsure where to put her until I remembered the old rabbit hutch which was still at the back of the house. I heaved the hutch round to the front of the house then I half carried and half dragged it down the garden and with some difficulty crammed it into the duck's side of the duck hut. I then installed Crow in the hutch with her clutch of eggs. Being in the duck hut Crow would have some company and being in the hutch the eggs would be safe from interference. In the mornings once the ducks had been let out and the hatchlings were old enough I would be able to lift them out of the hutch and let them have more room on the floor of the hut and on fine days I could open the little side door so they could go out into the run with Crow. The only other egg to hatch from that particular mixture of ducks' and hens' eggs was a little yellow chick and the two youngsters thrived.

The first time the little duckling went into the run it made a bee line for the old stone sink which was full of water. Crow squawked with horror but the duckling ignored her warning jumped in the sink and began to swim. Clearly unhappy with the behaviour of her rather strange and disobedient offspring Crow – with some resignation – also climbed into the sink and stood in the water looking like a lady paddling in a river holding her skirt up to prevent it getting wet.

Despite the uncertainty of their parentage the chicken and duckling were inseparable and continued to thrive. On Nancy's suggestion I called the little chicken 'Chuck' and restrained myself from calling the duckling 'Dick' instead I named him Linford Junior after his dad.

Towards the end of July Lucy Goose, by then around 20 years old, was struggling to walk. One morning she was either reluctant to or unable to move at all. I carried her out of the hut and laid her on the grass in the sunshine for an hour or so while I got on with my jobs after which I put her back inside her hut. Early that evening when I shut up the poultry for the night I found Lucy dead. Mabel was clearly distressed and over the next few days she stayed close to the hut obviously missing her old friend. I spoke to Bill about getting her a new companion but he warned me that Mabel may not accept another goose and suggested that I wait for a few days to see if she settled down. I expected her to tag along with the ducks but instead she struck up a firm and lasting friendship with Emily sheep. The two of them spent all their time together. I continued however to shut up Mabel in her own hut at night partly for her own safety regarding the foxes but also to avoid the possibility of her being squashed by Emily as she slept. Already there had been a couple of occasions when Emily had unintentionally trodden on Mabel's webbed foot and was quite oblivious to the poor bird honking as she tried desperately to pull her foot free.

Every now and again while she was away on loan I had called round to check on Jessie. That month Jessica came with me. We were immediately concerned about the pony's condition, she was very scruffy and looked to have lost weight. Having voiced my concerns over the phone I arranged to see her again the following day. Next morning by the time I arrived Jessie had been groomed and looked a lot better than she had done the previous day so I decided to leave the situation as it was with the intention of checking on her more frequently.

Merlin the big grey gelding in the last stable stood at an impressive 17hh. He was one of two horses owned by Marion and Bernard who came on the yard back in February 2004. Although their horses were stabled on our yard they did not use our grazing; instead Merlin and Santa grazed on Steve Foster's land where they invariably stayed out overnight in summer and had more turn out in winter than I could provide.

One day towards the end of July Merlin developed colic whilst out in the field. The plentiful trees with their full summer foliage prevented us from being able to see the two horses from Jericho and so it wasn't until Marion and Bernard arrived early in the evening and saw Merlin lying down in the field that we realized something was wrong. By the time they got to him Merlin was in severe pain and distress. Somehow they managed to get the big horse to his feet and walked him slowly up the lane and along to his stable. The vet was called and did all he could. Marion and Bernard stayed with Merlin all night but the following day he had to be put to sleep. Santa reacted badly to being on his own so Bernard put him in our fields to graze with the other horses for several weeks until Marion got herself another horse. For months afterwards Santa was still watching out for his old companion and became excitable whenever a grey horse went down Shiloh Lane.

Throughout the summer whenever we had the time we continued to work on the new bathroom. Alan tiled the walls and built a new airing cupboard. I painted the woodwork and hung wallpaper and between us we fitted a suspended ceiling. By the beginning of October the room was finally finished. It had taken a long time but we were well pleased with the result.

Around this time drilling equipment was set up at the bottom of the winter field and soon afterwards drilling commenced providing us, eventually, with our own borehole water supply.

The concrete area beside the house where we had always parked our cars was surrounded on three sides by the remains of a double grey brick wall which was all that was left of a large garage, the roof of which had apparently been blown off in severe gales during the winter of 1986. Because of the severity of the winter weather and the detrimental effect it had on the cars we had intended, for several years, to build a new garage on the site of the old one. At the beginning of October that year Sam made a start on it. It was to be constructed out of concrete blocks within the boundary of the old grey brick wall. The two narrow walls at the front - which would stand one either side of the large doorway - were to be faced with stone that would match as closely as possible the stone of the house. Sam worked quickly and competently and made rapid progress at weekends, but by the middle of November keen frosts and falling temperatures put a stop to building work.

Having been driven indoors by the dark evenings and cold weather our attention was turned to the next major indoor project. The old poky bathroom could now be dismantled and the partition wall taken down to provide Sam with a good sized bedroom. While the work was being done he moved into the spare bedroom next to ours.

Taking out the old bathroom fixtures and fittings wasn't too bad but dismantling the partition wall was a messy job. Once all the debris had been removed the new room with four mullioned windows instead of just two was light and spacious. However now that the partition wall was gone we could see that the ceilings of the two rooms had been on different levels. Both of them were in bad condition particularly where the dividing wall had been so we pulled the lot down and arranged for a plasterer to put in a new ceiling.

November proved to be a productive month beginning with Sam passing his driving test. Outside, the antiquated and dilapidated septic tank was replaced with an up to date 'digester'. Inside, progress continued in Sam's bedroom. Malc put in some new wiring and the plasterer boarded and plastered the ceiling.

Despite having felt unwell for several days Alan was determined – now that the wiring was finished – to put back all the floorboards and fit new skirting boards. It was taking him far longer than I expected to complete the job so I went upstairs to investigate. He was working in Sam's bedroom doorway on his hands and knees surrounded by tools and had just fitted the last piece of floorboard when I got there. Slowly he stood up and after steadying himself against the wall I watched him measure and re measure a length of skirting board. Clearly there was something wrong. I was concerned and told him to leave the skirtings until he felt better. He struggled on for a bit longer then stopped and put down the tape measure and after telling me that he felt dizzy and couldn't see what he was doing he crawled off down the landing and went to bed. It turned out that he had Labyrinthitus – a disorder of the middle ear – which forced him to spend the following week in bed.

Despite that setback and the time spent enjoying the Christmas festivities we managed to finish Sam's room before the end of December and fitted a new carpet just before the New Year. Before moving back into his newly refurbished bedroom Sam had a good clear out of all his belongings. Any unwanted clothing and other items were crammed into several black bin bags which he left clumped together on the new upstairs landing.

2006

The first few days of January were cold and Jericho was enveloped in damp, swirling mists full of indistinct and shifting images. I kept all the poultry locked in their huts. Emily bleated mournfully in her solitude.

National newspapers and television news programmes were dominated by reports of Bird Flu which was spreading across Turkey. Already it had reached Ankara and Istanbul and it was feared that it would spread to Europe.

After the New Year bank holiday I loaded up my car with all the black bags from the upstairs landing and drove to the council tip where I hurled them all into a large skip. I kept busy replenishing the log baskets in the barn room and refilled the shelves in Alan's work room with logs which had been stored under a tarpaulin outside. I cut up the wood which I'd collected from timber yards in the weeks leading up to Christmas and stacked it on the shelves next to the logs. Some of it I chopped into kindling which I brought into the barn and put into a wooden box beside the big stove.

We were well into the second week of January when Sam asked me if I'd washed any of his clothes recently. I ferreted about in the ever increasing pile of ironing and found very little which belonged to him. His dirty linen bag was practically empty and it soon became apparent that along with the numerous unwanted black bags which I had flung into the skip I had also thrown two bags full of dirty washing which included two pairs of denim jeans, his best shirt, several t-shirts and a new sweatshirt which he'd been given for Christmas!

An evening prize giving ceremony was held that month at Oldham College and I was presented with a special award for my course work. It was completely unexpected and I was well chuffed to receive it.

That night the wind picked up and continued to get stronger throughout the following day. Working down at the stables I was aware of the increasing severity of the wind. I had to fasten open the barn door to prevent it slamming shut and shield the water as it flowed into the bucket from the tap. Suddenly there was a loud crack. I looked up the garden and scanned the area in front of the house to try and pinpoint the source of the noise. My eyes settled on the hen hut which had tilted and was now swaying in the wind. The last gust must have snapped the wooden anchor straps which Alan had fastened onto the corners of the hut when he had built it back in 1996. As I progressed through my jobs on the yard I kept an eye on the hen hut. Every time there was a strong gust of wind the hut moved more freely. A large and dense thorn bush which was growing beside the hen hut had quadrupled in size since I had planted it about six years ago and its bulk was now giving the hut limited but vital support.

I went up the garden to weigh up the damage. As I had suspected both the anchor straps at the back of the hut had snapped. This resulted in the rear of the hut lifting every time it was battered by the wind. The degree to which the hut was tilting worried me and on closer inspection I realised that the two straps at the front of the hut, although still intact, had rotted over the years. This had not been a problem while the rear anchor straps were still fastened but now that they had snapped the front ones would be unable to take the strain.

After another prolonged gust the degree to which the hut listed was becoming serious and I feared for the hens' safety. It was moving far too freely for my liking and I had to make the decision whether or not to move the hens to a safer place. The last thing I wanted was to see the hen hut - complete with occupants – bounce across the garden and end up over the wall in Taylor's field like the bike shed had done years ago.

The small hen hut which Oliver and his two black hens occupied at the bottom of the garden was relatively sheltered and thankfully unaffected by the gales. I decided to transfer the hens from the hen hut at the top of the garden into Oliver's hut. The strength of the wind continued to increase. The top hen hut was creaking loudly. I was convinced that if it weren't for the dense evergreen bush growing beside it the hut would already have broken free and would have been at the mercy of the wind.

I soon realised that the rescue was not going to be straightforward. The roof at the front of the hen hut was leaning down towards me. I slid open the bolt and pulled the door open then ducked under the roof and stepped inside. The hens were squawking and flapping their wings as they tried to keep their balance on the sloping roosts. On the floor the corn bin was rolling around on its side and their water had spilt. I grabbed the nearest three hens. Gripping them firmly I withdrew from the hut and pushed the door shut with my knee. I managed to catch the bolt without dropping any of the hens and then clasping them close to me I ran down to Oliver's hut opened the door and threw the startled hens inside.

I returned to the top hut. By this time it was tilting even more its weight pushing heavily against the evergreen bush as it was battered by yet another strong gust of wind. Because the hut was leaning over so much I had to push myself against the sharp branches of the bush and duck down beneath the edge of the roof. The hut was standing askew now which made the door difficult to pull open. I crouched down wriggled through the doorway and stood up. Most of my body was now inside the hut although I was still standing outside it. Unable to balance on the roosts any longer the frightened hens were jumbled up together on the opposite side of the hut which was now pretty much where the floor used to be. The wind was blowing as strong as ever. It occurred to me that if there was another really strong gust the hut could break free completely and drop down trapping me inside it with a bunch of hysterical hens! With that in mind I grabbed the remaining four hens and stuffed them under my coat. Leaving Worthington alone inside the hut I ducked back out of the doorway and jammed the door shut. Once again clutching my coat close to me I braved the wind and hurried down the garden. I opened the door of Oliver's hut and flung the flustered hens through the doorway. Oliver was strutting about squawking loudly as the four large hens hurtled past his head. I slammed the door and bolted it then ran back up the garden endeavouring to rescue Worthington before the hut dropped down any further preventing me from opening the door. As I yanked the door open and ducked through the doorway Worthington slithered towards me his claws scratching frantically against the wood beneath his feet. I grabbed him, folded his wings close against his body and then holding him tightly I crawled out through the doorway relieved to be back outside.

As I approached Oliver's hut I could hear the hens squabbling. There were now 10 birds in a small hut less than half the size of the top hen hut. For a few moments I weighed up the risks of adding another adult cockerel into the mix. There were no windows in this little hut and so because of that and the fact that there were so many hens I hoped that Oliver wouldn't realise that Worthington was in there too. I decided that I'd rather risk the cockerels having a scrap than risk losing Worthington by leaving him in the top hut at the mercy of the gale – besides I had nowhere else to put him.

The wind died down considerably during the night. In the morning I opened the door of Oliver's hut. The hens tumbled out and quickly spread out across the garden. Oliver was one of the first to come out. Tentatively I looked inside. Worthington was standing at the back of the hut looking a little bemused but otherwise completely unharmed.

Surprisingly the top hen hut was still wedged against the thorn bush. The door had come off its hinges and the floor was buckled but apart from that it was still intact. Alan and Sam managed to heave the hut upright and carried out some major repairs particularly to the floor and door along with some modifications to the anchoring points. Before nightfall it was – at least for a temporary period – ready once again for Worthington and his hens to move back into.

Jess turned 21 at the end of the month and we met up with Malc's family and had a meal out to celebrate. Shortly after her birthday she left Jericho and moved into rented accommodation with Malc in Mossley.

As far as the weather was concerned January and February were not too bad and Sam was able to resume building the garage at weekends. Alan and I laboured for him and the building soon took shape. The weather deteriorated at the end of February becoming extremely cold with more gales and driving snow which forced me to keep all the poultry in for three consecutive days. The freezing conditions continued into March when the outside temperatures were measured at minus eight degrees. Freezing, driving rain welded itself to the window panes like pebble dashing.

Early in March I received a phone call from the people who were loaning Jessie. They told me that she was unwell and not eating properly. I went to see her and immediately called the vet. Jessie looked old and miserable had obviously lost weight and I couldn't believe that they had not yet had the vet to her. It turned out that she had a deep seated gum infection which had been troubling her for some time and had prevented her from eating. Thankfully she responded well to the treatment which she received from the vet and once the medication kicked in she began to eat again. I decided as soon as it was possible to do so, that I would bring her back to Jericho permanently. Sam was delighted at the prospect of his old pony coming home. The only problem was that all the stables were occupied including the lean-to stable at the end of the block where Emily sheep resided. After much thought we decided that the best thing to do was to build another lean-to against the existing lean-to. Emily would have to be ousted into the new smaller one and Jessie would have the original one.

We levelled the ground and laid some concrete flags for a base then Alan measured up and made a framework for Emily's new home. The oily boards which had previously formed the floor of the old hay barn were ideal to clad the frame with on three sides. We boarded and felted the roof and hung a door which had been used previously in the stable at the back of the house. I put down some clean straw and hung up a small hay net and it was ready for Emily. I then cleaned out and disinfected the old lean-to and got it ready for Jessie. Bernard offered to collect her in his trailer and at the weekend we brought her home.

Although she had been regularly shod and her vaccinations were all up to date the assurances which I had been given that Jessie had been well looked after and groomed regularly proved to be patently untrue. Her coat was dull, the hair tangled and full of scurf and grease. There was evidence of rain scald on her back, her ribs were clearly visible and I was sickened by the filthy and neglected condition of her. The last few times that I had called to see her she had been rugged up which had concealed the true picture. I was annoyed with myself for not having looked at her more closely.

Over the next couple of weeks I brushed her each day. Carefully I cut away the matted hair under her chest at the top of her front legs and where her girth had been all of which must have been hurting her whenever she was ridden. When the weather was warm enough I washed her and then I had her coat fully clipped. This was a slow and obviously painful ordeal for Jessie who previously used to stand quietly and make no fuss at all when she was clipped but this time she flinched frequently and put her ears back. The young girl who was clipping her was very patient and left the areas which seemed to cause the most pain for me to sort out later with scissors.

By the beginning of May she looked much more like the old Jessie that we had known and loved. We were all happy that she was once more living at Jericho where she will stay for the rest of her life. Nancy's daughter Georgina began to ride Jessie now and again to help get her fit. At first she rode her only as far as The Roebuck and back but Jessie was surprisingly forward going and before long they hacked round the reservoir. On reaching the woodland path Jessie's ears pricked forward undoubtedly recognising the bridle paths where she used to canter with Sam.

Life at Jericho

The white Runner duck, Linford Junior, was now one year old. Chuck, his devoted 'sister' refused to live in the hen hut with Crow and chose instead to live with Linford and the rest of the ducks in the duck hut. Despite living in the duck hut, due no doubt to his unusual upbringing, Linford appeared to regard himself as one of the hens and when all the poultry were out together he and Chuck spent their time with Crow and the rest of the hens scratching and rooting about in the shrubbery. As spring progressed Linford took even less notice of the other ducks and instead turned his amorous intentions towards the hens. Frequently, looking like an animated cartoon character, his legs and webbed feet pounding like waterwheels he could be seen persistently pursuing one or other alarmed hen rapidly across the garden, through the flower bed and round the oak trees before the hen, squawking loudly, would outwit him and flutter up onto the muck heap or onto a fence rail. Every now and again he would almost succeed in his mission to hump one of the hens, and this somewhat kinky behaviour was to continue each successive spring.

Mikey

And finally....

My diary entry for Thursday 11th May 2006 began... *'Have lived at Jericho for 12 years....'*

It had been twelve years to the day since we had obtained the keys to Jericho Farm on that cold May evening in 1994 when as a family we had ventured into our new home for the first time. Thankfully things are very different now. With each year that passes the light at the end of the tunnel grows a little bigger and a little brighter, and the time when one morning we will wake up to discover that there is no longer an endless list of jobs to be done is becoming ever closer. When that time comes we will be able to sit back and enjoy the fruits of our not inconsiderable labours in the knowledge that we have achieved something of which we are truly proud, and that our lives and those of our children have contributed to and are inextricably a part of that which is Jericho.